Endorsements for
Newark: City of Destiny

Newark is looking for a healing. We're trusting God for a healing. Newark is also a destiny city. Dr. Turner's book, which commemorates the 350th anniversary of the city, is an awesome piece of work. We're honored to have this piece of material. We're honored to have him our city, doing the work he's doing. And more importantly, we're honored that he titled this book, ***Newark: City of Destiny***. Let's be mindful of the fact that we must work together, that we must turn to God, that we must pray, and turn from all of our wicked ways, in order for our land to be healed.

Rev. Louise Scott-Rountree
Director of Clergy Affairs and Faith-Based Initiatives
City of Newark, New Jersey

Newark: City of Destiny has delineated the things that were essential when Newark was founded by the Puritans. Dr. Turner captures the spiritual essence of the city, which was created to be as close to the kingdom of God as possible. As an African-American pastor we have been tracing our Jewish heritage, and now we're finding out how we are also connected with the Puritans. Our destinies are entwined, one with another. Dr. Turner is also involved in the adopt-a-street prayer ministry, which is an outpouring of what was originated in those early days. Now today we actually going back to the spiritual heritage of Newark. We thank God for Lloyd and Joanne and for the spiritual anointing that is over Newark.

Dr. Gloria Harris
Senior Pastor, Beth El International Church
Newark, New Jersey

This year commemorates the 350th anniversary of the founding of the city of Newark. Newark was established to be a manifestation of God's kingdom here on earth. Through this book, ***Newark: City of Destiny***, we will be moved and motivated to get inspired by those who allowed themselves to be used of God so that the presence of God, through the servants of God, will be manifest in this city.

Dr. Bernard Wilks
President, The Resident Ministers Alliance (ReMA)
Founder and Overseer, Dominion Fellowship Ministries
Newark, New Jersey

This is an awesome book, and I am encouraging you to get the book, because you will be blessed as you dive into the history of our great city. As a pastor and overseer in the city of Newark, my passion is for those who are on the street, the homeless, the kicked out, the left out. My passion is for those who are out on the streets and won't come into a house of worship. Through our love they will know that our city cares for them. Yes, the city has a destiny, and we are looking forward to what God has in store for us. I thank God that Newark is a city of destiny. We will be the New Ark.

Apostle Gennie Holte
Ray of Hope Ministries
Newark, New Jersey

Newark is definitely a great place to be, because Newark is on the rise. There is a chapter in this book about having a dream. I felt one time that I had a dream, and now I am living my dream by serving as an ambassador for Christ. I compliment Lloyd for writing an excellent book. If you want to see your destiny, you'd better read this book!

Minister Jeffrey R. Brown
Kingdom Bound Ministry
Newark, New Jersey

I remember being a patient of Dr. E. Mae McCarroll. My girlfriend took me to see her when I was pregnant. I couldn't talk to our family doctor about this. She was an unusual doctor, because she listened to you, she counseled you, and she would really let you have it. She talked to my mother, which was the great part about it. She caused a new knitting between me and my mother, and she prayed for us. In addition she worked with the Keep Well Stations, which provided services for people who couldn't afford medical care.

Elder Betty Moon
Founder and CEO, Project Street Ladykeepers
Revival Center of Ministries
Newark, New Jersey

I'm excited about the book Dr. Turner has written, ***Newark: City of Destiny.*** I believe in it, and we at World Impact are staking our lives on it even, in terms of working in the hardest, toughest parts of the cities across America today. We know what Newark is today, and we're excited about what God is doing. We're looking forward to the restoration of this city in the future.

Minister Keith Wilks
Regional Vice President of Ministry
World Impact-Eastern Region
Newark, New Jersey

When I came to Newark, I worked for the Burch family for about six months. When I met the family, I found they were very cordial. But I thought Dr. Reynold Burch was a grouch, because he had such a growling voice. One day he got a telegram from the medical school in Boston, saying that he had passed the medical field exam, and he let out a big "Ho, ho." After that he came to me and apologized for being so focused on passing his exams. His partner (Mary) was just the opposite.

Elder Emily Brown
New Salem Baptist Church
Retired educator, Essex County Community College
Newark, New Jersey

Dr. Lloyd is a personal friend, and I'm intrigued about his new book. Newark is a city of destiny, and my part is prayer and intercession. The Puritans who founded the city were prayer warriors. We have a monthly Leaders' Intercessory Ministry meeting to unify pastors and leaders through prayer. God has laid on our heart that a powerful spiritual renewal will be coming to Newark. We are trusting that God will roll away the powers of darkness. The Lord sent me to this city and told me to go and interact with the leaders of Newark, so that peace and prosperity will return to the city through prayer. We need to bind together and pray that the power of the Holy Ghost will bring the city back to life again.

Dr. Jacobs Obamedo

Pastor, Ministry of the Word International
and House of Prayer
Newark, New Jersey

I am very proud for being able to see God's purposes advanced for the benefit of those who have been left out. I'm just thankful that God is not done with the city of Newark, and as Lloyd Turner's book points out, many people throughout history have done their part to advance the kingdom of God through their sacrifice, through their service, and through their faith. I'm going to encourage those of you who haven't seen this book to read it and see what you can learn about many people who have contributed to the advancement of Newark's destiny.

Minister Charles Smith

Educator and Advocate for the Arts
Newark, New Jersey

NEWARK

CITY OF DESTINY

---

by Lloyd Turner, Ph.D.
PrayForNewark

Newark: City of Destiny

Self-published with CreateSpace by Lloyd Turner

ISBN 978-1519576439
BISAC: Religion / Christianity / History / General

Acknowledgments
Cover Design: Steve Martin
Photo Selections: Dori Perucci

"The Spirit of the Lord is on me,
because he has anointed me
to preach good news to the poor.
He has sent me to proclaim freedom for the prisoners
and recovery of sight for the blind,
to release the oppressed,
to proclaim the year of the Lord's favor."

– Luke 4:18-19 (NASB)

Front cover images:

Clara Maass (1876-1901)	Donald Payne, Senior (1934-2012)
Edwin Leahy (1945-)	Mary Beasley Burch (1906-2001)

Contents

PREFACE..1

FOREWORD..9

Part One: Good News to the Poor..................11

1 Moses Newell Combs (1754-1834): Father of Newark Industry..*13*

2 Rachel Bradford Boudinot (1764-1805): The Newark Female Charitable Society.......................*21*

3 Seth Boyden (1788-1870): Transformation of Manufacturing...*33*

Part Two: Freedom for the Prisoners.............45

4 Theodore Frelinghuysen (1787-1862): Christian Statesman..*47*

5 Joachim Prinz (1902-1988): We Are All Neighbors..*61*

6 E. Alma Flagg (1918-): Newark's First Lady of Education..*77*

Part Three: Recovery of Sight for the Blind.....91

7 Edgar Holden (1838-1909): Public Health Advocate...*93*

8 Earnest Mae McCarroll (1898-1990): Pioneer Black Physician......................................*109*

9 Clara Louise Maass (1876-1901): No Greater Love..*123*

Part Four: Release for the Oppressed............137

10 Alexander MacWhorter (1734-1807): Newark's North Star...139

11 Elizabeth Stryker Ricord (1788-1865): The Newark Orphan Asylum....................................151

12 Edwin Leahy (1945-): Fighting Against the Street...165

Part Five: The Year of the Lord's Favor.........179

13 Marcus Lawrence Ward (1812-1884): Binding Up the Nation's Wounds....................................181

14 Mary Beasley Burch (1906-2001): The Leaguers..197

15 Donald M. Payne, Sr. (1934-2012): The Power of a Dream...209

NOTES..223

INDEX...251

PHOTO CREDITS..257

THE AUTHOR..258

PREFACE

As a young child I remember my mother reading stories to me about the lives of great men and women in history. The biographies of people such as George Washington, Abraham Lincoln, Christopher Columbus, Martin Luther and others from past centuries are still in my mind many years later.

The celebration of the 350th Anniversary of the founding of Newark is an appropriate time to reflect not only on the hopes and visions of Newark's original Puritan settlers but also on the progress that has been made to fulfill their desire that Newark should be "as nearly as possible a kingdom of God on earth."

As I have described in my earlier book, ***Proclaiming the Kingdom: City Transformation Through Prayer Evangelism,*** the Puritan's understanding of the kingdom of God drew heavily on Jesus's teachings in the four Gospels and other New Testament writings.

The Connecticut Puritans who founded Newark in 1666 had both spiritual and political objectives in settling in New Jersey. Their spiritual objective was to establish a 'pure' church that reflected kingdom values in their daily lives. Quite simply, they wanted to be able to worship—seven days a week—in a style of worship that was governed by biblical principles rather than mandated by religious leaders in the Church of England. They believed that the power of the Gospel could transform not only their worship services but also their daily lives.

At the same time, however, these Puritan settlers had a pressing need to leave Connecticut. In 1658 Oliver Cromwell died, and England was left without an effective government when his son Richard resigned as Lord Protector in the following year. In 1660 Charles II was crowned King of England and vowed revenge on Cromwell's supporters who were responsible for the execution of his father, Charles I.

The Connecticut Puritans must have looked at these changes in London with horror, because three of the judges who sentenced Charles I to death had taken refuge in New Haven for several years. If Charles II intended to restore the Roman Catholic rule in England, it could mean the loss of life and property for New Englanders who remained true to Puritan religious and political ideals.

With these concerns in mind Robert Treat, Jasper Crane, Samuel Swain, and the other Founders sailed from Connecticut in May 1666 to establish a city in New Jersey that would be free of British rule. Following the lead of theologians like John Cotton and John Davenport, they sought to establish a Puritan theocracy that would ensure that they were able to worship freely in the Congregational manner. They chose to drop anchor at the place we now call Newark, which was far removed from other cities by natural barriers of rivers and marshes.

And so for more than a century Newark remained as a small, peaceful settlement that sought to be isolated from national and international politics.

Like most utopian experiments, however, the Newark experiment in theocracy failed over time. The first church split occurred in the 1730's, precipitated by Colonel John Ogden's harvesting of his wheat on the Sabbath. By 1750 the Presbyterian Church and the Town Government were officially severed, and Newark was incorporated as a city in 1836. At the start of the Civil War there were more than forty churches in Newark, and this number had grown to more than eight hundred by 2000. Today it is quite obvious that Newark looks a lot less like a Puritan theocracy than it did to 17th and 18th Century residents.

But does this mean that that kingdom of God has failed to advance in Newark? Quite the contrary! If we go back to Jesus's teaching about the kingdom, he made it quite clear to authorities that "my kingdom is not of this world." (John 18:36) Jesus let it be known that He came to earth for a different purpose—"to seek and to save that which was lost" (Luke 19:10, NASB).

He emphasized that the kingdom of God was not about fame and fortune, but rather about discipling cities and nations according to kingdom principles (Matthew 28:19-20). He told his listeners that this transformation process would start very small and would advance slowly, like the growth of a mustard seed or the leavening of yeast (Matthew 13:31-32; Luke 13:20-21).

It would be like "treasure hidden in a field" and would

bring forth joy when it is uncovered. (Matthew 13:44). It would be about little children coming to Him, as well as caring for widows and orphans (Matthew 19:14, John 14:18, James 1:27). In addition the kingdom of God would expand without limit until Christ's future return (Isaiah 9:6).

This book tells the stories of fifteen men and women who caught glimpses of the kingdom of God advancing in Newark. These stories are organized into five parts, based on Jesus' teachings about his ministry in Luke 4:18-19:

- **Part 1: Good News to the Poor** – the economically disinherited.
- **Part 2: Freedom for the Prisoners** – the socially and politically disinherited.
- **Part 3: Recovery of Sight for the Blind** – the physically disinherited.
- **Part 4: Release for the Oppressed** – the morally and spiritually disinherited.
- **Part 5: The Year of the Lord's Favor** – a closer approximation to equality of opportunity for all.

I encourage you to read these stories and share them with young and old in your family and in your broader sphere of influence. God has done amazing things through His disciples in Newark during the past 350 years, but many of their stories remain buried in the field—like hidden treasures—that will bring great joy when they are rediscovered in the present generation.

Yes, my friend, read these stories about how God has

quietly continued to advance His kingdom in Newark, in fulfillment of the covenant promises He made with Newark's Founders in 1666.

Lloyd Turner

Lloyd Turner, Ph.D.
New Providence, NJ
May 2016

FOREWORD

Lloyd Turner in these insightful though brief biographies has captured the essence of the spirit of servitude exemplified in the lives of Newarkers. Such committed, caring, and compassionate spirit exhibited in the lives of those who came before us has laid and aligned the spiritual foundation of this city as the Ark of the New Covenant of the True and Living God.

Their lives and legacy serve as a testimony of discipline, dedication, and devotion to serving God and man. Such traits are admirable and are still essential today so that Newark will experience resurrection and restoration to former greatness as a city where love is exemplified, Jesus is edified and God is glorified.

It is hoped that the story of their lives will serve as a catalyst for igniting in us such love for God, and such commitment and caring concern for others, that we too will be moved with compassion to proclaim good news to the poor, healing to the broken hearted, deliverance to those in bondage, hope to those who have no vision, and liberation to those who have been crushed.

History affirms it was done by them. Today's urgency cries out that through us, and through the inspiration imparted through this book and the depiction of their lives, it will be done again.

Dr. Bernard Wilks, President
The Resident Ministers Alliance
Newark, New Jersey

Part One

Good News to the Poor

Good News to the Poor:

The Economically Disinherited

Newark was a small rural community with few needy persons during its first century. After the Revolutionary War, however, European immigrants came to Newark and other cities in search of employment and opportunity to become property owners. The people highlighted in Part One created skilled jobs for thousands of workers and pioneered new social institutions to care for the increasing number of needy individuals living in the city.

MOSES COMBS (1754-1834) was a shoe manufacturer who established the first vocational training school in America. His apprentices were young men who were agricultural workers during the growing season but were underemployed during the remainder of the year. An ordained pastor, Combs ministered to his apprentices while teaching them valuable vocational and classical educational skills. He taught new processes of shoe making that propelled Newark to national prominence as a center for the shoemaking industry.

RACHEL BOUDINOT (1764-1805) was instrumental in establishing the Newark Female Charitable Society, which was the third oldest charitable organization in America. The society was funded and managed by prominent Newark families and served the city's poor for more than 130 years.

SETH BOYDEN (1788-1870) was a brilliant inventor who developed new manufacturing processes in leather products, malleable iron, and steam locomotive engines. Through his genius and mentoring of young entrepreneurs, Newark rose to become the sixth largest manufacturing center in American by 1860.

CHAPTER ONE

Moses Newell Combs (1754-1834): Father of Newark Industry

During the winter of 1777-78 General George Washington and his army of 10,000 men camped at Valley Forge, Pennsylvania, on the outskirts of Philadelphia. Because of supply shortages, diseases, and exposure to the cold winter weather, however, only about 7,000 of these men were fit for duty by spring. On December 29, 1777, Washington wrote to the New Hampshire legislature requesting that they send supplies for their regiments. His specific request is as follows:

> "We had in Camp . . . not less than 2898 men unfit for duty, by reason of their being barefoot and otherwise naked. Beside this number, sufficiently distressing of itself, there are many Others detained in Hospitals and crowded in Farmers Houses for the same causes. In a most particular manner, I flatter myself the care and attention of the States will be directed to the supply of Shoes, Stockings and Blankets, as their expenditure from the common operations and accidents of War is far greater than of any other articles. In a word, the United and respective exertions of the States cannot be too great, too vigorous in this interesting work, and we shall never have a fair and just prospect for success till our Troops (Officers & Men) are better appointed and provided than they are or have been."[1]

One of Washington's soldiers was a 22 year-old Newark man named MOSES NEWELL COMBS, who enlisted in the New Jersey Militia in 1776. A tanner and shoemaker by trade, Combs recognized that a ready supply of shoes was a critical factor for the success of the Patriot's cause. This was a lesson he would never forget.

After Washington defeated Lord Cornwallis's army at Yorktown, Virginia, in 1781, Combs returned to the shoemaking trade and realized that the making of shoes was a 'cottage industry' with high labor costs. At that time a shoemaker was typically a single craftsman assisted by a journeyman and one or two apprentices. They typically worked out of their homes, living upstairs or adjacent to their shops. (This same cottage industry model also applied in other trades, such as clockmakers, silversmiths, and goldsmiths.) Wealthy customers had the option of hiring a shoemaker to live in their home for an extended period of time while he crafted shoes for all the family members.[2]

The Industrial Revolution began in England during the Eighteenth Century after Adam Smith and others discovered the principle of 'division of labor', which greatly improved worker productivity by breaking manufacturing processes down into subtasks that were performed by different individuals. To apply this concept to shoemaking, Combs' key insight was that the number of shoes produced per week could be greatly increased if the construction process was broken down into three-person teams. The first worker would concentrate on sewing the uppers, a second one would craft the soles, and the third would assemble the final shoe.[3] He set up Newark's first shoemaking factory at 77 Market Street and sold an order for 200 pairs of sealskin shoes in Savannah, Georgia, by 1790. This was the first reported manufacturing of shoes for a market outside of Newark.[4] It was also a widely recognized sign that Newark's economy was being transformed from agriculture to an industrial base.

In 1792 Combs set up a 'Free School' to provide education and training for apprentices. He spent his days assembling and selling his shoes. Then at night he ran a school above his shop, where he offered technical and liberal arts training to people in the community. Frank Urquhart describes this amazing school as follows:

> "Moses Combs did not build up a profitable manufacturing business for the sake of a personal gain. Money seems to have meant little to him unless he could do good with it. About the time he made his ever-memorable sale of shoes to a Georgia

> planter, Mr. Combs established his night school for apprentices.
> . . . It was not long before pupils were admitted to this school free. It was probably the first night school in the United Schools, and was one of the first free schools in the country (and probably the first). In that same year the ***New Jersey Journal***, recognizing Moses Combs' free school was something extraordinary, published the following: 'A worthy, industrious Newark mechanic in the town of Newark maintains at his own expense a School Master of a reputable character who teaches the English Language, Writing and Arithmetic to about forty children, among them the poor are taught gratis, at his annual expense of 20 pounds. Noble philanthropy! Honor to human nature and Christianity.'
> The Combs school was a place for the plain people, a place where working boys could fit themselves for a broader sphere in life if they chose. Not a few of the pupils of the school became men of influence in the town later on."[5]

His first apprentices were agricultural workers, who had paid jobs only during the growing season and were underemployed the rest of the year. As his business grew, however, apprentices came to Newark from Jersey City and other communities, and dozens learned the shoemaking trade through his apprenticeship program. During the next decade Newark became celebrated for its excellent boots and shoes. Combs helped many of his apprentices set up their own shops, and by 1806 Charles Basham (an instructor at Newark Academy) reported that one-third of all Newark workers were employed in the shoemaking industry. Basham's so-called "Shoemakers Map" was the first published map of Newark, and it displayed the locations of every shoemaker in town.[6]

Combs' "Free School"
77 Market Street

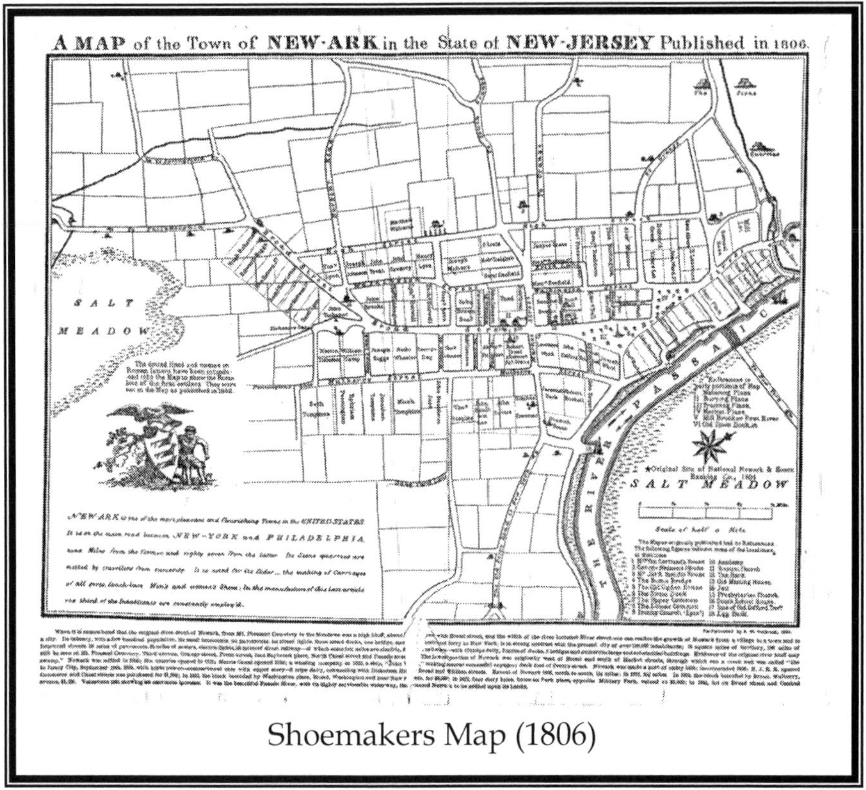

Shoemakers Map (1806)

His success in establishing the shoemaking industry is the reason why he is considered to be the "Father of Newark Industry" by Urquhart and other historians. Urquhart describes Combs' achievements as follows:

> "But it was, after all, the making of shoes that attracted the eyes of the outside world to Newark. It was shoemaking that laid the actual foundations of Newark's industrial strength, that created the fundamental though unwritten laws for the advancement of Newark as a centre where useful things were well made and at a reasonable price. The making of shoes to sell to people outside the Newark neighborhood seems to have first appealed to one far-seeing, hard-thinking man, Moses Newell Combs. . . . But it was not so much his skill at making

shoes that make it possible for Moses Combs to put Newark's industries upon a new and profitable basis as it was his masterful genius for organization.

It is a most significant fact that the apprentices' indenture for at least the first half of the last century [the 19th Century] showed evidence of being drawn up along the lines pursued by Mr. Combs in his business practice. 'The universal condition of apprenticeship,' said a Newark writer in the ***Daily Advertiser*** in 1863, 'was not only to be taught the trade, art and mystery of the business, but apprentices were to be provided with good and wholesome food, washing and lodging, a certain number of quarters of night-schooling, and to be found good and comfortable apparel, or an allowance of a certain specified sum of money in lieu thereof, with a perfect control of their boss over their morals.'"[7]

Combs was not only an outstanding entrepreneur but was also a deeply spiritual man who was committed to social reform and justice for the disadvantaged. He saw his work as a form of worship and encouraged moral behavior by all his workers and students. In an 1865 article about Combs, a writer for the Newark ***Daily Advertiser*** wrote,

"Mr. Combs, having several apprentices, was in the habit of calling them together after the hours of labor for the purpose of study and for moral and religious instruction. . . . Moses Combs strenuously advocated three things many years ahead of his time: emancipation of the slaves, temperance, and universal education. . . .

He was a regularly ordained preacher. He was a liberal contributor to the building funds of the First Presbyterian Church, the one now in use, and which was erected chiefly though the endeavors of Pastor MacWhorter. So far as can be learned the only church over which Mr. Combs presided was that which he himself erected [above his factory] on Market Street, as just described. He disapproved of some phases of the religious teaching of the First Church and he and his associates withdrew and for a period attended the First Presbyterian Church in Orange. . . . After a time the Combs religious society was disbanded and most of its members went back to the old First Church fold."[8]

Combs taught a generation of Newark apprentices how to become successful business owners and marketplace ministers.

Moses Combs and the other leading citizens fostered a spiritual climate in Newark that emphasized personal piety, a solid work ethic, and patriotism. He "invested his money in various public enterprises and from purely patriotic motives, as was the custom of the leading men of his time, when the money lust had not yet become offensively evident in the little community."[9]

Some of his other civic and philanthropic activities are summarized in this closing statement by Urquhart:

> "He was treasurer of the Springfield-Newark Turnpike Company in 1806, and the same year was giving his money, with others to improve the old ferry road (now Ferry Street) and to reopen the old ferry connecting with that road, which had fallen into some disuse since the opening of the bridges over the Passaic and Hackensack Rivers. In 1812 he offered for sale four building lots at the junction of what are now Springfield and South Orange Avenues, for money or in barter 'for seal or upper leather.' He was in the group who established Jersey City, buying up the land in great stretches and developing it.
>
> He was among the founders of the Newark Fire Insurance Company, and one of its directors. He was actively identified with the organization of one of the first of Newark's banks. When he came to die he did not leave a vast estate, even for his day and generation. He had worked quite as much for the betterment of Newark as for his own prosperity, in fact more. He was a remarkable and most valuable man to Newark, and well

deserves the space given him here. His best service, of course, was the providing of ways and means for poor but industrious youths to make more out of themselves than would have been possible had he not extended to them the privileges of education."[10]

CHAPTER TWO

Rachel Bradford Boudinot (1764-1805): The Newark Female Charitable Society

One Sunday morning the pastor at Newark's Old First Presbyterian Church announced that interested persons would be meeting at the residence of Judge Elisha Boudinot on January 31, 1803, "to devise some means for caring for the poor and distressed persons in the village." At that meeting the "Newark Female Charitable Society" was birthed, with Mrs. RACHEL BOUDINOT elected as the Directress of this first benevolent society in the State of New Jersey. In addition to Mrs. Boudinot, the Society appointed three other Board members and six managers and received one hundred seventeen subscribers. Thus began *systematic aid* to the needy, which continued until after World War II.

In the minutes of the Society's meetings it was reported that "not an ounce of flax, or yard of homespun was given without consent of the Board."[1] As Newark grew from a small village into a major U.S. city, the Society supplied increasing resources to meet the growing needs of the poor, generation after generation.

The revival of religion at the beginning of the Nineteenth Century came to be known as the Second Great Awakening. Across America there was a renewal of interest in spiritual matters, which led to the formation of numerous charitable organizations run by lay leaders, both male and female. Elias Boudinot, for example, was the President of the Continental Congress and was also the organizer of the American Bible Society. (Elias was the uncle of Judge Elisha Boudinot of Newark.) Other major charitable organizations founded during the Second Great Awakening included the Board of Commissioners for Foreign Missions (the first U.S. missions society), the Baptist Missions Society, and the American Sunday School Union.

At Newark's Old First Presbyterian Church Pastors Alexander MacWhorter and Edward Dorr Griffin exhorted their congregation to get involved in alleviating poverty and other social problems. In the 1790's three major events occurred that caused the population of needy persons to increase dramatically. The first was the growth of manufacturing, which started in 1792 when Moses Combs organized the first assembly line to produce shoes. As Combs' methods were copied by other Newark shoemakers, the demand for manufacturing workers rose rapidly. Many of these early shoemakers immigrated from Europe and had limited financial resources when they arrived in America.

Second, the opening of the Harrison bridge over the Passaic River in 1795 provided easy access to the village by outsiders. Newark suddenly became a transportation hub connecting travelers between New York, Philadelphia, and other East Coast cities. Newark officials could no longer limit the flow of persons who came to the village for business or personal reasons.

Thirdly, three epidemics of yellow fever broke out on the East Coast between 1791 and 1803. Almost 10 percent of Philadelphia's population died from yellow fever between August and December in 1793, and the disease spread quickly to Newark, New York, and other major coastal cities. These epidemics caused an immediate need for nurses and home-based caregivers and left many families destitute throughout the region.

The revival of religion, combined with these three major social events, caused Newark's leaders to recognize the need for an organized community response to the rising needs of the poor. In just two decades Newark went from casting out the poor to having more than a hundred leading families voluntarily contributing to address their needs. The 1784 Town Records clearly stated Newark's strict policy to exclude the poor. At the annual town meeting, held at Newark on March 9, 1784, the following motions were approved by village leaders:

Newark Policy on the Poor (1784)

"Voted, that the poor be farmed out.

Voted, that to Prevent Disputes, if any Person or Persons of the poor shall be adjudged by the Justices to be Removed for Non Residence, that the Expense shall fall on the Town and not on the farmer.

Voted, that Two hundred and fifty pounds be Raised the ensuing Year, for the Support of the poor.

Benjamin Coe, Farmer of the Poor at One Hundred and Ninety Six pounds. . . ."

—***Newark Town Records,*** *1784.*[2]

By these votes the Town authorized 196 pounds to Benjamin Coe to remove the poor from the community, if they were found to be non-residents, but only 250 pounds were allocated to address the needs of poor residents.

Although the spiritual awakening in that season led to a growing concern for the needs of the poor and destitute, two major hurdles hindered public responses to these needs. The first hurdle was the reality that all the village officials were males who worked full-time to support their families. Only a small number of wealthy and retired men had significant amounts of time to care for the needy.

The other major hurdle was the fact that local governments had very limited resources at that time. Newark had been devastated by British attacks during the Revolutionary War and needed to be rebuilt from the ground up. After the War ended the federal government also imposed heavy taxes on property owners to pay off massive debts that were owed to the war veterans. For these reasons village officials were unwilling to approve tax increases to meet the growing social needs.

As they prayed about the increasing community needs, Pastors MacWhorter and Griffin realized that the best solution to these problems would be to create a benevolent society managed by female caregivers. Both men gave sermons and public addresses describing how female benevolent societies had recently been established in Philadelphia and Boston.[3] They prayed and exhorted the female leaders in the Old First congregation to launch an outreach program to address the needs of Newark's poor and destitute.

Rachel Bradford was a granddaughter of William Bradford, who came to Philadelphia with William Penn in 1682 and established the first printing shop in Pennsylvania. In 1789, when she was 25, Rachel went to work as household manager for her brother William and his wife, Susan Vergereau (Boudinot) Bradford, at their home in the Rose Hill section of Philadelphia. In the following year William's responsibilities increased when George Washington asked him to serve as Attorney General in the new federal government.

In 1795 Rachel was devastated when her brother William died from yellow fever at his home. Rachel had been the chief nurse for William during his illness and witnessed his death. Shortly after her brother's death she wrote a note to Samuel Bayard, William's former law partner, that

> "My friend, my guide, my counsellor, my protector my companion, my idol, my earthly all—oh gracious Heaven have you suffered me to live to say it, my brother, my all is gone . . . [who] for 20 years has been my soul's centre, the Alpha and Omega of every plan."[4]

Two years later Elisha Boudinot's wife Catherine died in Newark from yellow fever, and Elisha himself fell ill with the fever in 1798. Fearing yet another loss in her family, Rachel went to the Boudinot home in

Newark to serve as the nurse to Elisha during his illness. After Elisha's recovery he proposed to marry her, and they were married after a short courtship.

They had a very egalitarian marriage, in which each honored the gifts and skills of the other. Elisha was the judge who was in charge of prisoners in the State of New Jersey. Rachel had gifts in nursing and household administration and agreed to care for Elisha's six children from his previous marriage. While visiting with uncle Elias Boudinot and his family in Burlington, New Jersey, in 1799, she wrote to Elisha,

> "Kiss my dear children for a parent, that loves them with a love that will show itself through Eternity."[5]

Both Elisha and Rachel were fervent Christians and were active members of the Old First Presbyterian Church in Newark. When Pastors MacWhorter and Griffin made pulpit appeals to address the problems

Site of Boudinot Home
74 Park Place

of poverty and destitution in the community, Rachel was eager to take the lead. At the founding meeting of the Newark Female Charitable Society on January 31, 1803, she hosted other prominent women from the congregation at their home at 74 Park Place and was unanimously chosen moderator and Directress of the Society.

Rachel organized the Society into officers and managers, with each manager responsible for addressing poverty and destitution in one of the city's districts. Boudinot and the other officers established criteria for distributing aid to the poor in kind, never in cash. Each of the 117 initial subscribers paid one dollar in annual dues. The Society's motto was, "To Help the Poor to Help Themselves," and it became a model for female benevolent institutions throughout New Jersey and surrounding states. The manager's role was to find schools for the children and paid jobs for the adults under their care.

The Newark Female Charitable Society was the third oldest charitable institution in America.

Rachel Boudinot died in 1805 and was laid to rest in the Boudinot family plot at the First Presbyterian Churchyard in downtown Newark. But the Society she helped to launch continued to serve the community faithfully decade after decade. One of the first fruits of the Society was a positive change in the spiritual climate in Newark. In his "Centennial Sermon" in January 1800, Dr. Alexander MacWhorter described the first church split in Newark's history, which arose over a dispute about Colonel Ogden's harvesting of grain on the Sabbath in the summer of 1733.[6] Pastor MacWhorter noted that the effects of resulting rift between the Presbyterians and Episcopalians had continued for more than seventy-five years. But in the year after Rachel's death there was a melting of hearts between these two congregations. In the December 26, 1806 minutes of the Society we read:

"Through the benevolent exertion of the Rev. Willard, thirty-

> five dollars was collected in the Episcopal Church, in this offering on Christmas Day, and presented to the Female Charitable Society."[7]

The pioneering work that Rachel Boudinot and her female colleagues began had not only benefited the poor and the destitute, but it had also healed a bitter church rift that had continued for more than seventy-five years!

During the century and a half of its existence, the Newark Female Charitable Society saw Newark's population grow a hundredfold--from 4500 to more than 450,000—by the middle of the Twentieth Century. As Newark expanded from a small village to one of America's largest cities, the number of managers in the Society was increased from 6 to

Former Site of Newark Female Charitable Society
350 Halsey Street

55, and the numbers of families served increased year by year. By 1903 the Society was caring for more than 600 families a year and had an annual budget in excess of $5,000. The scope and significance of the Society's work is well illustrated by this extract from the 1889 Annual Report:

> "The eighty-sixth year in the history of the Newark Female Charitable Society has been completed, and we bring our reports and statistics, though only a small portion of the work done can be represented by these. The records are kept elsewhere of the burdens borne, the cups of cold water given, the hungry fed, the naked clothed, the wounds bound up, the dying comforted. In the great Hereafter only will these books be opened; meanwhile our faithful band continue to minister to the sick, cheer the discouraged, and lead the little children into paths of virtue and knowledge. Our active members have never flagged in zeal and unremitting devotion, and for us to ask has been to receive, for in the hearts of our charitable citizens God has placed a readiness to bestow with love."[8]

On January 28, 1903, the Rev. Dr. David Frazier opened the Centennial Celebration of the Newark Female Charitable Society with these remarks:

> "The oldest of all of our local institutions—for it is the oldest—this historic old church, extends a greeting to the oldest charitable society. The old mother, rejoicing in her two hundred and thirty-six years of life, stretches forth both hands to the daughter, glorifying in her centennial of good works. In this old home, redolent with the memories of the past, and from which one hundred years ago went forth a goodly company of women to form the Female Charitable Society, we give you a most cordial welcome tonight. I congratulate you, not only on reaching your one hundredth anniversary, but for the record you have made, and I pray God that the future, by the marvel of its gracious work and well-doing, will be even more glorious than the past."[9]

Several other speakers gave their congratulatory remarks on that occasion, including New Jersey's Governor Murphy and Rev. Dr. Timothy Frost, who stated,

> "The Newark Female Charitable Society is to be congratulated for many reasons. There are few institutions organized in the early part of the Nineteenth Century which have lived to celebrate their hundredth anniversary. Most of them were gathered unto their fathers long ago. But this Society has lived. Indeed, it has never lived so effectively, so extensively, as now. It has never been so youthful. . . .
>
> I hope that the Twentieth Century will be the last century in which charitable work as it is now conceived and conducted will be needed or tolerated. The one who said, 'Ye have the poor always with you,' also said, 'Blessed are the meek, for they shall inherit the earth,' and 'Blessed be ye poor; for yours is the kingdom of God.'
>
> When the kingdom, which is a kingdom of human brotherhood, shall have fully come this Society shall not die, for its work is of the sort which makes for immortality and eternal life. It shall emerge through some gracious evolution into a larger ministry of some kind. . . .
>
> But let us hope that as long as this city shall endure a society or order of charitable women operating in the line of the last century's effort shall not cease to be busy about their Father's work."[10]

In the final address of that evening Mrs. Joseph Knowles, the President of the Society at that time, summarized the Society's accomplishments as follows:

> "Born in 1803, proud to tell her age, in her eyes the deep light of the wonders she has seen in the great Nineteenth Century, what memories are hers! . . . The philanthropic idea is a Christian idea. Its root is in the grand precept of Jesus, 'Thou shalt love the Lord thy God with all thy heart, and thy neighbor as thyself.' Its perfect exemplification is in the life and work of the Master Himself. . . .
>
> But organized charities belong to the Nineteenth Century. In

1803 the present long list of organized societies for all forms of benevolence, so long that it wearies us even to count their number, was undreamed of, and in that state of society, uncalled for.

As the country opened and the population increased, in the thirties and forties the old order of society rapidly changed and dependent and needy persons increased, and various organizations were formed under institutional and church supervision for improving the conditions of the poor. Foreign populations brought with [them] miseries and necessities among the unfortunate and the shiftless. So, with the growing need to relieve has grown, until the study of *how* to relieve and at the same time preserve in every soul its birthright of self-respect, self-help and self-development engages now the earnest thought of the most careful students of sociology, morals, and religion.

'Blessed is he that considereth the poor.' Surely this beautitude belongs to present day philanthropy. We count our work but half done when we relieve only the material and immediate necessity. We recognize the higher needs of the mind and the soul, and the relation of every man, woman and child to the social fabric of which he is a part. . . . It has been well said that 'It is nature's inexorable law that undisciplined charity shall not bless; that unwise love shall never be beneficient; that wisdom is born of experience.'

Philanthropy cannot be divorced from education nor from religion. Any system of caring for the poor or unfortunate which does not seek to lessen their number is deficient in the first requisite of a good system.

With these advancing views the Newark Female Charitable Society has kept pace. Its motto, 'The truest charity trains the poor to help themselves,' is put to practice in all its departments of work."[11]

In 1949 the Newark Female Charitable Society was formally dissolved, as many of its social welfare functions had been taken over by other public and private relief agencies. But its former headquarters at 350 Halsey Street in downtown Newark was converted into a day care center that continues to serve residents of the Central Ward. This building is a remembrance to Rachel Bradford Boudinot and hundreds of other women whose hearts burned with the fire of revival, and who believed that Christian love must make a tangible difference in the lives of the poor and destitute in our community.

CHAPTER THREE

Seth Boyden (1788-1870): Transformation of Manufacturing

In the early 1800's July 4 was always a special day in Newark. Newarkers, like Philadelphians, had vivid memories of the momentous events that occurred in their city during the Revolutionary War. Every year Independence Day would begin at sunrise with the firing of cannons, followed by a magnificent parade and religious exercises that went on for hours. On that day two or three companies of local militia—a troop of horse, artillery, light infantry, and others called the "Independence Corps"—would lead a procession starting at 8AM, followed by representatives of Newark's various trade groups.[1]

Newark held a very special Fourth of July celebration in 1826, which commemorated half a century since the signing of the Declaration of Independence. After the usual procession down Broad Street starting from the Presbyterian Church, a commemorative stone was dedicated by the old "Liberty Pole" in Military Park, bearing the following inscription:

> "The citizens of Newark, in grateful commemoration of the 50th anniversary of American Independence, have, on this Fourth day of July, A.D., 1826, deposited this stone as a foundation of a monument here to be erected; and when the dilapidations of time shall discover this inscription to future generations, may the light of the Gospel illuminate the whole world."[2]

Today we can still see this stone, which is adjacent to Gutzon Borglum's magnificent bronze "Wars of America" statue.[3] When the parade ended, the citizens of Newark returned to their homes without knowing the full impact of the events of that day. Only later would they learn that Thomas Jefferson, the Author of the Declaration of Independence, had quietly died at his home in Monticello, Virginia, at 1PM. Just five hours later, John Adams passed away at his home in Quincy, Massachusetts. It was the only time in American history that two Presidents died on the same day. The Colonial era was quickly coming to an end, and only one signer of the Declaration—Charles Carroll from Maryland—lived to participate in another Fourth of July celebration.

But a new era in Newark's history also began that day in the rear of a harness shop on Broad Street. For it was on July 4, 1826, that an inventor named SETH BOYDEN discovered a process to convert iron bars into malleable iron. This discovery revolutionized manufacturing in America and raised Newark into a position of prominence among America's industrial cities.

Seth Boyden's malleable iron process raised Newark to a position of prominence among America's industrial cities.

Seth Boyden was born in Foxborough, Massachusetts, on November 17, 1788, and was the youngest of five children raised by Seth and Susan (Atherton) Boyden. As a youth he worked on his father's farm and occasionally assisted his grandfather, Uriah Atherton, who owned an iron furnace and had reportedly made the first cannon in America. Uriah was a fervent patriot who manufactured mortars, swivels, bombs, and all manner of war munitions for several years. From these early experiences young Seth learned how to make a wide variety of products out of cast iron.

The people of Foxborough quickly discovered young Seth's mechanical genius. By age five he was the unpaid village mechanic, who restored watches, clocks, spinning wheels, and guns that did not work, just for the fun of it.[4] Despite having only a few months of formal schooling, he acquired a vast knowledge of optics, electricity, geology, botany, and natural philosophy. He applied this knowledge by building telescopes, microscopes, air guns, and various machines for making nails and files.

In 1809 Seth married a local woman named Abigail Sherman, and together they raised a family of six children. By 1815 Boyden had invented a sophisticated machine for splitting hides and other substances. He continued to refine this device until it produced several smooth and high quality leather products from a single cow hide. Having become bored with routine farm work, he and Abigail moved to Newark, which had become well known as a center for the manufacturing of shoes, harnesses, and other leather items. He freely shared his leather splitter prototype with other leather manufacturers, who eagerly learned how to make personal fortunes off Boyden's ingenuity. But Boyden himself quickly tired of splitting leather and became interested in more challenging manufacturing problems.

In August 1817 he was employed by Andrew Wilson, who owned a factory on Washington Street that plated bell-bands for wheel hubs—an item that was in high demand at that time. Mr. Wilson handed him a piece of patent leather, which he had received from a coach maker in New York. Wilson told him that patent leather was made in Germany by a proprietary process and was very expensive to import into America. He encouraged Seth to figure out how to make patent leather locally and offered him two hides and a workshop in the back of his factory to get started.

Boyden proceeded to build a one-story shop, as well as an oven and a drying frame. In less than a month he developed a patent leather process that was superior to the German sample he had seen. By the end of that year Boyden and one assistant were able to process a hide every day and sell it to local leather manufacturers.

When he outgrew the small shop on Washington Street, he purchased a lot on Bridge Street, where he built a larger factory and a small house for his growing family. Soon he was employing several workmen for building harnesses, moldings, and ornaments out of patent leather. As he had done with the leather splitter, he trained many others to make patent leather so that his mind was free to move on to new inventions.[5] By 1835 there were 155 Newark establishments that used Boyden's process to manufacture patent leather products.[6]

When the labors of the day were done in his patent leather factory, he used the forge in his plating-room to melt and refine small quantities of pig iron, which he annealed in a small furnace containing anthracite coal. By designing a small air furnace, he was able to make the first malleable iron produced in America.[7] Malleable iron was first invented in England, but Boyden took the art of making malleable iron to a higher level. One writer describes his improvements as follows:

> "What is called malleable iron was known before Boyden discovered it, but he invented it as truly as ever a man invented anything wholly new and previously unknown. Cast iron was so brittle that many articles of common use were therefore made of wrought iron which was costly. It happened when working in a furnace in his youth the fire bed was torn down for repair and Boyden discovered that part of a cast iron bar which had long been embedded in the hot brick work had become annealed and could be worked upon an anvil. He realized that an unknown process had given part of the bar fibre and softness, and his experiments resulted in the great discovery on Independence Day, 1826.
>
> Boyden describes it thus: 'The improvement consists in mixing rosin, pitch, or tar, with bituminous coal, and applying it as fuel for melting and converting crude or pig iron to malleable castings; the coal is pulverized or broken in pieces of a size suited in the furnace grate, and mixed with rosin, pitch, or tar, in a proportion as the intensive heat is desired, and applied in quantities, diminishing in proportion as the rosin is increased.'"[8]

His malleable iron business grew exponentially in the next decade, and in 1837 he partnered with a Boston firm to create a corporation called the Boyden Malleable Cast Iron & Steel Company. When Boyden sold out his share in the company for $25,000, it was manufacturing more than a thousand different metal products.

Malleable Iron artwork
from Boyden's High Street Foundry

The Franklin Institute in Philadelphia awarded him with an exhibit of buckles, bits, and other malleable iron products, which were said to have been outstanding for their smoothness and beauty.[9]

Over the years Boyden hired dozens of young men as apprentices and trained them to be skilled manufacturers of leather and metal products. The last of his apprentices was a young lad named Levi Broadbent. He described his training under Boyden as follows:

> "Night after night he worked in his shop experimenting with some new invention. Although often hard pressed for money,

mostly due to his own carelessness, for his inventions would have brought him a fortune if he had patented them, he always saw that his men were promptly paid. When I first entered his shop I was so small that I could not reach the bench, and Boyden had a special chair made for me, so that I could climb upon it and work.

The next apprentice in rank to me was Jim Smith, who afterward became one of the supervisors for the Pennsylvania Railroad. Boyden frequently took us boys in his office, and lectured us on little things, especially when we broke any of the set of rules, which were printed and hung in the place."[10]

All over the city manufacturers prospered by capitalizing upon Seth Boyden's inventions. This unkempt but generous man enjoyed wandering through the Newark streets. He frequently visited the offices of his one-time apprentices who were busy making products out of patent leather, malleable iron, steam engines for locomotives, and other Boyden inventions. He helped them fix troublesome machines and waved aside their offers to pay him for his services. He built an excellent telescope, grinding the lenses himself, then donated the finished product to local schoolboys who came by his shop. He provided free assistance to Samuel F. B. Morse, who consulted him about mechanical difficulties he was having with his telegraph.[11]

After the Civil War the Boydens moved to a small farm house in Hilton, NJ, which is now part of the Newark suburb of Maplewood. When he was too old to operate his own foundry, he worked as a factory laborer for $1.50 an hour in order to pay for food and other living expenses. Friends who had profited from his inventions were appalled by his poverty and tried to make a collection for him, but Boyden refused to receive contributions for his personal needs.

During his last years he avidly practiced horticulture and studied botany, intrigued by the possibility of developing a strawberry the size of pineapple—with no loss in flavor. His biographer summarized this experiment as follows:

"He became famous for his improvement in the strawberry,

producing the finest variety known, which is called the Boyden or the Hilton strawberry. Fifteen specimens of one variety weighted 16 ounces and all his varieties were distinguished for their flavor as well as size. . . . Boyden began their cultivation with a large fruited sour berry and a small fruited sweet one. These he hybridized carefully, and then submitted a fine specimen to a 48 hours' winter in a freezing mixture so that he could produce seeds and plants the same season. These new plants he gave generously to all his neighbors."[12]

One of the last people to visit Seth Boyden was Sanford B. Hunt, the editor of the ***Newark Daily Advertiser***. Shortly after Boyden's death in March of 1870 Hunt published this article about his interview at his home in Maplewood:

"When I first knew Seth Boyden he was a very old man. As I entered the gates I saw the traditional Jersey style of house, with wide clapboards painted white, and the usual green shutters made of plank. To the rear, extending down a well-kept garden, were long rows of peculiarly shaped grape-trellises, laden with the young fruit of unknown hybrids. Near them were a host of wonderfully thrifty strawberry plants, and among these stooped a most singular figure of a man who had once been tall, but was now bowed with age, though still strong in appearance.

On this bright summer morning he was bare-footed, bare-headed, and clad in a remarkable suit of fustian, a sort of "overall" in a single garment, fitting closely to his ample person, and tied behind with strings at the mysterious opening where he must have crawled in. . . .

Above this queer costume towered a square-built, massive, leonine head, with thick gray hair, and kindly blue eyes—looking out from beneath shaggy brows; but I noticed most a rough, homely weather-beaten face, singularly devoid of the outlines of care or affliction, but marked and scored by the heavy impress of thought and tireless research. There was not a suggestion of a soured life or a disappointed ambition. The whole expression was one of quiet content, mingled, as I learned to know afterwards, with a humorous wonder that he had accomplished so little of what he thought should be the purpose of a life."[13]

Boyden was an eccentric genius who had a heart for all of God's creation. He had Universalist convictions and believed in the fundamental goodness of all men and all creatures. His entire life was a celebration of love for his fellow man, including not only his family and workers but also those whom others might have considered competitors. Like Moses Combs, he promoted a moral form of capitalism that benefited both entrepreneurs and workers. In so doing, he demonstrated four outstanding personal characteristics that inspired everyone in Newark who knew him.

First, he constantly demonstrated that *labor is worship*. He believed that all work is noble and purposeful. He emphasized that work is not dull labor, but rather that it is producing something that has value in the marketplace. In so doing, he elevated the artisan class to a high level.

Second, his life overflowed with *love for all of creation*. At the unveiling of the Seth Boyden statue in Military Park in 1890, General Theodore Runyon said of Boyden,

> "His experiments and discoveries were not made as a means of gaining wealth. There was nothing sordid in his nature. What he did sprang from the very highest motives, and love of knowledge and the desire to promote the public good. He relinquished to others the benefit of his achievements and his discoveries almost as soon as they were made. . . .
>
> When he made a useful discovery he announced it, and, giving it to the world, set at work to make another. His nature was full of benevolence. He served his Maker by serving his fellow men. It has been well said of him that his anvil was his altar. He was of a kindly nature. He loved man and bird and beast. The little bird whose nest was in the branches of the tree near his house, tamed by him, would take food from his hand and feed it to her young. He taught the fish in his pond to come to him and be fed, and they became so familiar with him that they would not shrink at his touch. Even some of the wilder animals [that] would flee at the approach of others, learned to treat him as their friend."[14]

Third, his life was characterized by *great generosity*. At his funeral service in 1870, the Rev. A. A. Thayer had these comments about Boyden's impact on America and his generosity:

> "As a man and a citizen, his praise was on every lip. He was absolutely without avarice, as he was without wealth.
>
> 'His grand ideas,' wrote another at the time of his death, 'were scarcely perfected before they were applied, frequently with profit, to others. His was a quiet, natural life, without great trouble or sorrow. He was respected by every one that knew him, his kindly nature and genial disposition rendering him a friend to all.' And yet another has said, with equal justice, 'Few men have lived lives of more unobtrusive usefulness, or been more regretfully remembered at death, than he.'" [15]

And fourth, we see his *deep patriotism* in the following editorial that he wrote to the returning soldiers of the Second New Jersey Volunteers, in which one of his sons served during the Civil War:

> "Though your ranks are now thinned, and your comrades are cold as the earth in which they repose and silent as the green sod that covers them, yet their memory is warm in our breast and vocal as a festival, and as enduring as the monument that soars toward Heaven where their spirits rest; and the archives of the nation will glow with their deeds while history has a page. Their honored parents, their wives, their little ones and friends feel the vacancy, but know it is filled with that sacred glory that cannot be purchased with gold. Our country owes them a debt which I trust will not be dishonored."[16]

Seth Boyden built upon the manufacturing foundation developed by Moses Combs and brought jobs and prosperity to thousands of Newarkers. By the time of his death in 1870 Newark was America's sixth leading industrial city.[17] Although it is impossible to calculate the economic impact of Seth Boyden's contributions, it was undoubtedly a major factor in Newark's rise among American manufacturing centers. In addition, he helped create a culture of innovation, much like we find today in California's Silicon Valley. Inventors and entrepreneurs like Thomas Edison and Edward Weston came to Newark during Boyden's lifetime, and in 1875 the United States Patent office issued more patents from Newark than from any other American city.[18]

Boyden was a pioneer in the development of industrial brads, patent leather, malleable iron, daguerrotypes (early photographic plates), locomotive engines, steam machinery, and the Hilton (Boyden) strawberry. In addition his methods of research and development were copied by entrepreneurs in dozens of other industries for which Newark became famous in the late Nineteenth Century.[19]

Seth Boyden Statue

In 1890 the citizens of Newark erected a monument to Seth Boyden in the center of Washington Park, adjacent to the location of his first malleable iron factory. The original marker simply said, "Seth Boyden, Inventor," which was a marvelous understatement of his contribution to Newark and to American manufacturing.

At the dedication ceremony, Miss Grace V. Halsey wrote a beautiful poem to summarize the life and impact of this extraordinary inventor. Listen to the first two verses of this poem:

SETH BOYDEN

by Grace V. Halsey

This carven bronze! In face and form it stands
To honor him, a son of toil so true.
That from his brain, and never-tiring hands
Labor was crowned with dignity anew!
For him dull iron welded firmest bar,
And steam, and gold gave out a secret lore.
The round sunlight beams sent him from afar,
And silver wielded best of molten ore.
He sleeps in peace, upon that hillside fair,
And dear his statue, in our city's square.

With cunning tools he fashioned, wondrous, true,
Earth's many forms; for near to nature's heart
He dwelt, and ceaseless gave, who never knew
How great the learning of his life's low part.
A barefoot boy! He loved the earth's brown breast,
And ever found new beauties in each flower,
Her fruits she yielded to him first, and best
Growth of the sunshine, dews, and quickening shower.
He sleeps in peace, upon that hillside fair,
And dear his statue, in our city's square.[20]

On November 17, 1926, the citizens of Newark gathered again at Washington Park to celebrate Seth Boyden's birthday and to commemorate the 100th anniversary of his discovery of malleable iron. A bronze tablet enumerating all of his major inventions was dedicated at that time, and among those present were Thomas A. Edison, Dr. Edward Weston, Dr. John Cotton Dana from the Newark Public Library, and numerous city officials. On that occasion many memorable statements were made about the life and impact of Seth Boyden, including these remarks by Edison:

> "Seth Boyden was one of America's greatest inventors and one who never received proper credit for his many great and practical inventions. They have been the basis of great industries which have spread over the entire world and give employment to millions of people."[21]

What a great tribute by Edison, who learned much about inventing by following in Boyden's footsteps! We close this chapter with the final verse of Miss Halsey's poem, which is a fitting tribute to all the working men in Newark whose lives were elevated by his life and gifts:

> Seth Boyden! Dear thy bronzed form, and face,
> No grander words ere spake, or writ by pen
> Than these, which unto thy loved name we trace:
> "A working man, who loved his fellow men!"[22]

Part Two

Freedom for the Prisoners

Freedom for the Prisoners:
The Socially and Politically Disinherited

The Founders of Newark purchased land from the Hackensack Indians when they settled along the Passaic in 1666. They set up a closed community based on the English plantation system. As Newark grew into a modern city, old prejudices against Native Americans, African-Americans, and foreign immigrants needed to be addressed. In Part Two we highlight three individuals who dedicated their lives to resolving these issues.

THEODORE FRELINGHUYSEN (1787-1862) was a lawyer who became a staunch defender of the social and politically disinherited. Serving as a Newark lawyer and mayor, he advocated for African-Americans in civil disputes. In his term as U.S. Senator he was also an outspoken critic of Andrew Jackson's campaign to remove the Southern Indian tribes from their native lands.

JOACHIM PRINZ (1902-1988) was a German rabbi who spoke out against Adolf Hitler's rise to power during the Weimar Republic. He immigrated to America in the 1930's and became the leader of Newark's Temple B'nai Abraham. He was a personal friend of Dr. Martin Luther King, Jr., and saw a close parallel between the struggles of German Jews and African-Americans in the United States.

E. ALMA FLAGG (1918-) was the first female African-American to serve as principal of a public school in Newark. She was a courageous fighter for employment opportunities for black educators and also authored three volumes of poetry. She was perhaps proudest of the establishment of the E. Alma Flagg Scholarship Fund and the dedication of the Dr. E. Alma Flagg School.

CHAPTER FOUR

Theodore Frelinghuysen (1787-1862): Christian Statesman

All eyes in the United States Senate were on the young Senator from New Jersey on April 6, 1830. Who was this audacious man who was standing up to challenge President Andrew Jackson and leaders of the Democratic Party on the matter of Native American rights? THEODORE FRELINGHUYSEN cleared his throat and began to speak:

> "God in his Providence planted these tribes on this Western continent, so far as we know, before Great Britain herself had a political existence. I believe, sir, that it is not now seriously denied that the Indians are men, endowed with kindred faculties and powers with ourselves; that they have a place in human sympathy, and are justly entitled to a share in the common bounties of a benignant Providence. . . .
>
> As the tide of our population has rolled on, we have added purchase to purchase. The confiding Indian listened to our professions of friendship, we called him brother, and he believed us. Millions after millions he has yielded to our importunity, until we have acquired more than can be cultivated in centuries—and yet we crave more. We have crowded the tribes upon a few miserable acres of our Southern frontier; it is all that is left to them of their once boundless forests: and still, like the horse-leech, our insatiated cupidity cries, give! give!"[1]

Frelinghuysen's impassioned six-hour oration did not win many votes that day, as was evidenced when both houses of Congress ratified the Indian Removal Act a month later. Andrew Jackson and his party succeeded in expelling the Cherokees, the Choctaws, and other tribes from their homes and forced them to relocate to lands west of the Miss-

The Indian Removal Act of 1830

21st CONGRESS.
1st Session.

S. 102.

IN SENATE OF THE UNITED STATES.

February 22, 1830.

Mr. White, from the Committee on Indian Affairs, reported the following bill; which was read, and passed to a second reading:

A BILL

To provide for an exchange of lands with the Indians residing in any of the States or Territories, and for their removal West of the river Mississippi.

Indian Removal Act docket

issippi River. More than five thousand Indians would later die on the "Trail of Tears" march as they were rounded up and marched west to Oklahoma.[2]

But Frelinghuysen's distinguished colleagues in the U.S. Senate—Daniel Webster, Thomas Hart Benton, and Vice President John Calhoun among others—were impressed by the moral force of his argument as well as by his eloquence. His boldness in speaking out on the key social issues of the day—Indian rights, slavery, tariff reform, currency regulation, veterans' benefits, and the powers of the federal government—resulted in his receiving the title of "Christian Statesman."

Like his role model William Wilberforce in England, Frelinghuysen was frequently attacked by his political opponents and by the popular press for his refusal to be politically correct. During his six-year Senate term he became the champion for Native Americans, African-Americans, and other disenfranchised groups. But why, you may ask, did this young New

Jersey Senator stand up for groups and causes that were politically out of favor? What would drive a man to risk his political career by openly challenging the policies of the President and many prominent Senators?

Young Theodore was convinced that he wanted to become a farmer. At age thirteen he was bored with school in his hometown of Millstone, New Jersey, and wanted to drop out. He shared his desire with his father Frederick, who was open to his interest in pursuing a career in agriculture, as generations of Dutch settlers had done in the Raritan Valley. But his stepmother Ann was dead set against Theodore's plan. She saw the potential for him to become an influential leader, like his father and grandfather had been.

Theodore was named after his grandfather, Theodore Jacobus Frelinghuysen, who had been an outstanding spiritual leader in the Great Awakening in New Jersey in the 1730's. His father Frederick served as a New Jersey delegate to the Continental Congress and rose to the position of major general in Washington's army. According to one account Frederick had fired the shot that killed the Hessian commander, Colonel Rahl, at the historic battle of Trenton in 1776. He was regarded as one of New Jersey's greatest Revolutionary War heroes. Ann Frelinghuysen was determined that her son would get a rigorous classical education and would uphold the family tradition of excellence in leadership.

One day, when Theodore's father was out of town on business, she told him, "You're going to the Basking Ridge Academy to get a classical education." He was "greatly vexed" by her announcement but had no recourse. His father was not available to support him, and so he had no choice but to pack up his bags and enroll in the Academy. Years later he realized that this abrupt change in his plans was a major turning point in his life.

At Basking Ridge he was mentored by Dr. Robert Finley, who had established the Academy in 1795. Finley had been a brilliant student at Princeton under John Witherspoon and was later ordained as a Presbyterian minister. After assuming the role of pastor at the Basking

Ridge Presbyterian Church, he was inspired to set up a classical school that provided excellent training in foreign languages, history, moral philosophy, and theology. Moreover, he had a strong gifting to love and nurture each of his students.

Theodore bonded with Dr. Finley and soon abandoned his plan to become a farmer. He also made strong friendships with his classmates, many of whom became leaders in business and public affairs. He immersed himself in study and thrived under Dr. Finley's mentoring. In a short time Ann Frelinghuysen was proud of her son's academic achievements at the Basking Ridge Academy, although she regretted that he did not give his heart to Christ in that season.[3]

After graduation from the Academy Theodore continued his classical studies at Princeton College, where he achieved high honors and was chosen by his classmates to give the valedictory address in 1804. After completing his studies at Princeton he decided to go into law and became an apprentice to his brother John in Millstone. Then in 1808 he accepted a position at Richard Stockton's law firm in Newark. At that time Stockton had more than twenty years of experience in law and was a leading New Jersey attorney and politician. He had become a U.S. Senator in 1796 when Theodore's father Frederick resigned from politics for family and professional reasons.

Stockton was known as New Jersey's leading Federalist, having a high admiration for the U.S. Constitution and a desire for a strong central government. Theodore thrived in Stockton's firm and became sympathetic to Federalist political views at that time. At age twenty-one he was admitted to the bar and became involved in a wide variety of cultural pursuits in Newark, including the organizing of a debate society for young men. In the following year the War of 1812 broke out, leading Frelinghuysen to volunteer for the army and serve as a military captain over troops from New Jersey.

Theodore worked diligently in Stockton's office but was not well known as an attorney until 1812, when the New Jersey court system asked him to defend a poor black man who was charged with murder.

We don't know the name of this man, but he was described as a "penniless, friendless drifter".[4] The man pleaded innocence of the crime but had no resources to hire his own legal counsel. Knowing that the man was likely to get the hangman's rope, Frelinghuysen agreed to take the case and worked diligently to prepare for the trial. During the trial he appealed to the act of self-defense and to the court's sympathies for the poor man. His presentation of the case was so eloquent and so logically organized that it amazed all who were present in the courtroom, and the jury unanimously decided that the man was innocent of the charges presented against him. One observer noted, "I shall never forget the impression made upon me by this address of Mr. Frelinghuysen. . . . [Its impact] has never left me, and ever since I have regarded him with intense interest, from the feelings which his pathetic eloquence then excited."[5]

Frelinghuysen's reputation as a lawyer quickly grew after the word spread about his successful defense of this poor man. More and more clients asked him to represent them in court, and his practice became quite lucrative. Unlike most attorneys of his day, however, Frelinghuysen only accepted clients if he thought their case was valid; clients who approached him to defend questionable cases were referred to other Newark attorneys.

A colleague once remarked that Frelinghuysen had a remarkable ability to extract fine points of law from cursory readings of legal journals. Time and time again, he saw Frelinghuysen reach for a journal from the library, spend a few minutes reviewing one or two opinions from relevant past cases, and then draft a clear summary of the salient points as they related to the case at hand.

During court proceedings his clear, mellow voice, manly appearance, eloquent and fine flow of language, and acute knowledge of human nature allowed him to become the most popular advocate at the bar in Eastern New Jersey.[6]

His court presentations were so honest, sincere, and persuasive that juries generally agreed with his arguments and voted accordingly. Opposing attorneys sometimes complained that the jury was biased, because they were overly influenced by Frelinghuysen's presentation

Theodore Frelinghuysen

of the case.

By 1817 Frelinghuysen was regarded as a "rising star" in the New Jersey legal establishment. Although only thirty years of age at that time, he was asked to accept an appointment to be the New Jersey Attorney General. This was the first of several political appointments and honors that were conferred upon him without any solicitation on his part. In the next thirty years he served as a U.S. Senator, Mayor of Newark, Chancellor of the University of the City of New York (today New York University), President of Rutgers College, and Vice Presidential running mate for Henry Clay in 1844. He also served as president or officer of numerous charitable institutions during those years. As these and other opportunities were presented to him, he quietly prayed through these requests to see whether God was leading him to accept the office or position at hand. [7]

During his years in Newark he was a founding member of the Second Presbyterian Church, which was located at Washington and James Streets. There he served as an elder and also as superintendent of the Sunday School. Despite his busy and demanding professional schedule, he eagerly listened to the sermons of Dr. Edward Dorr Griffin, who was nationally known as a preacher and revival leader. He gave his profession of faith at the Second Presbyterian Church after his move to Newark in 1808.

Although he had been successively mentored by his stepmother, by Dr. Robert Finley, and by Dr. Griffin prior to his profession of faith, the turning point in his spiritual life was the death of his brother Frederick in November 1820. Frederick had been Theodore's childhood playmate, schoolmate, and closest friend. Both boys were lukewarm to the Gospel as teenagers, but Frederick accepted Christ into his life and renounced his former indifference toward spiritual things shortly before his terminal illness. On his deathbed Frederick gave a strong testimony about the grace of the Savior whom he now served. When Theodore asked him what Christ meant to him in his suffering, Frederick replied, "Oh Theodore, Theodore, I have not language to describe it. The enjoyment of this hour is greater than my whole life." When urged to refrain from speaking in order to preserve his strength, Frederick replied, "Why? I am much happier than if I were asleep, and what I say may also do good hereafter."[8]

Frederick's deathbed testimony had a transformative impact on Theodore's life. According to his nephew, "The impression it made upon Theodore was decided and indelible. It was so pervading as to render him, in the judgment of his friends, almost another man." A close friend added, "From that time down to his last moment on earth, the character of Theodore Frelinghuysen [had] a simplicity and singleness of goodness such as I have never seen in any other human being." Through this experience Frelinghuysen became a new man, filled with the love of Jesus Christ and the power of the Holy Spirit.

In 1828 Frelinghuysen worked vigorously for the re-election of President John Quincy Adams, and after Adams' re-election the New Jersey Legislature appointed him as a U.S. Senator. Although he was not interested in political power or status, he saw this as an opportunity to bring his Christian vision and values to Washington, D.C.

His defense of Native Americans was widely admired by his colleagues in the Senate as well as by the New Jersey legislature. Because of his high moral integrity, winsome personality, and his outstanding oratorical skills, he emerged as the Senate's principal moral leader. He was at his best when he was excited about a speech. On those occasions, a friend remarked,

> "His soul took fire. His logic was red hot. His appeals were irresistible. Before his audience were aware, they found themselves borne away at a master's will, and every thought and feeling absorbed in the rushing flow of the orator's voice. . . . [Words] tripped like nimble servants at his bidding."[9]

But Frelinghuysen's career in the Senate lasted only one term. In 1834 the Whig Party lost control of the Senate, and leading Democrats were upset at Frelinghuysen's strong advocacy of the Bank of the United States, his desire to end mail delivery on Sundays, and other issues. In 1835 the New Jersey Legislature decided to strip away his Senate seat, and so he returned to his private legal practice in Newark that year.

The loss of his Senate seat marked another turning point in his life. At age forty-eight, he now questioned whether he should leave his promising career in law and politics and become a pulpit minister. When the doors closed to his vision to transform Washington, D.C., he wondered whether God was calling him to abandon politics and go into full-time ministry. To answer this question, he sought advice from Dr. Gardiner Spring, who was a prominent New York City clergyman. Like Frelinghuysen, Dr. Spring had been trained as a lawyer but left the legal profession to become a Presbyterian pastor. They talked and exchanged several letters before coming to the following conclusion: Frelinghuysen should continue to serve as a lawyer, a politician, and a public servant rather than as a pastor. One of Spring's letters succinctly summarized the matter:

"Your present influence and standing at the bar and in civil life are against the change. Influence and character are plants of slow growth. . . . I have my doubts whether you can do as much for the cause of the blessed Redeemer in the ministry of reconciliation as you now do in your present and kindred relations. Our Master needs laborers in Church and State. Such is the feeling and such are the institutions of this country that ministers of the Gospel can get very little influence on the state, and therefore, there is the more need for men who are qualified and have the spirit of ministers to retain their political influence."[10]

In 1836 Newark was finally incorporated into a city—170 years after its founding. William Halsey was appointed the first Mayor and served a one-year term. At the next election the Whigs (Republicans) persuaded Frelinghuysen to be their candidate for Mayor, and he was elected as Newark's second Mayor in October of 1836.

His term as Mayor was most challenging. A great fire broke out on Market Street a week before the 1836 election and caused extensive damage to the downtown business district. Then in 1837 a financial crisis overwhelmed Wall Street and led to numerous bank closings. The impact on Newark and other cities was devastating, particularly to manufacturing firms and charitable organizations.

Frelinghuysen always had a heart for the poor and the disabled during his Newark years, and he spent every Saturday afternoon walking around the city to help those in need. As his income rose, he increased his charitable giving to 10% and then eventually to 50% of his income. Now, as Mayor, he reached out to charities such as the American Bible Society, the Sunday School union, and local temperance organizations to raise funds that were lacking after the Financial Panic of 1837. During his two years as Mayor he also added new public schools and championed a new water project that was needed to support Newark's growing population. Although a staunch conservative, his personal integrity and winsome personality allowed him to move the city forward while avoiding charges of being dogmatically conservative or liberal.[11]

After two difficult years as Mayor, Frelinghuysen became weary of politics and the heavy duties of the bar. He had always loved young people and saw the field of education as a high Christian calling. In 1839 he resigned as Mayor of Newark when the University of the City of New York's council unanimously called him to become Chancellor of that institution. The council stated,

> "[Frelinghuysen] was chosen because it was desired to place at the head of the institution a man of character so eminent in consistency of Christian virtues, combined with wide and honorable experience in public career, as to endow the . . . College with a prestige derivable from no other source."[12]

He served as Chancellor for eleven years and saw an increase in the student population as well as improved faculty quality, drawing distinguished educators from the Presbyterian, Episcopalian, and Dutch Reformed denominations among others. The University's Medical College began during Frelinghuysen's administration and was a great source of satisfaction to him and to the community.

In 1844 Henry Clay invited Frelinghuysen to be his Vice Presidential candidate in the Whig Party. Clay was the overwhelming choice of the Whigs that year because he sought to return the party to their ideological roots: well-regulated currency, a limited but efficient government, protection of domestic labor and industry, and opposition to usurpations of power by elected officials. The only real issue at the party convention in Baltimore was whom to select as Clay's running mate. Henry Clay had a reputation of being a very worldly man—one who engaged in heavy drinking and gambling, violent behavior, and taking revenge on his political opponents.

As a gesture of unity Clay agreed to let the convention select his Vice Presidential candidate. After three ballots the delegates chose New Jersey's favorite son to be his running mate. By that time Frelinghuysen was the preeminent Christian leader in American public service, and he was an outspoken evangelical in a country that was largely Protestant. His credentials added credibility and balance to Clay's reputation as a career politician. Commenting on the choice of Frelinghuysen as a Vice Presidential candidate, Daniel Webster said,

> "There is not a man of purer character, of more sober temperament, of more accessible manners, and of more firm, unbending, uncompromising Whig principles than Theodore Frelinghuysen; and not only is he all this, but such is the ease of his manners, such the spotless purity of his life, such the sterling attributes of his character, that he has the regard, the fervent attachment, and the enduring love of all who know him."[13]

But not everyone agreed with Webster's assessment of the Clay-Frelinghuysen ticket. Philanthropist Lewis Tappan remarked,

> "It is cynical for the Whigs to place 'the Christian statesman' on the same ticket as the 'reprobate' Henry Clay."[14]

The 1844 election was extremely close and ultimately saw New York as the swing state that gave the victory to Democratic candidate James Polk and his running mate George Dallas. When all the votes were counted, Clay and Frelinghuysen lost New York state—and the national election—by only 5106 votes. Polk campaigned hard to annex Texas to the United States as a proslavery state, which dragged Clay into a political issue he had tried to avoid. Propagandists also attacked Frelinghuysen because of His commitments to the American Bible Society, to foreign mission societies, and his personal contributions to support black churches in Newark.

After the 1844 election Frelinghuysen remained as Chancellor of the University of the City of New York until the state legislature withdrew most of its financial support for the College. Facing declining physical and emotional health, he resigned from the City College in 1850 and accepted the presidency at Rutgers College in New Brunswick, New Jersey. Returning to his Dutch Reformed roots, Frelinghuysen spent the remainder of his life building up Rutgers' reputation and finances. During that season Frelinghuysen gave numerous speeches to young scholars, urging them to integrate their faith with their professional work. Many Rutgers students at that time went on to gain national prominence in fields such as medicine and mathematics.[15]

Frelinghuysen drew no distinction between the sacred and the secular. He viewed all Christians as being ministers, in whatever sphere of influence they served.

Theodore's legacy as a transformational leader in business, education, and government was a rich one. In his first twenty years he was widely acclaimed as a brilliant and principled attorney. Men commented that it was foolish for him to leave a highly profitable and prestigious career as a lawyer to go into government and later into higher education. But his "moral compass" directed him into positions that served the public interest rather than personal wealth or professional status.

Throughout his adult life he was constantly involved in serving voluntary organizations. Clifford S. Griffin stated that Frelinghuysen was "the greatest hero that benevolent societies ever had."[16] The list of benevolent institutions that he served included the American Bible Society, the American Tract Society, the American Board of Commissioners for Foreign Missions, the American Sunday School Union, the Congressional Temperance Society, and the American Colonization Society. As President of the American Colonization Society, he repeatedly spoke out against slavery and was recognized by abolitionist William Lloyd Garrison as a great friend of African-Americans.

On a personal level Frelinghuysen was a devoted family man and always made his home available to visits by nephews and grand-children. Although he and his wife Charlotte had no children of their own, they adopted his nephew Frederick Theodore Frelinghuysen after his brother's untimely death in 1820. Growing up in his uncle's home in Newark, Frederick studied at Newark Academy and followed his uncle's footsteps by entering the field of law.

During the Civil War Frederick became Attorney General of New Jersey and was later appointed as U.S. Senator by Governor Marcus Ward. He also served as Secretary of State under President Chester A. Arthur (1881-85).

Living in an age of increasing secularism—like Twenty-First Century America—Theodore Frelinghuysen led a life that drew no distinction between the sacred and the secular. He viewed all Christians as being ministers, in whatever sphere of influence they served. His life purpose was to support organizations that would realize as much of the kingdom of God on earth as possible. Taylor Lee, a close friend of Theodore Frelinghuysen, summarized his life as follows,

> "His whole soul was in the pilgrimage to the New Jerusalem. . . . [He] was still but a 'seeker of salvation.' This was ever the form of his thought and the spirit of his language. . . . [He] regarded himself [and other Christians] as a company of earth-weary, heaven-seeking pilgrims, marching hand in hand . . . until at last the heavenly land is reached by all, the weakest as well as the strongest in the band."[17]

CHAPTER FIVE

Joachim Prinz (1902-1988): We Are All Neighbors

The date is August 21, 1963, and we are part of the quarter million people who are assembled at the Lincoln Memorial during the historic March on Washington. After an inspiring opening song by Mahalia Jackson, Newark Rabbi JOACHIM PRINZ stands up to give the first message to a crowd that has gathered for a peaceful demonstration to promote civil rights and economic equality for African-Americans. He begins by describing why the Jewish people are concerned about protecting the civil rights of African-Americans:

> "I speak to you as an American Jew.
>
> As Americans we share the profound concern of millions of people about the shame and disgrace of inequality and injustice which make a mockery of the great American idea.
>
> As Jews we bring to this great demonstration, in which thousands of us proudly participate, a two-fold experience—one of the spirit and one of our history.
>
> In the realm of the spirit, our fathers taught us thousands of years ago that when God created man, he created him as everybody's neighbor. Neighbor is not a geographic term. It is a moral concept.
>
> It means our collective responsibility of man's dignity and integrity."

He continues by stating what he believes is the most pressing problem facing the American people:

> "When I was the rabbi of a Jewish community in Berlin under the Hitler regime, I learned many things. The most important thing that I learned under those tragic circumstances was that

bigotry and hatred are not the most urgent problem. The most urgent, the most disgraceful, the most shameful and the most tragic problem is silence. A great people which had created a great civilization had become a nation of silent onlookers. They remained silent in the face of hate, in the face of brutality and in the face of mass murder.

America must not become a nation of onlookers. America must not remain silent. Not merely black America, but all of America. It must speak up and act, from the President down to the humblest of us, and not for the sake of the Negro, not for the sake of the black community but for the sake of the image, the idea and the aspiration of America itself."[1]

Today the 1963 March on Washington is remembered by Americans as the occasion on which Dr. Martin Luther King, Jr., preached his famous "I Have a Dream" message, which he delivered immediately after Rabbi Prinz's speech. But we should not forgot that there was great

Joachim Prince and Martin Luther King, Jr.
at Temple B'nai Abraham on January 17, 1963

solidarity between the Jews and the African-Americans during the Civil Rights era. As President of the American Jewish Congress from 1958 to 1966, Rabbi Prinz had a long-term friendship with Dr. King, who was the acknowledged spiritual leader of the African-Americans. Both leaders realized that their constituents had faced long-standing discrimination in America, and that advances by one of these minority groups would lead to the advancement of the other group as well.

America must not become a nation of onlookers. America must not remain silent.

Joachim Prinz was the oldest of the three boys born to Joseph and Nina Prinz in Burkhardsdorf, Germany—a small village in Saxony near the Polish border. His father was a prosperous businessman who owned the town's general store. Joseph Prinz was from an Orthodox Jewish background but only observed Jewish customs once or twice a year on holy days. Joachim described his father as a stern authority figure, who rarely showed intimacy or affection for his wife and children.

His mother, on the other hand, was very warm and loving, and always embraced her children with affection. She was not a practicing Jew either, but she had a great respect for God. In his autobiography Joachim wrote,

> "Somehow I knew that I was a Jew, but not because of any Jewish customs that were observed in the house. I remember that we had a Hebrew prayer book, but it was only taken out when there was a thunderstorm. I remember that whenever there was loud thunder and frightening lightning, my mother would take out our prayer book, open it to a certain prayer, put it on the table, and tell me that the prayer on that page would protect our lives. Evidently it did because the house was never struck by lightning."[2]

The first World War broke out in 1914, and Joachim remembers his mother delivering baskets of sandwiches and hot coffee to refresh the soldiers who were stationed at the bridge on the outskirts of town. She did this three times a week for an entire year, which made a deep impression on Joachim about her love and bravery. During that time she became pregnant. In the last weeks of the pregnancy she developed a serious kidney infection, for which there was no medical treatment available. She grew weaker day by day and died shortly after delivering the child. It was a girl, and Joseph named her Dorothea. Years later Joachim described his mother's death as the most important event of his life. He wrote,

> "It became more tragic because of my complete lack of relationship with my father. . . . [M]y relationship to him was nonexistent.[3] "I doubt that I would be the person I am without this great and tragic event."[3]

During those years the Prinz family moved to nearby Oppeln, a city of 50,000 people that had better schools as well as an established Jewish community. There Joachim developed a strong friendship with the local rabbi, Dr. Goldmann, who became a father substitute for him—someone with whom he could discuss all kinds of things. Joachim describes his relationship to the rabbi as follows:

> "My greatest and most important experience in the new town was the relationship with my rabbi. . . . He soon took a liking to me. Several times during the year he would ask me to get up in the morning at five o'clock and come to his house. In front of his house was a horse-drawn carriage loaded with packages. He came down smilingly and said to me: 'Get up there, I need your help.' Then the driver took us to the districts of the town where the poor people lived.
>
> Almost all of these people were Christians, but Dr. Felix Goldmann (that was his name) knew the names of the poorest of the poor. Whenever we stopped in front of a house, he would ask me to place one of the packages in front of it. Then we left. The packages contained food and clothing, and very often his own clothing.

These were unforgettable morning hours, for here was a man who practiced what he preached, and piety suddenly became an act of love. Love, not charity, for the first thing he made me understand was that one does not give charity. Giving was an expression of love for one's neighbor. It did not matter to him whether the neighbor was Jewish or not, a believer or an atheist. He was a human being. After these experiences. . . . I listened attentively to his sermons.

He was extraordinarily eloquent and had done away with the false solemnity and pathos of the Nineteenth-Century preacher. He talked in his normal tone of voice, and often was more forensic than anything else. This had something to do with the fact that he had also studied law. When he wanted to make a point, he did so clearly and unafraid of any kind of criticism, with a great deal of courage and a brave attempt to address himself to the problems of the time."[4]

Joachim was now fifteen years old and became deeply involved in Judaism. His mother's death, and his friendship with Rabbi Goldmann, fueled an intense desire to lead a life that honored his beloved mother in a very deep and meaningful way. To deal with his acute sense of loss, and with his increasing awareness of his Jewish heritage, he decided to attend the daily services that were offered in his synagogue. He wrote,

"There were daily services in our synagogue, which were held in the little chapel. So when my mother died, I decided to attend services every day. On a Monday morning, when the Torah was being read, we noticed we had only nine men. I had not yet celebrated my bar mitzvah and therefore was not counted among the minyan [quorum of ten Jewish men].

The rabbi looked at me and said, 'We have only nine men and you will not be bar mitzvah for a month. But I will follow an old Jewish custom.' He went to the little ark and took out a Torah scroll. He gave it to me to hold and sit with it during the service. It was a little scroll, not too heavy for a young boy,

> with a beautiful velvet mantle adorned with golden letters and symbols. It must have been pretty old.
>
> I was sitting during the service when suddenly my cheek touched the velvet. It was so soft. Suddenly, it reminded me of my mother's warm skin, which I had actually felt whenever, during our birthdays, we visited her when she was still in bed. I actually felt that I was sitting with my mother since the velvet was as soft as her skin. I celebrated some sort of wedding with her, the Torah becoming a symbol of my mother. I was determined to devote my life to her. The Torah and my mother—they had become one. Then and there I determined to become a rabbi."[5]

One day, while visiting the local book store, he came across a book by Theodor Herzl which was titled ***The Jewish State***. This book described the Zionist movement, which advocated the formation of a separate Jewish state. He was particularly struck by the last sentence of the book, which said, "If you will it, it will not be a fairy tale."[6] He found three other people in his community who were Zionists, although secretly because Zionism was largely rejected by the Jewish community. These men told him about a youth movement called the "Blue-Whites," who had their own Zionist flag and who taught that it was beautiful to be Jewish. While his family was absorbed in the daily news about the War, young Joachim became increasingly captivated by the literature and proceedings of the Zionist congresses.

At the beginning of 1918 his father arranged for Joachim to begin an apprenticeship at the largest commercial establishment in Breslau, a city of 500,000 people located an hour from Oppeln by train. While his father had hopes of him becoming a merchant and eventually taking over his family business, Joachim's mind was increasingly absorbed with the Zionist movement. After several months he became bored with his apprenticeship and returned to Oppeln to finish high school. During his last three years of high school he studied Hebrew and rabbinic literature in order to learn more about his Jewish heritage and how the Zionist movement fulfilled many of the prophecies of the Jewish scriptures.

Upon graduating from high school he enrolled at the Jewish Theological Seminary in Breslau, which was the first modern theological seminary in the world and the leading conservative Jewish seminary in Germany. There he studied philosophy and met a woman named Lucie Horowitz, who was the daughter of the most famous professor at the Seminary. They were romantically involved during his years as a student at Breslau, and later at the University of Berlin and the University at Giessen, where he earned his Ph.D. in 1924. The following year he and Lucie were married in Breslau.

That year Joachim and Lucie moved into a small apartment in Berlin, and he took his first position as rabbi at the Friedenstempel ("Temple of Peace"), a large synagogue that had fifteen hundred seats. He quickly established himself as a promising but unconventional rabbi:

> "When I preached my first sermon in the synagogue, the sanctuary was completely filled. I was twenty-three years old, talented and foolish, and people began to flock to me. I was flattered. I decided at that time that I would concentrate on working with the young people. My first gathering with them took place shortly after I arrived, and I decided to take them ice-skating. The community was up in arms. They had never seen a rabbi figure-skating with young people and considered it beneath rabbinical dignity. All my colleagues were in their fifties. Many of them had white beards. I was considered an outsider. On the other hand, many people began to love what I was doing, particularly the young people."[7]

Although rejected by his colleagues—most of whom were anti-Zionist –but extremely popular among the young people, Prinz quickly developed a reputation for being the most articulate Zionist leader in Berlin. He reported that all fifteen hundred seats were taken at every Friday night service, and the doors had to be closed half an hour before the service to avoid overcrowding. On Saturday mornings he presided over an average of three bar mitzvahs and sometimes up to ten in one day. He wrote, "All young people wanted to be with me rather than with the stodgy, solemn, old rabbis who did not quite understand them."[8]

Joachim and Lucie had many friendships with members of their synagogue and thoroughly enjoyed their ministry and social life in Berlin in those years. In 1930 they wanted to start a family. Lucie became pregnant and was scheduled to deliver the baby in January 1931. Two weeks before the baby was due, however, Lucie developed a carbuncle (i.e., a staphylococcus bacterial infection) on her arm. She delivered a baby girl on New Year's Eve, 1930 and "was hilariously happy" at the time. But the delivery exhausted her, and she developed a high fever. Shortly after the baby's birth, she died at twenty-eight years of age on January 14, 1931. Joachim was now a widower with a infant baby, which he named Lucie in remembrance of his wife.

After mourning Lucie's death Joachim courted a young girl named Hilde Goldschmidt, who was eleven years younger than he was. Hilde was a friend of Lucie's and had visited their home almost every day for several months. Hilde had German-Jewish origins which traced back to the Twelfth Century and came from a very proper and successful family. Prinz describes her as "quiet, very pleasant, and very pretty."[9] They were married the next year and had four children of their own. Their marriage lasted for fifty-six years, ending when he died in New Jersey in 1988.

Life became increasingly difficult for German Jews after Adolf Hitler was appointed chancellor of what would become the Third Reich in January 1933. In that year Hitler dissolved the Parliament, adopted the black swastika on a red background as the national flag, and filled the streets with Nazi storm troopers. These troopers wore brown uniforms with a black swastika on their armband, and they were given free reign to arrest or attack anyone they considered to be "anti-Nazi".

Soon Hitler stepped up his anti-Jewish campaign by forbidding Jews to hold jobs, by forcing them to change their names, and by requiring that they have a "J" stamped on their passport to identify that they were Jewish. The impact on the Jewish community was devastating. As Prinz describes, "The Jews were suddenly seized by a collective neurosis of fear and trepidation, and our services at the synagogues became a refuge for our people and a source of consolation and pride."[10]

In 1934 he wrote his most famous book, ***Wir Juden*** ("We Jews"), which sold more than 100,000 copies and became the "bible" for Jews living under the Hitler regime. In this book he summarized Theodor Herzl's arguments which rejected the liberal goal of Jews assimilation into the mainstream European community and advocated the formation of a separate Zionist state in Palestine. He described the wanderings of the Jewish people for more than three thousand years and stated that the Jewish people had "failed our Jewishness" (see Excerpt on next page).

One night he was invited to attend a meeting organized by a group of Protestant pastors. The meeting was highly secretive and was held at midnight, since Hitler had forbidden clergymen to meet with Jews at that time. As they started the meeting, a group of Nazi storm troopers were conducting their midnight exercises outside the church and began chanting anti-Semitic tunes. Pastor Rackwitz, who hosted the meeting, asked Joachim to begin with a prayer for all those who were in attendance. Prinz describes what happened next during this extra-ordinary prayer meeting:

> "I told him it was not in the Jewish tradition to say spontaneous prayers but that I was willing to read something to them. There was a big, well-worn Bible in front of me and I decided to open it at random. . . . Miraculously, the Bible fell open at the 23rd Psalm. I began to read, 'The Lord is my shepherd, I shall not want.' As I read, the storm troopers began to sing a new song. It was the famous anti-Semitic anthem praising the night of the long knives when all the Jews would be murdered. The knife had become a symbol of death to the Jews and the song spoke glowingly about the glorious moment of the blade and knife plunging into the heart of a Jew and the blood flowing from the body as though in an act of spiritual redemption.
>
> I stopped for a moment and then I began to read until I came to the sentence: 'Thou prepares a table before me in the presence of mine enemies.' I stopped there. I looked around and into the faces of the ministers. Then they began to understand, as I did, that this was no mere piece of poetry written some two thousand years ago but a very relevant piece to be read. 'In the presence of mine enemies, it says here, but

QUOTES FROM WE JEWS ("WIR JUDEN")

WE JEWS have been wandering in the world for more than three thousand years. Tall, wild Bedouins . . . tanned and strong . . . fought against desert and danger. Heroes struggled with giants. Kings ruled over princes and peoples. . . . The upward path of every nation has wound over the strong bridges of the Ten Commandments.

We have lost our own land. The vultures of trouble and disaster circled over the holy city of Jerusalem. Yet our journey from the homeland was proud and strong; within us there still lived the manly self-sufficiency of our Bedouin ancestors. . . .

Our life was a failure when we failed our Jewishness. Out of that failure arose the hatred of Jews against their own people. Others may have stopped hating us, but we still hated ourselves. Our ancient, sacred, strong tree bent low and struck its own far-spread roots as if wholly extinct.

WE JEWS, Bedouins, heroes, kings, prophets, poets of old, forgot ourselves, and our beliefs were crushed through this oblivion and became the great, aching question of the nations. Our warm, often yearning and tragic love for the nations did not soothe the wound.

WE JEWS seek our feeling.[11]

> they are not mine—not the enemies of the Jews, but the enemies of everyone.'
>
> 'And the table is prepared not only for me and my people; I can assure you that it is also prepared for you and yours. As we will go down during the many nights of the long knives, so will you, and as we perish, so will Christianity, for the meaning of our meeting is to understand this: that we are all in one boat. Unless you understand this you understand nothing and you don't deserve the title of a minister of Christ, who, after all, were he alive today, would be among the victims of my people.' I finished the reading of the Psalm....
>
> This was my first meeting with Christians. It was also my last. After that night in July 1933 not a single minister dared call me or, for that matter, any other Jew. The Christian church had succumbed."[12]

In the winter of 1937 a confidant who was a member of the Nazi party warned Prinz that he and Hilde needed to leave Germany. The Nazis had a thick file about him but were particularly incensed by a speech he gave in Leipzig, in which he stated that Jesus of Nazareth was an important figure in Jewish history.[13] That statement, of course, was in direct contradiction to the Nazi propaganda that the Jews were an inferior race.

By this time Prinz had befriended Dr. Stephen Wise, who was an eminent Jewish leader in America. Wise encouraged him to move to America and become a lecturer for the United Palestine Appeal. Prinz accepted his offer to give lectures about Nazism and the plight of the Jews living in Germany.

In July of 1937 Joachim and Hilde emigrated to the United States and rented a small house in Great Neck, New York. Stephen Wise arranged for Joachim to give a nationwide address through a well-known New York radio station, and he titled his address, "A Sermon to My Fellow Jews in Nazi Germany." The address was well regarded, and in the next few weeks he received more than five hundred invitations to lecture not only to Jewish audiences but also to American universities and churches. He spent the next two years following up on these invitations and spoke in forty U.S. states during that time.

As he traveled and lectured across America, Prinz was appalled at the fragmentation of American religious life and the isolationism of the American people. He was shocked that Americans had such a poor understanding of the situation in Europe and the dangers it posed to the free world. He could not understand why most Americans embraced democracy rather than socialism, and why they were so indifferent to the blatant discrimination against African-Americans.

At the end of this two-year period most of his speaking contracts ended, leaving him in a desperate financial situation. He went back to Rabbi Stephen Wise for help, stating that he was now willing to accept a position as rabbi at a local congregation if such a position became available.

Temple B'nai Abraham in Newark was the second oldest synagogue in New Jersey. Founded in 1853 by a group of Polish immigrants, the congregation originally met in the Bank Street home of merchant Abraham Newman. By the end of the Nineteenth Century Newark's Jewish population had grown from two hundred to several thousand as immigrants from many European countries flocked to the Greater New York region. By 1897 B'nai Abraham needed a larger synagogue, and so they constructed a 900-seat sanctuary on the corner of High Street (now Dr. Martin Luther King, Jr., Boulevard) and 13th Avenue. Under the leadership of Rabbi Julius Silberfield, B'nai Abraham became "one of the outstanding, one of the most progressive, one of the most forward-looking Jewish congregations in this country."[14]

Under Rabbi Silberfield's direction the congregation outgrew the High Street sanctuary by 1924 and moved into an immense "uptown" structure at Clinton Avenue and South 10th Street. At that time it was the largest synagogue building in New Jersey, providing a 2000-seat sanctuary, a dozen classrooms, a social center wing, a gym, and a swimming pool.

The 1929 stock market crash and the Great Depression that followed wiped out the fortunes of many major contributors who had unpaid pledges. The congregation's finances plunged over the next few years as many congregants lost their jobs and their homes. By the late 1930's B'nai

Abraham had a large operating deficit, and congregational leaders approached Rabbi Stephen Wise for advice. Dr. Wise told them pointedly,

> "There are only two people can save your congregation. I could do it and Dr. Prinz could do it. Unfortunately, I am not able to come since I have a congregation, but Dr. Prinz is free and I hope he will accept your invitation."[15]

After a short interview process the congregation extended an offer to him for a one-year contract with a $6,000 salary, which was not a large amount but was comparable to what other leading congregations paid at that time. Prinz accepted their offer, on the conditions that he would have no administrative responsibilities and that he would be the acknowledged leader of the congregation in every respect. Joachim and Hilde purchased a home in the Clinton Hill neighborhood near the synagogue that year and began their 38-year ministry at B'nai Abraham in 1939.

At the beginning of his Newark ministry Prinz instructed his congregation about the difference between a *Jewish organization* and a *Jewish congregation*:

> "I distinguished very clearly between a Jewish organization and a Jewish congregation. Joining a Jewish organization was a rather mechanical act. Membership in a Jewish congregation, however, was a declaration of Jewish and human commitment. This concept included every possible area of human interest and concern. It was the very opposite of a restricted ghettoized Judaism that was only involved with parochial Jewish problems and concerns.
>
> I never had any respect for what was called the sanctity of the pulpit. I excluded no topic—political, economic, literary, or anything else—from those to be discussed. The pulpit was a forum; the synagogue was not a church but a house of assembly for the Jewish people. I believed that the majority of the people were sick and tired of the cursed solemnity of both the sermons and the services. I rejected these notions and placed squarely before my people my own concept of an all-embracing, universal Judiasm that acknowledged the existence of the Jewish people as well as the relevance of the Jewish faith.[16]

Temple B'nai Abraham building at
620 Clinton Avenue (1924-1973)

It did not take long for the congregation to understand what Prinz meant by this distinction. When Charles Lindbergh began making anti-Semitic statements and established commercial relationships with Hitler, Temple B'nai Abraham was the only large synagogue in Newark that spoke out against supporting Nazi Germany. [17] At the same time he decried the arrogant attitude toward blacks that many Americans—including prominent Jews—held at that time. He began to see that Jewish Americans and African-Americans had much in common, and that the two groups needed to work together to achieve racial and ethnic justice in America. He was grateful that the leaders of B'nai Abraham understood and accepted their moral responsibilities for leadership in Newark and in the global community:

> "It helped me greatly that I had come to a congregation whose leadership understood that congregations, Jewish or Christian, could not afford to live on an island of their own parochial solemnity; but had to be active in building the community at large as well as the Jewish community."[18]

At the end of World War II Prinz agreed to serve as the head of the United Jewish Appeal of Essex County. In one year he increased the Appeal's budget from $200,000 to $1,000,000, which was an astounding amount of money for a Newark charitable organization. Through the Appeal and other initiatives he became recognized as a spiritual leader for the entire Newark Jewish community.

In 1958 he expanded his horizon by becoming President of the American Jewish Congress, a position which he held until 1966. During these years he became a close friend of Dr. Martin Luther King, Jr., and he invited Dr. King to speak at B'nai Abraham in January of 1963. At Dr. King's invitation, Prinz became a Founding Member of the March on Washington leadership team, which was planning the arrangements for this historical civil rights event in August of that year.

During the Civil Rights era thousands of Jewish and non-Jewish people left Newark and moved to the suburbs, and the B'nai Abraham congregation faced a difficult dilemma: Should they remain in Newark or relocate to the suburbs? By 1973 it was clear that there were very few B'nai Abraham congregants left in Newark, and so the congregation decided to build a new sanctuary in nearby Livingston. Rabbi Prinz had mixed feelings about this, as he stated in his final sermon at the Newark synagogue:

> "I conceived, as I do now and will until I die, of a Judaism and its contribution, its total dreams and visions, as part of the great dreams and visions of mankind. Therefore we remained in and were part of this town when this city, this community, went down. This is why I feel complete responsibility, and this may in fact be an irresponsibility, for our being the last large Jewish congregation to leave the city of Newark. . . . We do this with a clear understanding that we are not fleeing from it or trying to escape from it, but will continue to feel part of its problems, its nightmares, of its present, of its future, of everything that will remain part of this town."[19]

As the congregation prepared to move out of Newark, Rabbi Prinz knew that neither the Jewish people nor the African-Americans in Newark had completed the journey to a lasting freedom. He knew that although the Jewish people were better off than the African-Americans, both groups had a continuing obligation to help advance social justice for all in employment, housing, and other areas. He knew that the American ideal of equal opportunity for all would not become a reality for the Jewish people as long as African-Americans remained in bondage.

In 2013 Rachel Nierenberg Pasternak and Rachel Eskin Fisher of R-Squared Productions released the documentary film, "I Shall Not Be Silent," which chronicled the life of Rabbi Joachim Prinz.[20] The movie emphasized that to his dying day he remained a "rebellious rabbi" who repeatedly risked his life by speaking out against social injustices. In his view all people are our neighbors, and we cannot lead lives based on our narrow self interests. Dr. Prinz summarized this concept very eloquently in his ***High Holiday Prayer Book***:

> "We do not live alone. Nobody has a right to live in accordance with his selfish interests. We are part of the community of men, each of them, of whatever race and creed, or whatever station in life, created equal in the image of God."[21]

CHAPTER SIX

E. Alma Flagg (1918 -): Newark's First Lady of Education

Hannibal and Caroline Williams, along with millions of other black families, moved north during the Great Migration of the 1920's and 1930's to seek better economic and social opportunities.[1] Although blacks won important rights of freedom and voting in the Nineteenth Century, the continuing violence and discrimination in the southern states led them to believe that the North was the earthly "Zion" they were seeking.[2]

In view of these harsh realities, Hannibal and Caroline left their home in Virginia and moved their family to Pennsylvania in 1921 and then to Newark five years later. In 1926 they purchased a property at 71 East Kinney Street and established a sign and house painting business at that location.[3]

Although their two youngest sons died during their teenage years, their other three children grew up to become successful professionals. Their oldest daughter, Thelma Williams Gillis, became chief clerk of the Newark Municipal Court. Hannibal Allen Williams, their second child, earned a doctorate of ministry degree and became the founder and pastor of the New Liberation Presbyterian Church in San Francisco and later a moderator the Synod of the Pacific.

Their third child, ELOISE ALMA WILLIAMS, entered the field of education and became the first black principal to be appointed in the Newark public school system in 100 years. In this chapter we review the inspiring story of her achievements in education, literature, and community service. Despite her humble family beginnings, during the latter half of the Twentieth Century Alma made such important contributions to public education that she came to be known as "Newark's First Lady of Education."[4]

As a youth Alma was very bright and inquisitive and was promoted two grades during the years she attended Newark's Chestnut Street School. One of her proudest memories was receiving an award for good grades from her seventh-grade teacher. "Miss Gerber," she said, "encouraged me," giving her a book to acknowledge her outstanding achievements. She later said that this book, ***Nellie's Silver Mine***, became one of her fondest childhood treasures.[5]

But new hardships came to her family the following year, when her father unexpectedly died from asthma and heart problems. At that time Alma was only twelve years old and was about to graduate from eighth grade at the Oliver Street School. Not surprisingly, Hannibal's death threw the family into a crisis.

Caroline Williams was suddenly responsible for providing for her five children. She took jobs as a domestic worker to support the family, but the money she earned was barely sufficient to meet the family's financial needs. She was under great pressure to let others raise her children but was determined that this would not happen. By faith and the grace of God, the family stayed together and was able to make ends meet. During that season they received great encouragement from their pastor and congregants at the First Mount Zion Baptist Church at 186 Thomas Street. Reflecting back on those difficult years, Alma said,

> "Some people wanted to split us up, but Mother never gave that a second thought. She worked as hard as she could as a domestic to keep all five of us [children] together. Somehow we got by, but it wasn't easy."[6]

The Williams family had few personal possessions but always stuck together, according to her friend, Joan Henderson:

> "Family was and always will be important to Alma. She had

Dr. E. Alma Flagg

> very little as a child, very few material things, but the family was very close."[7]

The Williams family later moved to Brunswick Street in Newark's East Ward, where they lived while Alma attended East Side High School. She participated in track and field events at East Side and frequently wrote poems for the school newspaper. She also developed a strong interest in reading and spent many hours studying at the Newark Public Library on Washington Street. In high school she was a member of the National Honor Society and was active in dramatics and chorus.[8]

In 1935 she graduated from East Side and enrolled as a student at Essex County Junior College. She attended classes at the school's campus at 185 Broadway and was accepted as a transfer student at Newark State College two years later. She was one of only four black students in the Newark State Class of 1940 and experienced blatant hostility from her instructors as well as from other students. In a 2001 interview with Barbara Kukla she reflected on the racism she encountered in college:

> "When I did my first practice teaching as a junior, there were just three of us [black students]. In my senior year, a mature lady joined us, so there were four. There were few outright [discriminatory] acts, but there was always something there. . . . I also can remember the dean asking me how I accounted for my intelligence. When our grades were posted in the hallways, we were all listed as 'Colored'."[9]

Alma and her other black classmates generally ignored these insults, since there was no acceptable response. She said, "You couldn't go around fighting all the time, so whatever was said, was said and done with."[10] Racism also affected the career opportunities open to black teachers. Alma and her fellow black students were encouraged to do their practice teaching at Charlton Street School in Newark, where most of the students were black. Schools in white neighborhoods were off-limits to black teachers at that time.

In May of 1864 James M. Baxter, Jr., graduated with honors from the Institute for Colored Youth in Philadelphia. That fall he accepted a teaching position at the State Street Public School in Newark. Just two months later the Newark School Board promoted him to principal, although he was only nineteen years old. He proceeded to restructure the school's curriculum and upgraded the condition of the school building. Over the next forty-five years Baxter "developed the school, and it became a very large one, ranking with the best in that city . . . he kept pace with all the modern systems of teaching and was rated by the educational authorities as a teacher of rare value."[11]

After the Civil War ended Baxter opened up a night school so that older

African-American workers could also receive a primary school education. At that time Newark students were separated by race, religion, and ability. There were separate schools for white boys and white girls, but the State Street School admitted black children of both genders in order to save money. Furthermore, Newark's only high school accepted only white children from Protestant families. Black students were excluded, as were Germans, if they were from Catholic backgrounds.[12]

In 1871 the Newark superintendent of schools urged the Board to open up high school admissions to all students, noting that it would prepare Newark for "the time that is surely coming" when public school education would be colorblind.[13] But it was Baxter's impassioned pleas for justice that eventually opened up Newark's High School to blacks. In 1872 one of his students, Irene Pataquam Mulford, became the first African-American to enroll at the school.

Baxter served the Newark Public Schools with distinction and was considered the "Dean of Newark School Principals" when he retired from service as an educator. When he died in 1909, the New York ***Times*** carried a lengthy obituary concerning his life and accomplishments in Newark. An excerpt from this obituary is included on the next page.

James Baxter was the only black principal to be appointed by the Newark Board of Education during the Nineteenth Century. It would be 100 years before another black educator was chosen to serve as principal in the Newark public school system.

Alma wanted to find a teaching position in Newark when she graduated from Newark State College, but the Newark school system did not conduct a teacher's examination in 1940. She heard, however, that the Washington, D.C., school system had teaching opportunities and offered the teacher's exam that year. She successfully took the exam in Washington and was offered her first teaching position in that city. But her heart was set on returning to Newark, and so she continued to look for Newark teaching opportunities while she pursued a masters

J. M. Baxter Was Dean of Newark School Principals—Served 45 Years

James M. Baxter, who had the distinction of being the only colored Principal of a public school in Newark and was the Dean of the Newark staff of Principals upon his retirement, died suddenly of heart disease at his home in that city yesterday. Mr. Baxter had completed forty-five years' service in the Newark educational system, and to him was given much credit for the opening of schools for colored children in Newark.

His death recalls a lively contest as to the right of a colored child to enter High School upon graduating from Grammar School. The controversy ended with a decision in favor of the negro race after an earnest plea from the colored Principal. He insisted that colored Grammar graduates have the same privilege of entering the Newark High School as others who had met the requirements of the Grammar grades, and the first negro pupil to be so admitted was graduated under Mr. Baxter. His last official position was as Principal of the Market Street School in Newark, an institution exclusively for colored children.[14]

—The New York ***Times***, December 29, 1909

degree in education from Montclair State College.

During that time she met her future husband, Thomas Flagg, at the St. James AME Church (then located at Lafayette and Jefferson in the Ironbound), where they both worshipped. Thomas had been an honors student and track star at Barringer High School in Newark and later at Montclair State, where he earned a masters degree in chemistry. They were married in June 1942 at the First Mount Zion Baptist Church in Newark.[15]

Thomas was drafted into the army shortly after their marriage and was assigned to duty in Liverpool, England. His unit crossed the English Channel on D-Day on June 6, 1944. He was later assigned to serve in the Medical Corps in France until the end of World War II.

While Thomas was assigned to overseas duty in Europe, Alma passed the local teacher's exam and was appointed to her first teaching position in Newark. She was assigned to teach third grade at the Eighteenth Avenue School in the fall of 1943 and was tenured three years later. Eleanor Crutchfield, one of her first students, had the following memories of Alma's early years as a teacher at that school:

> "To this day, I marvel at Dr. Flagg's ability to remember every detail from the time I was in third grade. Not only can she remember the names of students in my class, including some I've long forgotten; she can remember exactly where they sat in the classroom. These are things that happened in 1944!"[16]

In 1949 the Flaggs had their first child, Thomas Lyle Flagg. At that time Alma wanted to teach at a higher grade level, but all of the teachers in the upper grades at Elizabeth Avenue were men. In 1952 she requested a transfer and was assigned to teach seventh grade at McKinley School, which was located in a white neighborhood. That year she experienced blatant bigotry at McKinley:

> "At my arrival, I had several unpleasant experiences. . . . [Black students at McKinley] had a difficult time. Most of them lived across the railroad bridge. Sometimes the white students would block the bridge so they couldn't get across to come to school."[17]

The student population at McKinley was declining at that time, and Alma was one of three teachers whose contracts were not renewed at the end of the year. When she became pregnant with her second child, Luisa, she requested time off for maternity leave.

The following year she was transferred to the Peshine Avenue School, where she taught third graders in a predominantly white and Jewish neighborhood. She was the first black teacher at McKinley as well as at Peshine Avenue, so it was not surprising that she faced discrimination in both of these European neighborhoods. When the Flaggs purchased an attractive, four-bedroom home at 44 Stengel Avenue in the South Ward, they were not welcomed by most of their white neighbors:

> "The neighbors were mostly Jewish, and we were not. Some neighbors were cordial, but no one embraced us with open arms."[18]

After moving into their new home on Stengel Avenue, the Flaggs joined the Elizabeth Avenue-Weequahic Presbyterian Church and were active members in the church for more than four decades. During that time Alma served as an ordained elder, choir member, Sunday school teacher, guidance chairman, and clerk of session at the Elizabeth Avenue church.

Their son Thomas attended Maple School and then Weequahic High School. After graduating from high school he earned bachelors, masters, and doctoral degrees in chemistry from the University of Michigan. Thomas went on to become a professor of chemistry at Adrian College in Michigan. In a 2001 telephone interview with Barbara Kukla, He fondly recalled his mother's strong dedication to her family and community:

> "My mother's always been reluctant about asking other people for help. She likes to do things herself. When my grandmother and father were both sick and died within a year of each other, my mother knocked herself out caring for them. Even when there was nothing more that she could do, she felt there was.[19]

Daughter Luisa had similar memories of her mother's determination:

> "Her sense of drive and determination comes from her mother, who had little education yet raised five children on her own. If you understand that, you understand the source of my mother's dedication to her family and to her community."[20]

After graduating from high school Luisa received an undergraduate degree from Bryn Mawr College in Pennsylvania and became a Spanish teacher at the Cherry Hill High School in south Jersey.[21]

In 1955 Alma received her doctorate from the Teachers College at Columbia University. She was now one of the most highly educated teachers in the Newark public school system but felt that her skills were underutilized in her current position. For years she had wanted to get into guidance counseling but was blocked for advancement due to racial politics in the Newark school system. In an interview with Barbara Kukla she stated,

> "There I was with a doctorate, teaching third grade."[22]

She felt it was time for advancement and expressed her desire to get into remedial reading. This time the School Board agreed with her and transferred her—without a promotion—to teach remedial reading at two schools, South Tenth Street and South Seventeenth Street. She held this position from 1957 to 1963.

In 1959 several black teachers applied for an opening for vice principal, but all of them failed the oral examination. When it became apparent that none of the black applicants ever scored high enough on the oral exam to win an appointment, Flagg and several of her black colleagues filed a discrimination suit against the Newark Board of Education. They appealed to the State Educational Commissioner, who dragged out the case for years and eventually sided with the school administration.

In September 1962, however, a black educator, Carrie Epps Powell, was appointed vice principal at Hawthorne Avenue School, and Flagg was appointed vice principal at Garfield School the following March. Then in September 1963 Gladys Berry Francis was also appointed vice principal at South Eighth Street School. Within one year the Newark Board of Education had appointed three black vice principals.[23]

One hundred years after James Baxter's promotion to principal during the Civil War, Dr. Flagg broke through to become Newark's second African-American principal.

Then in August 1964 Alma Flagg was promoted to principal of the Hawkins School, becoming the first black woman to hold that title in Newark's history. At the same time she became the first African-American principal of an integrated school. ***The New Jersey Herald News,*** a black weekly publication, had this to say about her promotion to principal:

> "Down through the years, Newarkers have been clamoring for a Negro principal, they same as they did for a number of years to secure a Negro judge in this community. We recall the terrific struggle that Newark teachers had trying to become vice principals. They were most successful and impressive on the written examination, but for some strange reason, their minds went blank when taking the oral examination. It is shocking to think that qualified Negroes would be held back in our Newark school system. We are happy at last to see our school officials come of age and carry out the functions of their office without fear or prejudice. Our heartfelt congratulations go to Alma Flagg for achieving this goal."[24]

News of her appointment energized Newark's black community, and this was the beginning of several promotions of black educators into the administrative ranks. A hundred years after James Baxter's promotion to principal during the Civil War, Dr. Flagg had broken through to be-

Newark is Home

by Dr. E. Alma Flagg

What is a city and what is a home?
What makes each more than a place?
Skyscrapers stretching to dizzying heights?
Vehicles bent on a race?
Elegant Hepplewhite gracing a room?
Curtains resplendent in lace?

Shall we consider what makes each a fact?
Can we reach that which is real?
There is no building that fulfills our quest,
No car that shows what we feel,
Furniture neither that answers our need,
Fabric nor colors that heal.

Cities are made by people who live
Working and playing in turn,
Those who together in programs unite,
Focused on common concern:
Beauty, good health, and a bountiful life,
Peace and goodwill here to learn.

Homes are created by people who love;
Caring pervades every space;
Helping or listening or just being there
Sharing the family place;
Summoning memories out of the past
Memories time can't erase.

Newark is my city, and in it my home;
Here I developed through the years,
Seeing dear loved ones move out of this life,
Saying farewell through my tears,
Seeing newcomers arrive on the scene,
Banishing weakness and fears.

City, O city, I call you my own—
Blood, sweat, and tears make it true!
Friendships and good times are part of the whole,
With troubles and struggles no few.
People and purposes always in flux
Here, Newark, I'm staying with you.[25]

come Newark's second African-American principal. As predicted by the Superintendent of Schools in 1864, "the time that is surely coming" had arrived, due to the determination of Alma Flagg and her black colleagues who had endured years of racial discrimination.

During the next two decades Alma Flagg continued to push for improved educational opportunities for Newark students and minority educators. She was responsible for the inclusion of Aerospace Education in the curriculum and several other innovations in teaching. Over the years she assumed several other roles, including citywide administrator of summer reading programs, assistant superintendent of schools, and director of curriculum services.

She also found time to write poetry and was acclaimed as "Poet of the Year" by Las Amigas for her poems about Dr. Martin Luther King; Robert F. Kennedy; Newark's 300th Anniversary (in 1966); and Grace Baxter Fenderson, who followed in the footsteps of her father, James M. Baxter, Jr., as an outstanding educator in Newark for forty-two years.[26] One of her most touching poems, "Newark is Home," is printed on the previous page.

Most of all, however, Dr. E. Alma Flagg will be remembered as a role model who gave hope and encouragement to others. Her long-time colleague Geraldine Sims concisely summarized her leadership qualities in the following statement:

> "Alma gave everything she had to broaden opportunities for the rest of us. The woman was powerful, even though she was quiet. She was like a quiet storm. Frankly, many of us were awed by her. She had vision. And she was determined to keep going, no matter what. You had to be twice as good as anyone else to get anywhere, and Alma knew that."[27]

Charles Smith, a Newark educator and arts advocate, fondly recalls

Dr. Flagg's impact on his life and career aspirations:

> "My earliest reflections on Dr. E. Alma Flagg focus mainly on when I was her 3rd grade student at Peshine Avenue School in the Weequahic (South Ward) section of Newark in the mid-1950's. I had been an "average" C student until I entered her class, due mostly to a lack of motivation after my parents separated.
>
> Immediately, I sensed there was something special about this African-American woman who was my teacher. Not only did she appear attractive and smartly dressed every day, she greeted us every morning with a smile, perhaps a poem or a reading, and set us right to work with a fluid, disciplined approach to getting things done in the classroom. The tone of her voice could be both soothing and firm at the same time. Often, just a look from her was enough to stop any student misbehavior or inattentiveness. When I needed help, she took time to assist me personally, and sent notes home to say I was improving.
>
> That year, my grades improved from C's to B's and A's, and I gained a sense of accomplishment that boosted my self-esteem greatly. She instilled in me the thought that I could achieve whatever I set my mind and will to do. I have always held her memory dear as I succeeded to earn an undergraduate degree from Harvard University years later."[28]

Nathaniel Potts, a former principal at West Side High School, describes how she served others who sought to advance to the ranks of school administrator:

> "Dr. Flagg was a mentor to many of us. A group of us who wanted to become administrators used to stop by her house to talk about the principles of administration. The group included Bert Berry, who became principal at Thirteenth Av-Avenue School; Howard Caesar, who also became an assistant principal; the late William Brown, principal at Bergen Street School (William H. Brown Academy), who also be-

> came an assistant superintendent; and Ernie Thompson, principal at Martin Luther King and Burnet Street schools."[29]

After her retirement the Newark School System honored Dr. Flagg by naming a new elementary school after her. Today the Dr. E. Alma Flagg School on North Third Street is a living testimony to Dr. Flagg and the countless lives she touched as a teacher, administrator, and community worker. This was the first Newark public school to be named for a living educator.

We close with a poem that was written to honor Dr. Flagg for her many achievements:

Tribute to Dr. E. Alma Flagg

by Adamu Shaibu Braimah

Newark's finest woman of substance
Born with poise, dignity and grace
Educated at Chestnut, Oliver & East Side high
Discriminated against but persevered
You inspire both young and old.

Newark educator with intelligence
Departed to Washington, D.C for opportunity
Perfected her skills despite all odds
Taught all children and lessons with devotion
You inspire both young and old.

Newark teacher extraordinaire
Promoted to vice-principal
Celebrated as first Black principal
Elevated to Assistant Superintendent
You inspire both young and old.[30]

Part Three

Recovery of Sight for the Blind

Recovery of Sight for the Blind:

The Physically Disinherited

During the Revolutionary War there were no medical schools and very few trained doctors and nurses in America. Most people were born, lived, and died in their own homes, and epidemics were rampant. The Civil War created a health care crisis which led to the formation of Newark's first hospitals and advances in the training of health care professionals.

EDGAR HOLDEN (1838-1909) was a practicing physician at the Ward Hospital during the Civil War. He was a leading authority on the use of sphygmomanometers to measure blood pressure and conducted important research studies that led to a 50% reduction in Newark's mortality rate by 1920.

EARNEST MAE McCARROLL (1898-1990) was the first African-American physician to be hired by Newark's City Hospital. Her ceaseless efforts to break the racial barrier in health care opened the way for other African-Americans to serve in Newark hospitals and improved access to health care facilities in the city.

CLARA MAASS (1876-1901) was a staff nurse at the Newark German Lutheran Hospital who was appalled by the death toll from yellow fever and other infectious diseases. After she gave her life as a subject for an unsuccessful yellow fever study, the German Lutheran hospital was eventually renamed as the Clara Maass Medical Center in honor of her bravery and service to the sick and the dying.

CHAPTER SEVEN

Edgar Holden (1838-1909): Public Health Advocate

During the Nineteenth Century communicable diseases were major causes of death in Newark and other American cities, and the field of public health was in its infancy. Dr. EDGAR HOLDEN was a nationally recognized medical practitioner and pioneer in epidemiology who provided practical recommendations to improve public health practices and dramatically reduce Newark's death rate from preventable diseases.

In his 1878 annual address to the city, Newark Mayor Henry J. Yates advocated that homeowners run sewer pipes to the roof of their houses as a means to reduce the city's high mortality rates from cholera, diphtheria, scarlet fever, and other epidemic diseases. He was convinced that improperly constructed sewers and poor drainage leaked sewer gas into private homes and were responsible for much of the disease that was prevalent in Newark.[1] Mayor Yates's comments represented the popular view that sewers were dangerous to public health. The disease processes that actually produced high mortality rates in Newark and other major cities around the world, however, would not be discovered until many years later.

Drainage was not a significant problem in Newark's early days, because the topography of the city provides excellent runoff. From the Orange Mountains on the west, a gentling sloping plain extends to the Passaic River on the east and readily absorbs rain water into several streams and ditches. Most of the year these natural conduits provide adequate drainage to remove waste products from homes and small businesses.

As the city's population and manufacturing base increased, however, private privies and cesspools became increasingly inadequate for waste removal, particularly during times of drought. In 1857 the city authorized the construction of sewers after a petition was raised by a majority of property owners along the proposed route.[2]

The development of public sewers was slow, however, for three reasons. The first problem was that sewer construction was very expensive. Large sums of money needed to be collected to build sewer lines, and the costs were prohibitive in many neighborhoods. Secondly, the first sewers were poorly built. The earliest sewers were made of wood, brick, stone, or other porous materials, which tended to leak the contents into the soil after a few years. For this reason some sanitarians opposed sewers, referring to them as "elongated cesspools."[3]

The third reason for the slow adoption of sewer systems in Newark and other large cities was the belief that sewer gas produced atmospheric poisoning, which was viewed as a major contributor to disease. In the middle of the Nineteenth Century many people in the medical community believed that diseases were spread when noxious gases were released by the fermentation of organic matter in stagnant pools and accumulations of garbage. This view was referred to as the "miasmic theory," which purported to explain why congested urban areas frequently had high rates of disease and mortality. To the extent that sewers increased the concentration of sewer gas, the expansion of sewer systems was seen as posing a danger to public health. The miasmic theory was widely held by the medical community until discoveries by Louis Pasteur, Joseph Lister, and Robert Koch provided convincing scientific evidence for the "germ theory of disease" in the late 1800's.[4]

According to 1890 U.S. Census data Newark was "the nation's unhealthiest city."[5] In that year Newark had the nation's highest death rate for cities with over one thousand in population, and it also had the highest scarlet fever and infant mortality rates. Moreover, the city was also among the ten highest in terms of communicable diseases such as malaria, typhoid fever, tuberculosis, and diphtheria.[6] As Newark's population and manufacturing base grew during the mid-Nineteenth

Century, politicians, physicians, and business leaders were largely ignorant or indifferent about the city's vital statistics data, which were often manipulated to suit political purposes.[7]

From 1800 to 1890 the population of Newark exploded from 8008 to 181,830—an increase of more than 2000%. Wave after wave of immigrants from Germany, Ireland, Italy, and other European nations brought a steady supply of talented labor for Newark's factories, which at that time produced thousands of different products to meet the growing demand for manufactured goods in America. Public health expenditures, however, grew at a much slower rate. During the 1870's the average expenditures of the Newark Board of Health were about $9000—amounting to only seven cents per capita. During that decade there was only one meat inspector and four sanitary inspectors for the entire city, and the secretary of the American Public Health Association reported in 1875 that Newark's sanitary government was a "fiction."[8]

Between 1870 and 1890 Newark's overall mortality rate was higher than that of comparable Northern and Western cities in 18 out of 20 years.[9] In 1872, for example, the Newark ***Daily Advertiser*** disclosed that the Passaic River—the city's major source of water at that time—was "hopelessly polluted" and was befouled with sewage, animal carcasses, dead bodies, and industrial wastes.[10] The Newark Board of Trade acknowledged that water contamination was a "much-vexed question" but shelved and dismissed sanitary reform proposals as impractical after the city's economy was devastated by the depression of 1873.[11]

In describing the development of Newark's public health crisis, Cornell University researcher Stuart Galishoff summarized the situation as follows:

> "Once noted for its handsome thoroughfares and majestic elms, [Newark had become] a vast cesspool of human and animal excrement and industrial waste."[12]

During those two decades many Newarkers worked together to improve the water supply and sanitary conditions in the city, most notably Dr. Edgar Holden.

Edgar Holden was born in Hingham, Massachusetts, in 1838 and was the son of a foundry owner. His father, Asa Holden, owned the Eagle Iron Foundry, which produced castings for furnaces, window weights, and plows.[13] Asa's father was John Holden, a Continental soldier who was rewarded for his bravery during the Revolutionary War at the Battle of Bunker Hill. John Holden later served as a Captain under General George Washington and became a founding member of The Order of the Cincinnatus, a hereditary society that included direct descendants of the staff who reported to Washington during the War.[14]

Asa and Ana Holden had seven children, of which Edgar was their oldest son. They had a high regard for education and sent Edgar to private schools in Massachusetts and Long Island as a youth. In 1852 the Holden family moved to Newark when Edgar was fourteen years of age. They were attracted to Newark because of family connections and also because of Newark's growing prominence in manufacturing. In Newark Edgar and his siblings learned many stories about the legendary Seth Boyden and his contributions to industry (see Chapter Three).

At the end of his formal schooling Edgar went to work as a teaching assistant under the Rev. John Pingry, a Presbyterian minister who served as a private tutor for boys in nearby Roseville. Pingry's motto was "the greatest respect is owed to the boys," and his favorite scripture was Proverbs 1:7: "The fear of the Lord is the beginning of wisdom." (In 1861 he opened the Pingry School, which today has campuses in Short Hills and Basking Ridge and has provided outstanding preparatory schooling for thousands of young men and women who have excelled in numerous professions.[15]) Edgar worked diligently during his year with Dr. Pingry to prepare for the entrance examinations at Princeton College, where he matriculated as a sophomore in 1856.

At Princeton Holden was only an average student in mathematics, logic, and rhetoric. He was best known as the class poet and as a regular contributor to the ***Nassau Literary Magazine***, a monthly periodical produced by Princeton's senior class. He wrote several poems, including one titled, "Success," which he presented at his senior year Class Day exercises on May 16, 1859. His reading on that occasion was described ten years later by one of his classmates:

> "At 8 o'clock the Orator and Poet entered the chapel amid long and renewed cheers from the students. The Divine blessing having been invoked by the President, the Poet of the class—Mr. Edgar Holden—was introduced and received with loud applause. Nor was expectation disappointed. Mr. H's poem was of high order. His verses were concinnous [concise] and his ideas worthy of the subject. In satirizing the follies of the day, falsely styled successes, the speaker made some telling hits—provoking cheers even from those most sharply cut. The delivery was very fine—his gestures rhythmic and his manner easy and possessed."[16]

Success

by Edgar Holden

'Retired physicians' hang a showy sign,
And very humbly claim their powers divine;
Boast of some sov'reign balm for ruined health,
To give back hope and joy, and all but wealth;
That—with the very kindliest end in view,
They have good care, shall not get back to you;

To 'complish wonders is their occupation,
From curing headache, to—decapitation,
The larger is the lie, the more the crowd,
The more their ardor, and their praise more loud,
So it be smooth who dares to say 'a lie,'
'Twere easier to believe it, than deny.[18]

During those years he studied anatomy under Dr. John Stilwell Schanck, a practicing physician who was regarded as "the leading physician of Princeton." Dr. Schanck's successful private practice allowed him time to give regular lecturers and recitations at the College, where he taught for many years. In addition to maintaining his medical practice, he served as chairman of the Chemistry Department and also taught natural history, zoology, mineralogy, botany, and hygiene. Although his students at Princeton were described as "riotous and disorderly," Dr. Schanck grew accustomed to their shenanigans and reportedly "had the patience of Job."[17]

Through Dr. Schanck's teaching and summer internships with physicians in Newark, Edgar became interested in a career in medicine. In Newark he had contact with medical people of all persuasions, from respected physicians to irregulars and hucksters who promised cures for all sorts of medical ailments. He gathered memories from all these experiences and later wrote extensively about the deceptive practices of water-cure doctors, patent medicine hucksters, and unscrupulous medical doctors. His poem, "Success," alludes to some of the medical practices he encountered during his apprenticeships.

New Jersey had no medical schools until the middle of the Twentieth Century. In the 1850's an aspiring medical student needed to go out of state for training and then spend a year as a preceptor (or apprentice) with a practicing physician. In 1859 Holden was admitted to the College of Physicians and Surgeons in New York City, where he studied under Dr. John Call Dalton, Jr., and six other faculty members. Dr. Dalton was an outstanding professor of physiology at the College and revolutionized the teaching of physiology in America.[19] He taught Holden and his fellow students how to use the microscope as a tool for experimental physiology and how to apply scientific methods for the study of disease. His lectures on the physiology of blood circulation and the workings of the sympathetic nervous system proved to be invaluable to Holden in his later career. Holden graduated from the College of Physicians and Surgeons in 1861 and anticipated practicing medicine in New York City.

His first assignment after graduating was at the Kings County Almshouse in Brooklyn. The Almshouse hospital admitted over two thousand patients a year, of whom one out of every eight died in the hospital. As a young house physician Holden found daily opportunities to apply his diagnostic skills in that setting. At that time many patients died from tuberculosis, as well as other infectious diseases such as meningitis, pneumonia, and syphilis. One discouraging characteristic of the Almshouse population was high readmission rates. Holden and his colleagues noted that many patients discharged from the Almshouse hospital returned to the hospital with the same disease or with complications.[20]

Holden dreamed about doing postdoctoral studies and moving up the medical ladder when national events interrupted his life. The Civil War broke out in 1861 and provided a new medical and surgical training ground for Holden and hundreds of other young medical professionals. The Civil War battlefields became the post-graduate training program for these aspiring young doctors—"a professional baptism under fire."[21]

In January of 1862 Holden was commissioned as an active surgeon at the Naval Hospital in New York and spent a total of sixteen months at sea. In March of that year he was onboard the USS Maryland and was an eyewitness observer of the famous battle between the Union Monitor and the Confederate Merrimack at the battle of Hampton Roads. This famous "battle of the ironclads" was a draw, but it preserved the Union blockade of the Chesapeake Bay. After the battle Holden was appointed Senior Surgeon for the fleet, which included three warships.

Later that year he was transferred to the USS Passaic, which was one of the Union's first ironclad vessels. On that vessel the officers and crews lived in a "submerged, enclosing machine [that] confronted its inhabitants with a strange experience and simultaneously hid them from the rest of the world."[22] The early ironclad vessels were cold and damp in the winter and oppressively hot and humid in the summer, and the fumes and fetid air caused considerable sickness among the sailors. During that time Holden exercised his literary and medical skills by

Edgar Holden

writing three articles that were published for a popular audience in ***Harper's New Monthly Magazine***.[23] He later published a medical journal article about "ironclad fever"—an illness that appears to have been similar to which we refer to today as carbon monoxide poisoning.[24]

In October 1864 he left the naval medical service and assumed a post as acting assistant surgeon at the army hospital in Newark. This facility, which was named the Ward Hospital, was the first hospital in Newark and served as a model for several civilian hospitals that would be built in the 1870's and 1880's (see Chapter Thirteen). In this position he gained broad medical experience by treating hundreds of soldiers who had battlefield wounds and a variety of infectious diseases.

He and his wife Katharine also purchased a home in Newark and gave birth to two daughters. Katharine was from the prominent Hedden family in East Orange, NJ. Her health problems at this time (probably an early case of tuberculosis, from which she later died), plus Edgar's respect among the officers at the Ward Hospital, caused him to give up his dreams of practicing medicine in New York and to remain in Newark at the end of the Civil War.[25]

During the next twenty years Holden was a general practitioner and became one of Newark's leading physicians. In addition to running a successful private practice, he was a skilled surgeon and contributed to leading regional and national medical journals.[26] His specialties included insurance medicine (actuarial sciences) and the field of laryngology. Holden was a nationally recognized authority in laryngology through several inventions and was a member of several state and regional medical societies. As his career developed he became more interested in public health issues and sought to transcend the limitations of being a general practitioner.

He was particularly interested in the subject of home hygiene, which sought to create a residential environment that was free of germs and noxious gases. In the early 1880's leading medical experts believed that ill-ventilated houses and noxious gases were major contributors to the spreading of disease in poor and middle class homes.[27]

Building upon his wartime background of serving on poorly-ventilated ironclad vessels, it was a natural step for his interests to evolve into home health issues. One of his publications, "House-heating and Its Dangers," was published in the ***Sanitarian*** in 1885 and stated that home heating systems of his day created significant health hazards. In that article he stated that

> "[T]he powerful draughts from highly heated air in our houses draw the effluvia of water-closets and drains from the lower levels where they originate, and warming them into activity, we supply them to our families and friends.[28]

Undoubtedly, many people developed headaches and sluggishness by living in homes with poorly-designed heating systems, but the contribution of sewer gases to health problems remained a controversial topic.

In 1880, as the public debate over sewer gases raged, Holden decided to do a scientific study of the relationship between water and sewer systems and mortality rates from typhoid fever and other infectious diseases.

By 1880 Holden had given up his private practice and was working as the medical director at the Mutual Benefit Life Insurance Company. In that position he published a report, ***Mortality and sanitary records of Newark, New Jersey, 1859-1877***, which provided solid statistical evidence about Newark's poor health and mortality conditions.[29] This report stated that Newark had a higher mortality rate than New York and most other major U.S. cities, which he attributed to the excessive occurrence of preventable diseases—mainly acute communicable diseases, lung ailments, and bowel diseases.

To test the theory that sewer gas was responsible for cholera, diphtheria, scarlet fever, typhoid, and other epidemic diseases, he drew two disease maps of Newark, which plotted all deaths from preventable diseases for the years 1872 and 1876. In those years Newark had a general mortality rate of more than 30 per 1000 population. While he expected to find that the death rates were highest in neighborhoods drained by sewers, both maps revealed that the highest mortality rates were found in neighborhoods served by privies. To his great surprise, there was no statistical evidence that sewer development led to increased mortality—in fact, exactly the opposite occurred. His surprising conclusion in the report was this:

> "In summing up the investigation, I have been struck by the fact that theories, however plausible on the subject of a city's sanitary surroundings, are valueless against stubborn facts and figures."[30]

Having demonstrated convincingly that sewers were not the cause of Newark's mortality and infectious disease rates, he refocused the public's attention on a more likely culprit: contaminated water from polluted wells and from the Passaic River, which were the two major sources of water for the city at that time. Quoting Holden's report, an 1880 article in the ***Sunday Call*** stated,

> "We are told by physicians that the water we drink contains properties poisonous to our system, and we know that this must be true, because we know that our drinking water washes the front of two cities and carries off their sewage and refuse. We are told that much of the mortality of Newark is due to the use of Passaic water and we cannot doubt the statement for it comes from unquestionable authority and is based upon undisputed fact. . . . Viewed in the light of the public health, the water question becomes a problem that overshadows all other matters relative to the weal of the city. It is the one vital question that demands a solution immediately, that cannot be put off to a future day."[31]

In that same report Holden recommended that the Newark Sanitary Board be reconstituted and its budget increased to support public health needs. He stated,

> "A well-equipped Sanitary Bureau is a necessity as it is a refinement and blessing of modern times, and it is but poorly to the credit of a large manufacturing city that other and smaller towns have throughout the United States availed themselves of the modern improvements for cleanliness and hygienic supervision before it."[32]

In 1883 another prominent physician reported to the Newark Medical Association that the city's high mortality rate was caused by factors that were "evident to all who could see or smell." Both the Newark ***Daily Advertiser*** and the Newark ***Daily Journal*** also ran articles that year exposing the city's sanitary problems and the threat they posed to public health. The ***Daily Journal***, for example, stated that each of Newark's 10,000 cesspools was "a generator of disease and the cause of much of the sickness and death in the city"[34]

Holden's landmark report produced the first evidence in a U.S. city proving the beneficial effect of sewers. This report set into motion a series of actions that led to a dramatic reduction in Newark's mortality rate over the next three decades. In 1881 the chief health physician of the Newark Sanitary Bureau complained about the "limited means and powers" his agency had to address Newark's growing public health needs.[35]

Public awareness and support for improved sanitation facilities increased quickly in the years following Holden's 1880 report, at which time there were only sixty miles of sewers in the entire city. In 1884 city engineers began work on an intercepting sewer and pumping station in Newark's meadows. This was called the Great Intercepting Sewer, which was completed three years later at a cost of $600,000. During the next quarter-century more than two hundred miles of new sewers were built. By 1919 more than 95% of Newark's developed land was served by sewers, and the city's mortality rate had dropped by nearly 60%.[36]

In addition to his 1880 mortality report, Holden also conducted an exhaustive study of deaths from outbreaks of typhoid fever, which frequently occurred during the summer months. He produced a chart which clearly demonstrated that typhoid deaths were concentrated around the town pumps, which had become polluted by the infiltration of raw sewage from privies and surface water. A 1909 obituary emphasized the pivotal role of Holden's epidemiological study on the causes of typhoid fever:

> "Newark was one of the first of the cities, and probably the first, to discover the intimate connection between the public and typhoid fever, and it was Dr. Edgar Holden who made the practical demonstration and saved hundreds of lives."[37]

In 1891 Newark had its last major typhoid fever epidemic. In that year more than 100 out of every 100,000 residents died from this disease. Then, in 1893 the city started receiving 100% of its drinking water from the Pequannock Reservoir rather than from the Passaic, and the typhoid

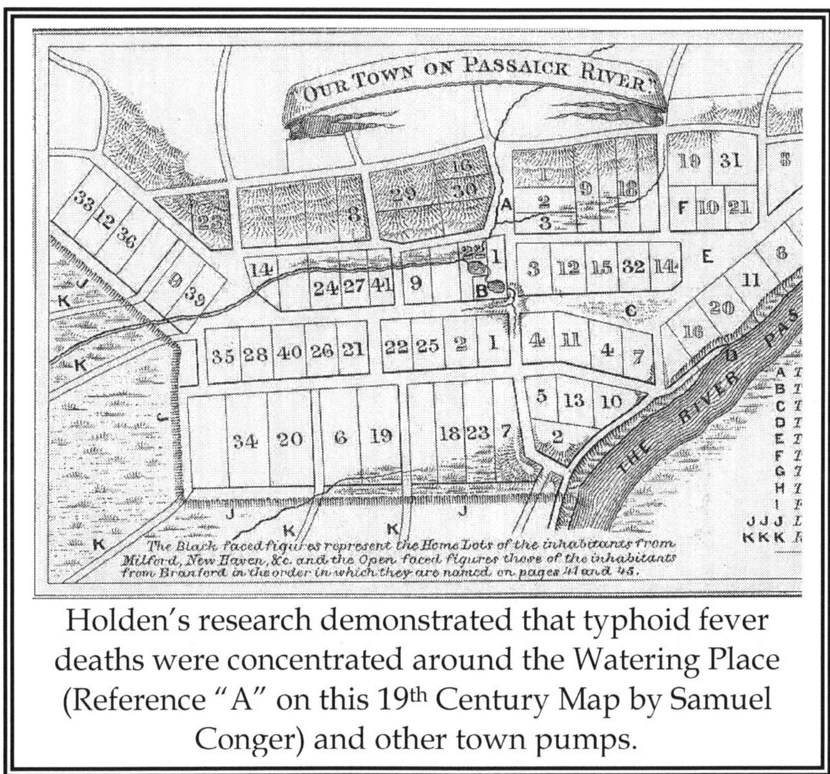

Holden's research demonstrated that typhoid fever deaths were concentrated around the Watering Place (Reference "A" on this 19th Century Map by Samuel Conger) and other town pumps.

fever death rate fell to less than 30 per 100,000 residents. Between 1890 and 1920 the city's death rate from typhoid fever dropped by 90%, and the overall mortality rate dropped from 27.2 per to 13.2 per 1000 residents—a decline of more than 50%. In that year Newark was no longer "the nation's unhealthiest city," but actually had a lower general mortality rates than two-thirds of American cities with more than 100,000 population.[38]

Edgar Holden was a medical pioneer who helped to raise public health and medical care standards in Newark and across New Jersey. In her 2014 biographical sketch of his life, Dr. Sandra Moss wrote,

> "Edgar Holden [transcended] the local medical culture to occupy a modest national stage in the fields of general medical and surgical practice, sophisticated physiological research, insurance medicine, and the new specialty of laryngology."[39]

He was a multi-talented man who was involved in numerous local and regional medical societies, served as an elder at the Second Presbyterian Church in Newark, and was also a devoted family man. His son, Edgar Holden, Jr., also received his medical degree from the College of Physicians and Surgeons and was an attending orthopedic surgeon at the Newark City Hospital, the Home for Crippled Children, the Newark Memorial Hospital, and the Newark Babies' Hospital. He also consulted as an orthopedic surgeon at several regional hospitals in the Greater Newark area.[40]

Holden's research helped stimulate public awareness of the causes of disease and actions that the Newark Sanitary Bureau could take to dramatically reduce Newark's general mortality rate.

The New York ***Times*** obituary for Edgar Holden (Sr.) called him a "Prominent Newark Physician,"[41] and the ***National Cyclopaedia of American Biography*** described his life in the following manner:

> "Dr. Holden was a man of great culture and refinement and one who had supplemented a broad and liberal education by constant reading and study not only in matters connected with his profession but also in the whole realm of history and literature. He had a talent for painting and sculpture and his few hours of recreation were largely devoted to work in those arts…
>
> Although possessing the poise and dignity of true genius and ability, Dr. Holden always manifested such a sincere affection for those around him and such a personal interest in their welfare and his life was so filled with good works and deeds that he enjoyed the full confidence of everyone and was always held in

affectionate regard by his friends and business associates and by the community generally in which he lived the greater part of an honorable life."[42]

CHAPTER EIGHT

Earnest Mae McCarroll (1898-1990): Pioneer Black Physician

For ten years Dr. EARNEST MAE McCARROLL made an annual visit to Newark City Hospital to apply for a medical staff position. The first time she applied, she was told that she was ineligible because she was not a member of the American Medical Association ("AMA"). "But the AMA doesn't permit Negro members," she explained.

Friends from the Phyllis Wheatley Society urged her not to give up. Every year McCarroll and her friends piled into an open-air car and drove down to City Hospital to submit a job application. Year after year, however, there was no response to her applications, nor was there any public awareness of her efforts.

Late in 1945, however, a reporter from the Newark ***Evening News*** wrote an article about her struggle to integrate the medical staff at City Hospital. When asked why she continued to apply for a staff position at that institution, she told the reporter,

> "I do so because I know that someday someone like me, some person of color, will be appointed if we persevere. If you are determined to do something, you cannot give up. We are tired of leaving our patients at the hospital's front door."[1]

Newark's first hospital for African-American patients was the Kenney Memorial Hospital, which was established by Dr. John A. Kenney, Jr. He was a successful physician who had opened the John A. Andrew Memorial Hospital at the Tuskegee Institute in Alabama in 1913. This was the nation's first full-service hospital for African-Americans. Dr. Kenney was the personal physician for Booker T. Washington (Founder of the Tuskegee Institute) and for George Washington Carver (the famous botanist and inventor). He was also the founder of the National Medical Association ("NMA"), which was established "to advance the art and science of medicine for people of African descent through education, advocacy, and health policy to promote health and wellness, eliminate health disparities, and sustain physician viability."[2]

Dr. Kenney moved to Newark in 1923 after threats from the Ku Klux Klan in Alabama, who resisted his goal of having the Tuskegee hospital be completely staffed by African-Americans. When he learned that the Klan was plotting to burn down his hospital and attack him, he moved to Newark to pursue his dream of providing better medical services for black families. On September 1, 1927, he opened the doors of the Kenney Memorial Hospital at 132 West Kinney Street with funding from his personal assets. From the beginning the Kenney Hospital lacked resources to purchase much-needed equipment and to hire enough dedicated doctors and nurses to care for the growing number of patients, so Dr. Kenney ended up doing much of the work himself. He would frequently rise at 3 or 4 AM to perform surgeries, then work until dark doing the administrative and building maintenance chores required to operate the hospital.

The Kenney Hospital was hard hit by the Great Depression in the 1930's, which necessitated major staff layoffs. As the Depression deepened, he felt that the hospital could not continue to function unless it became a community-owned resource. And so, on Christmas Eve 1935, he gave the residents of the Third Ward a remarkable gift—their own community-run hospital. Because it was donated to the community, the neighborhood residents called it the "Community Hospital."[3] The Hospital continued to struggle financially for years and closed its doors permanently in 1953.

During the 1930's and 1940's the Newark Interracial Council worked hard to improve health care opportunities for African-Americans. This Council gathered widespread support from clergy, politicians, and other community leaders to integrate Newark's City Hospital. A 1939 government report, for example, concluded that the New Jersey state government had been a "complete failure" in protecting black citizens from racial prejudice in health care. Regarding the City Hospital, the report stated,

> "Despite the fact that City Hospital is supported by public funds and because of unhealthy living and working conditions, Negroes are forced into ill health. The School of Nursing has no Negroes among its ninety students, nor has it ever had one. Neither has it a Negro physician on the staff, nor does it provide facilities for Negro interns."[4]

As Newark's black population grew, and as the resources of the Community Hospital continued to be inadequate, John Kenney's dream of adequate medical services for black families appeared to be fading by the time of the Second World War.

Earnest Mae McCarroll was born in Birmingham, Alabama, in 1898 and was the fourth of eight children born to Francis Earnest McCarroll and Cornelia Burrell. Francis was a teacher and postal employee who worked hard to support their large family. Like many of her siblings, Mae (as she preferred to be called) was an excellent student and had the opportunity to attend college. After graduating from Talladega College in 1917, she completed chemistry and physics courses at Fisk University and was accepted to the Women's Medical College at the University of Pennsylvania in 1922. She was one of only three black students in the College's Class of 1925.

After serving an internship in Kansas City, she returned to Philadelphia to practice medicine for two years. During that time she married James Leroy Baxter, who was a graduate of Penn's School of Dentistry. He was from a prominent Newark family and was serving in the New Jersey General Assembly as the state's third black legislator (1927-29). After their wedding she moved into Leroy's house at 54 Hillside Place in Newark's South Ward. Barbara Kukla described the couple as follows:

> "The Baxters made a dashing couple. She was lanky, beau-

> tiful, and full of energy. He was charming, politically adept, and the son of one of Newark's most highly regarded citizens. His father, James Baxter, a revered educator, had been principal of Newark's Colored School from 1864 to 1909."[5]

Leroy's sister, Grace Baxter Fenderson, was a founding member of Newark's branch of the NAACP in 1914 and introduced Mae to many civil rights leaders. Fenderson held NAACP meetings at her townhouse at 17 Elm Street and hosted prominent local and national leaders, including Roy Wilkins (National executive director of the NAACP) and Thurgood Marshall (who became the nation's first black justice to serve on the U.S. Supreme Court).

Mae opened up her private medical practice in 1929 at their home on Hillside Place and ran a successful medical practice there for forty-four years. Through her patients she became aware of the increasing incidence of sexually transmitted diseases and was determined to eradicate these diseases in Newark. In 1934 she was appointed as a clinical physician in the Venereal Disease Division of the Newark Department of Health. She was later appointed as assistant epidemiologist for the city of Newark. Gwen Cooper, who worked for years as McCarroll's nursing assistant, described how she balanced her private medical practice and public health roles:

> "Mae worked long hours. She made her hospital rounds in the morning and then went downtown to spend most of the day at the city clinic, where she was an epidemiologist. After that, she'd come to the office to see her patients. Then, she would make house calls all over the city, generally two or three a night. I lived nearby, so I would go along with her."[6]

In addition to these day-to-day responsibilities, she took graduate school training in public health at the College of Physicians at Columbia University, where she received an M.S. degree in 1939. After that she enrolled in post-graduate training at Harvard University, where she continued her research on sexually transmitted diseases. Her article, "Standard Curative Treatment of Early and Late Syphilis," was published in the ***Journal of the National Medical Association*** in July of 1941.[7]

Shortly after the previously mentioned ***Newark Evening News*** interview appeared in 1945, Mae received a phone call from the head of the medical staff at City Hospital. He was a proctologist (i.e., a specialist in colorectal medicine) who was looking for an assistant. He asked if she would be willing to accept this position. McCarroll discussed the opportunity with her friends and decided to take up his offer. She explained her decision this way:

> "A lot of people said I should not accept his offer because proctology was not a field for women. They thought the offer was a ploy—that the doctor and his colleagues were being patronizing because they were convinced I would never take a position in proctology. My feeling about the matter was entire-

E. Mae McCarroll

ly different. The chief of staff was a man I respected. I thought he was quite sincere and sensitive to the issue at hand. Breaking down racial barriers and stereotypes was not an easy thing. The news article helped. It was such an embarrassment to the hospital that it opened the doors to me as a Negro physician. It gave the good doctor an opportunity to hire me."[8]

She started work at City Hospital on January 3, 1946, becoming the first black physician to break the racial barrier in Newark's public hospital. As might be expected, her appointment created controversy. Some of Newark's black male doctors supported her appointment, but others thought the first black to be hired should be a man. Others were sensitive to receiving care from a black physician or sharing facilities with people of color. Rosetta Lee, who served as a nurse's aide at City Hospital during that time, commented,

"When women of color had their babies, they had to stay on the first floor of the hospital away from the white women. When their husbands came to see them, the men had to stand outside and talk to their wives through the windows. They couldn't come inside."[9]

On January 3, 1946, McCarroll became the first black physician to break the racial barrier at City Hospital. "What I did, I did for our patients, not necessarily just for the doctors. But they benefited too. Everyone benefited."

But Mae was not discouraged by the criticism she received for accepting the staff position at City Hospital. In a news article that appeared shortly after her appointment she said,

"What I did, I did for our patients, not necessarily just for the doctors. But they benefited too. Everyone benefited. I wanted to be able to stand on my own two feet, to be my own boss, and to be in a position to help overcome intolerance. Everyone has been very nice to me at the hospital and at the clinic, and I'm very happy with my work."[10]

Leroy Baxter was twenty years older than Mae and had a niece named Julia. She was raised on the family farm in Far Hills but often came to visit her dad and Aunt Mae at their home in Newark. In an interview with Barbara Kukla, Julia Baxter Bates described these happy times:

> "The first time I met Aunt Mae I was about seven or eight years old. Uncle Leroy brought her out to the farm in Far Hills, where my father had a veterinary practice. She was very warm and friendly. She gave me a hug. I guess I liked her because I didn't get much affection. Our family was a bit standoffish. I can't remember my father ever kissing me. My mother died when I was three, and my stepmother and I didn't get along."[11]

Like her Aunt Mae, Julia was a very diligent student and made history as the first black student admitted at Douglass College, which was the women's undergraduate college at Rutgers University. Although her application included the required photo, college officials were surprised to find that this light-skinned applicant was an African-American. The embarrassed admission officers suggested that she might be "more comfortable" at another college, but Julia and her father stood their ground, and so she studied four years at Douglass. After Dean Margaret Corwin unsuccessfully lobbied for her to live on campus with the other students, Julia moved in with Aunt Mae and her uncle. "It was easier for me to take the train from Newark to New Brunswick than it was to commute from Far Hills," she explained. "I also liked living with my aunt and uncle."[12]

Julia graduated magna cum laude from Douglas in 1938 and then earned a master's degree in education from Columbia University. After teaching a few years at Dillard College in New Orleans she returned to the Northeast as research director at the NAACP's national office in New York. During the time she had spent living with Aunt Mae, she was introduced to Roy Wilkins and Thurgood Marshall and became friends with these national leaders.

She served twenty-five years as the NAACP's research director and was Marshall's chief researcher for the historic *Brown v. Topeka Board of*

Education case in 1953, which outlawed segregation in the nation's schools. This landmark civil rights case brought national fame for Thurgood Marshall and helped him to be appointed to the U.S. Supreme Court. But Julia never mentioned her critical role as a researcher, even to her close friends. They had to pry this information out of her years later.[13]

Mae's marriage to Leroy ended after fifteen years, but she continued to live on Hillside Place and maintained her medical practice at home. Carol Cooper Cross, who was another niece, also had fond childhood memories of Aunt Mae:

> "She was a very determined woman. She didn't demand respect, but you had to respect her. What impressed me most when I was a teenager was that she didn't have office hours. She stayed open late, and people just wandered in."[14]

She also remembered that her aunt enjoyed the finer things in life. She drove a pink and black Lincoln, to match the color scheme of her bedroom. She was also the first person in her neighborhood to have a walk-in closet. But the most distinctive feature of her home was the white living room carpet. It was a symbol of her lifestyle, but visitors were always afraid of spilling something on it. Cross also remember that Aunt Mae was an excellent cook and loved to prepare her own meals when her busy time schedule permitted. "She was good at it. Everything she made tasted terrific. But there was always a certain formality to it. We always sat in the dining room," she added.[15]

In 1958 Mae married Bob Hunter, an outgoing young man who worked at the Howard Bank. One of her friends, Ruth Crumpton Dargan, said that Mae and Bob were very compatible:

> "Mae told me that she married again because she was tired of going to conventions where all the other women physicians had doting husbands. Bob was much younger than Mae, but he was very loving and took wonderful care of her. She'd get off an elevator and there he would be with her mink coat, waiting to escort her."[16]

Mae was also a woman of great faith. During her first marriage she and Leroy Baxter belonged to St. Philip's Church, which later became Trinity & St. Philip's Cathedral, an Episcopal church where the Baxter family were long-standing members. After her marriage to Bob Hunter she converted to Roman Catholicism. Monsignor Patrick McGrath, who was a priest at the Blessed Sacrament Church (located at 610 Clinton Avenue) at that time, remembered them well:

> "Somewhere in the 1960's they appeared in the rectory, asking to take classes and join the church. They began coming to see me once a week. Mae was a delightful person to know. She also was the most intelligent woman to whom I ever gave instructions. I can distinctly recall her taking notes each week. No one else had ever done that."[17]

McCarroll's commitment to social justice was a strong component of her faith. After successfully fighting to integrate Newark's City Hospital, Mae and her friends decided to take on the downtown business establishment, which was blatantly discriminatory toward blacks at that time.

Following Thomas Edison's invention of the motion picture at his laboratory in West Orange, theaters began opening up in Newark and all across America. In 1915 Proctor's Palace opened its doors to the public at 116 Market Street. It was an immense "double decker" theater which had 2,300 seats on its lower level. In addition the top four floors contained a smaller cinema that had 900 seats. After a busy day of working and shopping downtown, Newarkers enjoyed coming to Proctor's Theater to watch their favorite actors in live performances or on a big screen.[18]

Like other Newarkers Mae McCarroll and her friends enjoyed these performances, but they were offended that the downtown theaters required blacks to sit in the balconies. They considered this treatment to be an insult to their dignity and humanity. So one day Mae and other black women community leaders staged a protest in front of Proctor's Palace. They marched around with signs in their hands and let it be known that the downtown theaters should allow blacks to enjoy the performances from any seat in the house. They also made sure that the shoppers at nearby Bamberger's and other retail stores were aware of their protest against racial discrimination by downtown businesses.

Shortly afterwards all the Newark theaters ended their discrimination against blacks, which was a significant step toward ending segregation in Newark's central business district.[19] A few years later Proctor's Theater was sold to Radio Keith Orpheum, and its name was changed to RKO Proctor's. By the early 1960's RKO Proctor's was featuring black artists and poets, including Newark's own Amiri Baraka. His play, "Black Mass," had its premiere performance at RKO Proctor's in 1966.[20] The nonviolent protest by McCarroll and her friends had opened doors to black artists and entertainers as well as theatergoers.

Mae's medical practice grew year after year, and she became one of Newark's most highly respected physicians. She was totally committed to her profession and to her family and friends. In a 2001 interview Carol Cross reminisced,

> "Sometimes when I came to the office, I'd find her asleep at her desk. Day after day, she kept up a frantic pace."[21]

But her reputation as a physician went far beyond Newark. After joining the National Medical Association in 1929, she served thirty-two years on its Publication Committee. During those years the ***Journal of the National Medical Association*** became known as a first-class medical periodical. She also served on the NMA's Board of Directors for sixteen years and was chairperson of several NMA committees in the 1930's through 1970's. When she retired and closed her private medical practice in 1973, the NMA held a retirement party and referred to her as the "First Lady of the NMA." Although she never sought the presidency, some male physicians believed that she could have been the first female president of the NMA:

> "[T]his quiet lady of soft and mellifluent voice, was her own woman. With no persuasion she stood always steadfast in the faith. This strength of character was not as widely known in the

> Association as it would have been had she chosen to allow her name to have been placed in nomination for the presidency of the NMA. There is no doubt, however, that the respect in which she was generally held within the organization would have made her its first woman president had she elected to run. The NMA—past, present, and future—is in the permanent debt of its "First Lady" who has radiated so much good, so far and so long."[22]

After her retirement from medicine in 1973 she moved to Florida but made several trips back to Newark to visit friends and to participate in community events. One of these trips was for the dedication of the Haskin-McCarroll Building on May 5, 1982. This new public health facility was the largest building constructed by the City of Newark since before World War II and was built at a cost of $4 million. It was dedicated to Dr. Aaron H. Haskin and Dr. E. Mae McCarroll, each of whom dedicated more than twenty years to improve public health in the City of Newark.[23]

At that dedication ceremony Newark Mayor Kenneth A. Gibson gave a speech praising Haskin and McCarroll for their commitment to public health, saying:

> "The New Haskin-McCarroll Public Health Building is another example of Newark's commitment to the health and well-being of its citizens. Protecting our citizens from disease and illness is an honorable duty which we are proud to perform and from which we will never deviate."[24]

Mae listened politely while the Mayor and other prominent politicians gave long-winded orations. When it came time for her to speak, Mae rose and said simply,

> "Thank you for the honor." Barbara Kukla asked her later why she had not given an acceptance speech that day. "The program was very long and it was getting too hot in the sun," was McCarroll's reply. But Mae's niece Julia gave a different account: "I think it was because the politicians spoke for so long there was no time on the agenda for Aunt Mae."[25]

Haskin-McCarroll Building
110 William Street

Kukla later obtained a written copy of a three-page acceptance speech that McCarroll had labored to write the night before the dedication:

> "This occasion marks, in one sense, a new beginning—a rededication to the health goals all communities should seek—a happy childhood for all youngsters, hearty, outgoing adolescent school days, fruitful work, fulfillment during the vigorous middle years, and serene contentment for those who reach life's true prize."

She recalled with fondness the years she had served under Dr. Charles Craster (the city's chief health officer), Dr. Julius Levy (head of the Child Hygiene Division), Dr. Robert Sellers (in charge of the Venereal Disease Division), and Dr. Aaron H. Haskin (who ran the public health clinic). She wrote,

> "It was a privilege to serve under the direction of these dedicated and farsighted physicians. Those of us who did were the envy of

> our colleagues. Payment was unthinkable. The opportunity afforded us to work in their shadow, which was greater than remuneration."

She went on to describe how Dr. Levy had enabled her to serve at his neighborhood Keep Well stations:

> "Mothers would bring their tiny babies, many of whom bore the unpleasant consequences of untreated conditions—sightlessness and other physical deformities. How strongly we prayed in those days for some means of educating our neighborhood communities in the dangers to life and health that venereal infections bring with them."

We close this chapter with the conclusion of the acceptance speech that she never delivered to the public:

> "The social health of any city is measured by the extent to which its citizenry remains protected, informed, and educated. The dedication of this building today is, in its silent way, a measure of the distance Newark has come, and of the distance Newark must go."[26]

CHAPTER NINE

Clara Louise Maass (1876-1901): No Greater Love

CLARA MAASS was neatly dressed in a black woolen skirt and a white blouse as she rode the trolley to the campus of the Newark German Lutheran Hospital. She got off the bus at Newton and West Bank Streets and walked through fresh snow to Trefz Hall, which was being dedicated that day. It was Thanksgiving Day, 1893—the day that changed Clara's life.[1]

"I would like to see Head Nurse Anna Seeber," she said to the receptionist. "Be seated," invited the woman, who rose and delivered the message to Miss Seeber. In a few minutes Clara heard the rustling of crinoline skirts as the receptionist returned. Clara was surprised that the Head Nurse had come in person to meet her. Miss Seeber extended her weathered hand to Clara, who took it and curtsied briefly.

"You wanted to see me?" Miss Seeber inquired.

"Yes, I'd like to enroll to become a nurse," Clara replied.

Miss Seeber studied her carefully.

"You're very young," she replied in her usual stolid manner. "We usually don't take girls until they are twenty. Some nursing training schools don't admit applicants until they are twenty-five." She gave a quiet laugh and added, "In fact, some folks believe that only middle-aged women should apply, after they have been tamed by marriage and the troubles of raising children."

"I am young," Clara admitted, "but I have raised many children already even though I'm not married yet. I am seventeen now and have served as a housekeeper at the Newark Orphan Asylum for the past two years. I work there seven days a week but have taken off today to attend your celebration to dedicate Trefz Hall. Working at the Orphanage has been a very valuable experience to me, but my heart is set on becoming a nurse."

Miss Seeber looked at Clara's simple but well-pressed clothes, her slight frame, her serious blue eyes and her hair pulled back tightly into a knot. She replied wryly, "It's been said of nurses, that those who look the most worn out, and who give themselves tirelessly for others, never thinking of themselves, are the best nurses." At length she said, "Come with me to my office. We will talk further."

Clara glanced around the hall, peeking into examining rooms, the bathrooms, and the apothecary as she walked with Miss Seeber to her office on the second floor of The Training School of Nurses in Trefz Hall.

Miss Seeber's office was an attractive, homey room with white painted doors and woodwork and with wallpapered walls. There were straight-backed wooden chairs with attractive carving, and an inviting rocking chair for visitors to occupy. There was an odd brown wooden box on the wall, which Clara concluded was probably a telephone. She thought to herself, "I wonder if they'll teach me how to use it?" . . .

"You know German, of course?"

"Yes, and English too," Clara replied.

"You'll need German more—this is a German hospital. All the lectures will be in German and some in Latin."

"I had two years of Latin in high school."

"Good," replied Miss Seeber. "Nursing is not an easy career. Florence Nightingale said that instructors cannot put into students what is not already there. Our training will enable you to use and develop the ability you already possess."

Clara's heart leaped with joy. She thought to herself, "Why, that's exactly what I want! I know I can do much more than I've been doing." . . .

Miss Seeber continued, "The doctors here are very demanding. I don't know how many students will finish the training program." She smoothed her already smooth apron and added, "You are aware, of course, that nurses are not re-

Clara Maass

garded highly enough to be paid well. You will probably receive less than a laundress." She shot an inquiring look at Clara. Clara said nothing but thought to herself, "It surely must be more than the $10 a week I've been paid at the orphanage."

"If you graduate," Nurse Seeber said, "you do private duty. You'll be working at least 56 hours a week and probably more. When you work in a patient's home, you'll need to be able to respond day and night. Your salary will probably be $15 a week."

Clara gasped and thought to herself, "Fifteen dollars a week—I'll be rich! I will be able to send Mama more money to help her take care of my brothers and sisters."

"Private duty nurses," Miss Seeber added, "take care of patients recovering from fevers: typhus, typhoid, and the most dreaded of all when it appears now and again—yellow fever. Tuberculosis is perhaps our greatest enemy, along with pneumonia. We need graduate nurses here to train the probationers. And there are also opportunities to serve wounded soldiers in Cuba. Florence Nightingale has been stirring up support for properly organized and equipped military hospitals for the wounded. No nation can afford to go to war without adequate plans for medical aid."

She continued, "Your first year will be spent in the classroom and the wards. In the second year we send you as a private nurse to homes to gain further experience. The salary you earn that year will be sent to the hospital, of course, since you are in training. But there's a $100 bonus you will receive at graduation." . . .

Anna had several more questions for Clara: Was she willing to place herself unquestionably under the supervision of the Head Nurse for the next two years? Was she willing to work hard and follow the doctors' orders, to keep their confidence, and to administer drugs with the utmost caution? Was she able to work under doctors who were difficult to get along with?

Clara answered affirmatively to each question, feeling her stomach knot up after each answer. She wondered what Miss Seeber was thinking about her responses.

After all these questions, Anna Seeber relaxed her stiff mouth long enough to crack out a brief smile. "Arrange with the orphanage to leave as soon as you can. As soon as you move in, we shall begin to train you."

Clara Maass was born on June 28, 1876, in East Orange, New Jersey, and was the oldest of nine children. Her parents, Robert and Helwig Maass, were devout Lutherans who immigrated to America with few material possessions. After Clara's birth they had four boys and four more girls in short order. As the oldest child Clara was expected to care for her younger siblings and quickly became the family's unpaid nurse and housekeeper. When she was twelve years of age, her parents moved to a farm in nearby Livingston, and Clara was enrolled in a small school near her home. Her classmates remembered Clara's honey-blond hair and unfailing optimism.

After struggling for several years to make a living on the farm, her father took a factory job and moved the family back to East Orange.

Clara attended the East Orange High School for three years and became proficient in English at that time. At age fifteen she dropped out of high school and took a full-time position at the Newark Orphan Asylum, where she earned a salary of $10 a week. Every week she sent at least half of her salary to her mother, to help meet the family's living expenses.(See Chapter 11 for more about the Newark Orphan Asylum.)

Her position at the Asylum involved caring for children seven days a week, which was physically and emotionally demanding. Through this position she gained valuable experience in dealing with the emotional and physical challenges of orphans. The work was rewarding but was also very demanding for a young woman in her circumstances. As she cared for these young people, she developed a yearning to be in a profession that would make a significant improvement in people's lives. She heard stories about Florence Nightingale and decided to give nursing a try.

In December 1893 she left the Orphan Asylum and became a full-time student at the Trefz Nursing School in Newark's Central Ward. At that time approximately one third of Newark's population was German, and these immigrants were concentrated in Newark's Central and North Wards. The Trefz Nursing School was affiliated with the Newark German Hospital, which was one of Newark's first hospitals when it opened in 1870. Unlike other hospitals in the area, the German Hospital was committed to providing health care services to people from all classes, nationalities, and creeds.

During her orientation interview Dr. Charles Lehlbach spoke with Clara about the "founder's spirit" that his father and two other doctors had when they established the hospital. "The founding fathers of our hospital," he said, "were men committed to bringing hope and comfort to the oppressed at any personal cost. They were willing to risk all in caring for others. 'The grave is secure,' one of them quoted, 'but terribly dull. Let us live life to the full, for others—little brown brothers, or big black brothers, or grimy white brothers. All are to be cherished as God's people.'" Dr. Lehlbach continued, "Now if you girls, our nurses, can imbibe the spirit of the founding fathers of our hospital and be willing to risk all to alleviate the suffering of others, we shall be proud of you. We shall honor you and remember you."[2]

Clara never forgot Dr. Lehlbach's impromptu lecture to her about the "spirit of the founding fathers," and she worked hard to graduate in the Nursing School's second class in 1894. One day she remarked to a classmate, "My goal is to become the best nurse I can and lead a worthwhile, significant life. But I give my energy to the work of the day, whatever it is: cooking, cleaning, nursing, or studying."[3]

During her studies Clara read about a typhoid epidemic that had broken out in the South in the summer of 1878 and quickly moved up the East Coast to New Jersey. By the end of that summer more than 74,000 typhoid cases had been reported, and the financial losses in American cities was calculated at more than $100,000,000. New Orleans alone reported 4,600 deaths to typhoid that summer.

In the summer of 1894 the Newark German Hospital admitted a man who had contracted typhoid fever. One day Clara noticed that the bed where he had been was now empty. She was devastated when her roommate told her this man with typhoid fever had died. An anger welled up in Clara's heart about all the diseases that attack and kill human beings—particularly typhoid fever, pneumonia, and yellow fever.

> "Is there no way?" she puzzled, "to conquer these murderers?" She dug her clenched fists deep into the palms of her hands. And then, even as her anger burned hot and fierce, a shiver rippled through her slight frame. A chilling premonition swept over her, a premonition that the battle to conquer these fevers would be only at a fearful cost, not only to one, but to many, and the cost may well be lives. But little did Clara guess that one day it would involve her too."[4]

Clara completed all of her nursing requirements and attended the graduation ceremony in October 1895. During the ceremony she and her classmates repeated the Florence Nightingale nursing pledge:

> *I solemnly pledge myself before God and in the presence of this assembly to pass my life in purity and to practice my profession faithfully.*

I will abstain from whatever is deleterious and mischievous, and will not take or knowingly administer any harmful drug. I will do all in my power to maintain and elevate the standard of my profession, and will hold in confidence all personal matters committed to my keeping and all family affairs coming to my knowledge in the practice of my calling.

With loyalty I will endeavor to aid the physician in his work and devote myself to the welfare of those committed to my care.[5]

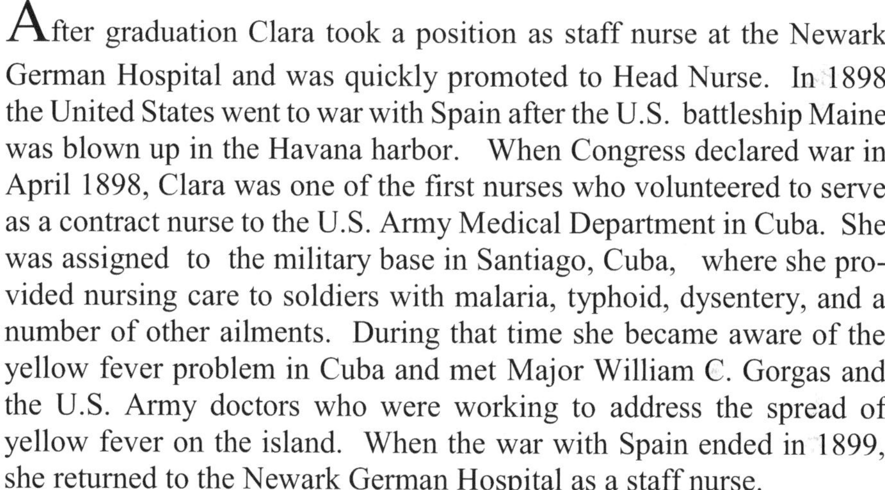

After graduation Clara took a position as staff nurse at the Newark German Hospital and was quickly promoted to Head Nurse. In 1898 the United States went to war with Spain after the U.S. battleship Maine was blown up in the Havana harbor. When Congress declared war in April 1898, Clara was one of the first nurses who volunteered to serve as a contract nurse to the U.S. Army Medical Department in Cuba. She was assigned to the military base in Santiago, Cuba, where she provided nursing care to soldiers with malaria, typhoid, dysentery, and a number of other ailments. During that time she became aware of the yellow fever problem in Cuba and met Major William C. Gorgas and the U.S. Army doctors who were working to address the spread of yellow fever on the island. When the war with Spain ended in 1899, she returned to the Newark German Hospital as a staff nurse.

In 1900 the United States government launched a systematic program to eliminate yellow fever in Cuba. Under the direction of Dr. Walter Reed, the U.S. Yellow Fever Commission set up a research center to identify the process by which yellow fever was transmitted. One theory was that yellow fever was spread by filth that covered the streets of Havana. A competing but more controversial theory was that yellow fever was transmitted by infected mosquitoes. Under the leadership of Major Gorgas, the Yellow Fever Commission was funded to do research to identify which of these competing theories was true. His personal belief was that yellow fever was transmitted primarily through unsanitary living conditions and that a "sanitary, spotless town" would eliminate the spread of yellow fever.[6]

When Dr. Gorgas issued an announcement for nurses to attend to yellow fever patients in Cuba, Clara quickly volunteered to join his team. On October 14, 1900, she received a cryptic telegram from Havana: *Come at once*. It was signed, "Gorgas, Chief Sanitary Officer." She saw that this was an opportunity to use her nursing skills to fight the dreaded disease of yellow fever. In that same week she sailed for Cuba to serve on staff at the civilian hospital at Las Animas.

At Las Animas Clara reported for duty and met with Dr. Gorgas and a number of other men, including Dr. Walter Reed. They explained to her that one of their team members, Dr. Jesse Lazear, had recently died of yellow fever after being bitten by mosquitoes that had been infected by the virus. His death, along with the deaths of two others who had voluntarily been bitten by the infected mosquitoes, had provided convincing evidence that the primary pathway for transmitting the disease was through mosquito bites.[7]

In the winter months there were fewer patients at the Las Animas Hospital, allowing the staff to take time off duty on a regular basis. One Sunday Clara had the opportunity to attend a worship service at the local Episcopal church. When she walked into the sanctuary, she was surprised to see Dr. Gorgas sitting up front in the vicar's chair. That day he had been asked to give a short sermon on Paul's letter to the Philippians. Paul, he explained, was an old man at that time and was confined to prison in Rome. The Philippians had sent Epaphroditus, one of their members, to Rome to bring a love offering to Paul and to encourage him during his time in prison. Shortly after Epaphroditus arrived, Paul came down with a serious illnesss and wrote later that he had been "nigh unto death." Paul said that God had sent Epaphroditus to console and care for him, even though by doing so "he risked his very life for me."

Dr. Gorgas went on to note that the early Christians had a name for those who risked their lives for others—*Parabolani*, or "The Gamblers." The *Parabolani* visited the sick in wretched places, in prisons, and especially in caring for those who had contagious diseases. In A.D. 252 Cyprian, the Bishop of Carthage, called the *Parabolani* to assist in caring for victims of a plague that was threatening the city. These brave Christian caregivers risked their lives by caring for the sick, burying the dead, and comforting the bereaved. Their selfless care had helped to avoid a widespread epidemic that might have wiped out the city of Carthage. Dr. Gorgas stated that the world still needed Christians to serve as *Parabolani*:

> "As for me," he assured them, "I hope I can go on pouring out my life for others until the very end. I hope," and his dark eyes twinkled, "like the old soldier, I can die with my boots on." He declared that he had no fear of death, because he expected to live beyond the grave because of the sacrifice of his Lord. . .
>
> As she returned to the Las Animas Hospital Clara could not get Dr. Gorgas' message out of her mind. Her heart was profoundly stirred as she meditated about the courage of the early Christians who served as *Parabolani*.[8]

Now that the Yellow Fever Commission doctors knew the role that mosquitoes played in causing yellow fever, their next major goal was to eradicate the disease in Cuba. In June 1901 Dr. Gorgas and his colleague Dr. Juan Guiteras hypothesized that a person might be immunized from yellow fever by allowing them to contract a mild case of the disease under controlled hospital conditions. To test this hypothesis they set up an experiment in which volunteer subjects would be bitten by infected mosquitoes. Each volunteer was offered $100US for participating in the program—a large sum of money at that time. If they contracted yellow fever, they would be given another $100 and would receive prompt medical attention at the Las Animas Hospital. This was one of the first informed consent clinical trials ever conducted by the U.S. government.

Clara was the only female who volunteered to participate in the study. Two of the six male participants died of yellow fever, but Clara only had a mild fever and was back to work the following week. She offered to provide a blood sample to Dr. Guiteras, thinking that she was now immune to the disease. But Dr. Guiteras thought that her case was too mild to provide immunity. Two days later she showed up in Dr. Guiteras' laboratory and said she wanted to participate in another mosquito trial. Dr. Guiteras was reluctant to have her again as a subject but eventually gave in when he saw that she was determined to repeat the trial.

On August 14, 1901, Clara bared her arm and allowed herself to be bitten twice by an infected mosquito. Four days later she woke up at 6 A.M. and was shaking violently. By 2 P.M. her temperature was up to 102 degrees and her pulse was 115. Dr. Gorgas visited her and remarked that "It really got you this time. You're going to have to fight back with all you've got."[9]

That evening she began vomiting but felt better afterwards. She asked her nurse for some stationery and a pen. Then she proceeded to write a note to her mother, who was now widowed and caring for her two youngest daughters back in New Jersey.

> "Good-bye, Mother. Don't worry. God will care for me in the yellow fever hospital the same as if I were at home. I will send you nearly all I earn, so be good to yourself and the two little ones (her younger sisters). You know I am the man of the family now, but do pray."[10]

On August 24 Clara died, a martyr in the battle against yellow fever. That evening Dr. Gorgas sat down at his desk and picked up the telephone to send the following telegram:

> "A wire please to Mrs. Robert Maass, East Orange, New Jersey. It should read—" His voice broke. He struggled for control, then went on, 'Miss Maass died twenty-fourth, six-thirty.' Sign it Gorgas."[11]

On August 25 the New York ***Journal*** carried a front-page article about Clara's death, followed by a New York ***Times*** editorial that same week. After the ***Times*** editorial, a public outcry against trials with human subjects forced the U.S. government to stop all ongoing experimental research on human subjects. The Yellow Fever Commission then launched a massive campaign to remove all the places where mosquitoes could breed. With fastidious attention to detail they succeeded in completely eradicating yellow fever from Cuba by May of 1902. A few cases of yellow fever occurred in 1905, but they were quickly handled using Dr. Gorgas' methods.

Dr. Gorgas next went to Panama and eradicated yellow fever there in 1906. After that he went on to Rio de Janeiro, Vera Cruz, and Guayaquil, Ecuador, and removed the threat of yellow fever in all these cities.

After Dr. Gorgas's death in 1920 researchers discovered that twenty different species of mosquitoes could carry yellow fever, and they eventually isolated a virus that was responsible for causing the disease. Several scientists and volunteers died before a vaccine for yellow fever was discovered in 1949. But Clara Maass was the only woman and the only nurse who died in this decades-long quest for a cure for this most dreaded tropical disease.

On February 20, 1927, Miss Leopoldine Guinther picked up the Newark ***Evening News*** and glanced at the "25 Years Ago Today" column. In this article she read, "The body of Clara L. Maass, who died in Cuba, has been shipped to Newark and buried there with military honors." Miss Guinther was the Superintendent of Nursing at the German Hospital, which had been renamed as the Newark Memorial Hospital in 1919. She had seen portraits of Clara Maass at the hospital and was vaguely aware that she had died in Cuba, but she was astounded to learn that she had received a military funeral when her body was buried in Newark. She was determined to learn more about this courageous young staff nurse who had given her life for the advancement of science.

Miss Guinther found Clara's eighty-year old mother, who was then living in a home for the aged. From the mother she was able to find Clara's grave, which by then was covered with weeds in Newark's Fairmount Cemetery. After that she made a trip to Cuba at her own expense, to learn what she could from scientists and government authorities at the Las Animas Hospital where Clara had died.

After returning home from Cuba Miss Guinther launched a campaign to raise money for a new grave marker for Clara Maass. By 1930 she had collected enough money to purchase a pink granite headstone for Clara's grave. On the headstone she placed a bronze tablet with a portrait of Clara and a paragraph about her life. At the bottom of the tablet she had instructed the engraver to write the inscription, "Greater love hath no man than this."[12]

On August 24, 1951, the Cuban government issued a two-cent stamp on the 50th anniversary of Clara's death. Three million of these stamps were issued, containing a portrait of Clara Maass and drawings of the old Newark German Hospital and the Las Animas Hospital. At the bottom of the stamp was the message, "For Science and Humanity—In Peace and in War." Pastor Arthur Herbert of the Newark Hospital—which had been renamed to the Newark Lutheran Memorial Hospital—and three of Clara's surviving sisters traveled to Cuba to participate in the ceremony for the issuing of the stamp.

Pastor Herbert continually pressed the Hospital to increase public awareness about Clara's ultimate sacrifice for medical science. Finally, on June 19, 1952, the Hospital was renamed again as the Clara Maass

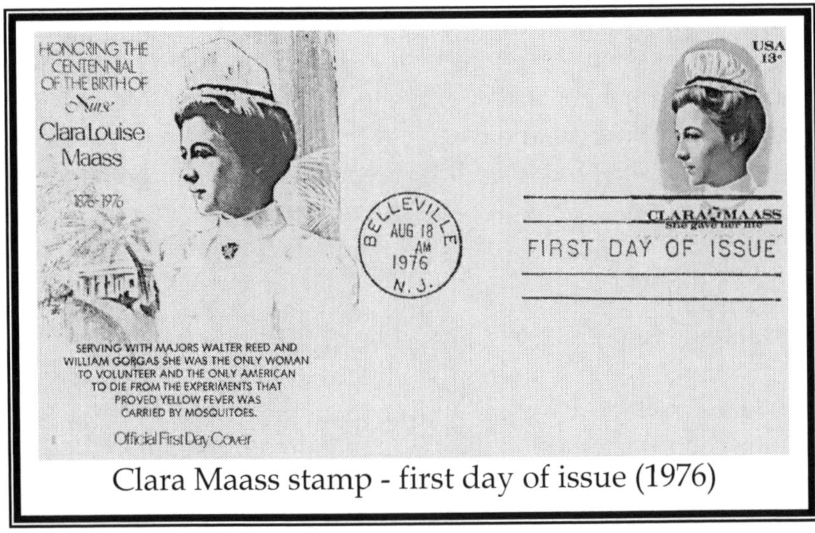

Clara Maass stamp - first day of issue (1976)

Memorial Hospital. The Hospital had been in financial distress for many years, and a campaign to raise funds for a new building had begun shortly after the end of World War II. In 1954 a private matching grant of $1 million was pledged, and a larger site was selected for the new facility in nearby Belleville. In August 1956 the new facility was opened with 125 beds. Twenty years later the U.S. Postal Service issued a Clara Maass stamp to commemorate her 100th birthday.

The Clara Maass Medical Center was the first U.S. hospital to be named after a nurse.

Today the Clara Maass Medical Center is part of the RWJBarnabas Medical System and is a 469-bed acute care center that serves Belleville, Newark, and many other communities in Northern New Jersey. It has a staff of 700 physicians and 2000 employees and serves more than 19,000 patients every year.[13] It continues the tradition of medical excellence that the Founders began in 1868. It was the first New Jersey hospital to use antiseptic methods and to perform Caesarian deliveries and other innovative procedures. The Hospital continues to receive commendations for its excellence in cleanliness and other categories of medical care.

The Clara Maass Medical Center was the first hospital in the United States to bear the name of a nurse. This outstanding medical facility continues to be a remembrance to the courageous young German-American nurse who became a Twentieth-Century *Parabolani* by caring for those who suffered from infectious diseases.

Part Four

Release for the Oppressed

Release for the Oppressed:

The Morally and Spiritually Disinherited

Newark and other major American cities have thousands of residents who lead lives of hopelessness and desperation. These problems are always present but are intensified during wars and civil disturbances. The individuals presented in Part Four gave hope to men and women, orphans, and youth living in Newark.

ALEXANDER MacWHORTER (1734-1807) was a Presbyterian pastor who served on General George Washington's War Council during the battles of Trenton and Princeton. After the Revolutionary War he spearheaded the construction of the current First Presbyterian Church and led the church during several waves of religious revival. In his later years he promoted the establishment of numerous charitable organizations to benefit the disadvantaged.

ELIZABETH RICORD (1788-1865) was the first American woman to write books on psychology and philosophy. She founded and directed an innovative female theological seminary in Geneva, New York, for several years. When her health declined, she moved to Newark to live with her son Frederick and became one of the founders of the Newark Orphan Asylum. Frederick was a noted historian who also served as Mayor during Newark's Industrial Exposition in 1872.

EDWIN LEAHY (1945-) is currently Headmaster of St. Benedict's Preparatory School. After the school closed in 1972 due to declining enrollments, Father Leahy and his colleagues cast a vision to reopen the school to educate young men from all backgrounds based on Benedictine standards. The school's resurgence since 1973 has been called "the miracle on High Street."

CHAPTER TEN

Alexander MacWhorter (1734-1807): Newark's North Star

In November 1776 the Continental Army suffered a disastrous loss at Fort Washington, New York, during which nearly 3000 of Washington's troops were taken captive by the British army. After failing to hold Fort Washington and Fort Lee, New Jersey, Washington's remaining army of 3500 soldiers crossed the Passaic River and marched south to Newark. With Lord Cornwallis' army in hot pursuit, the Continental army entered Newark by night on November 22 and tarried in the village for five days.

According to one account, a young soldier named Thomas Paine sat under a Sycamore tree in Military Park and penned the first of several letters that he called "The American Crisis."[1] He wrote,

> "These are the times that try men's souls. The summer soldier and the sunshine patriot will in this crisis, shrink from the service of their country; but he that stands by it now, deserves the love and thanks of man and woman. Tyranny, like hell, is not easily conquered; yet we have this consolation with us, that the harder the conflict, the more glorious the triumph. What we obtain too cheap, we esteem too lightly; it is dearness that gives everything its value.[2]

These five days that "try men's souls" gave Washington and his troops the brief rest they needed to continue fighting despite the overwhelming advantages held by the British Army. According to one historian Washington set up his headquarters at the Eagle Tavern on Broad Street, while his troops made camp at Military Park and various other locations around the village.[3] It was there that Washington reconnected with his friend and compatriot, Pastor ALEXANDER MACWHORTER. Their friendship grew even stronger in that season, which historians now refer to as Washington's "Retreat to Victory."[4]

At the outbreak of the Revolutionary War Newark was a charming village that was isolated from the day-to-day events in the cities along the East Coast. Except for occasional outbreaks of diseases like smallpox and yellow fever, Newarkers led their lives relatively free of outside influences. One hundred years after its founding, Newark was a small village with about 1200 inhabitants. Commenting on life in Newark in the 18th Century, one historian remarked that "it drowsed and dreamed in peace and quiet, content to stay as it was. . . ."[5] The same historian continued,

> "Its people do not seem to have cared much to be rich nor did they wish to see their town made big. They were born, grew up, married, lived their span of years in peace and quiet and moderate labor, died and were buried in the old burying ground back of the fire-engine houses on Broad street near Market street—or in the churchyard that you may still see back of the First Presbyterian Church—like their fathers and grandfathers before them.[6]

All of this changed quickly, however, in the year 1776. Suddenly the people of Newark were forced to take sides—to declare their allegiance either to King George or to the Patriot's cause. Like the rest of New Jersey residents, when the war started Newarkers were split between Patriots, Loyalists, and those who were politically neutral. The Patriots were most strongly represented by the Presbyterian churches, who had been part of the Dissenter movement in England for more than a century. The Loyalists, on the other hand, were aligned with the Episcopal church, the American counterpart to the Church of England, which was nominally headed by the King. And then there were many farmers and craftsmen who were disinclined to have any political allegiances and wanted to lead their lives free of British or Patriot involvements.

Lord Cornwallis and his army entered into the north end of Newark on November 28, 1776—the same day that Washington's army was marching south to Elizabethtown (or Elizabeth, as it is called today) en route to Pennsylvania. The British tarried in Newark until December 1, which was a stroke of good luck for Washington and his army but was a disaster for the residents who lingered behind in Newark and Elizabethtown.

Alexander MacWhorter

MacWhorter and his colleague, the Rev. Jacob Van Arsdale from Springfield, retreated to Pennsylvania with Washington and became part of the War Counsel that planned and executed the Continental Army's strategy to attack British outposts along the Delaware River. On Christmas Eve Washington and his troops crossed the Delaware and captured the Hessian outpost at Trenton. A week later they made a surprise attack on the British garrison at Princeton and then escaped safely to their camp in Bucks County. These back-to-back victories astonished King George and helped to persuade France to join the American cause.

When MacWhorter returned to Newark four months later, he was appalled at the devastation caused by the British soldiers. In a letter to the ***Pennsylvania Evening Post***, he wrote,

> "Great have been the ravages committed by the British troops in this part of the country, as to what has been done by them in Trenton, Princeton, &c., you have seen. Their footsteps with us are marked with desolation and ruin of every kind. I, with many others, fled from the town, and those that tarried behind suffered almost every manner of evil. The murder, robbery, ravishments, and insults they were guilty of were dreadful. When I returned to the town, it looked more like a scene of ruin than a pleasant well cultivated village. . . Their plundering is so universal, and their robberies so atrocious, that I cannot fully describe their conduct. Whig and Tory were all treated in the same manner, except such who were happy enough to procure a sentinel to be placed as a guard at their door."[7]

These and other similar accounts persuaded many New Jersey people to join the Patriot cause, seeing that the British had no regard for either Patriot (Whig) or Tory residents or their personal property. Ben Franklin's observation that "we must, indeed, either hang together, or most assuredly we will hang separately," must have rung in their ears as they surveyed the devastation the British army caused as they passed through New Jersey.

The MacWhorter family knew the cost of religious freedom. Alexander's maternal ancestors were Scotch-Irish merchants who lived in County Armagh in the north of Ireland. His mother's grandparents were martyrs who died in the Irish massacre of 1641 during the English Civil War. His immediate parents, Hugh and Jane, were pious Christians who immigrated to America in 1730 and settled in Newcastle, Delaware. They had eleven children, of which Alexander was the youngest. He was born on July 15, 1734, and was given the same name as one of his brothers who had died a month earlier.

As a young child Alexander recalled that his parents had a custom of spending every Sabbath day raising up their children in the fear and admonition of the Lord. To the day of his death he remembered many long walks in the forest with his dear father, as well as his mother's importunate prayers about his spiritual condition. She frequently took the young lad to a private room, exhorted to him with tears, and entreated him with anguish to be reconciled to God. These early devotional times did not produce an immediate effect on the young Alexander, but they bore fruit in due season.[8]

In February 1748, when Alexander was in his fourteenth year, his father died and left Jane to care for their four youngest children. Since three of their eldest children had previously settled in Charlotte, North Carolina, Jane moved there to be near them. There the family was ministered to by a Mr. John Brown, a "New Light" (evangelical) preacher who taught them the horrors of death apart from the love and grace of Jesus Christ. Struck with grief from his father's death, and fondly remembering the long walks they had taken together in Delaware, young Alexander retreated every day to the pine woods near his brother's house and repeated the same prayers he had learned from his father. As his eulogist wrote,

> "Thus the seed of truth, which had been planted by a father's care, and watered by his mother's tears, was preparing to shoot."[9]

After living two or three years with his mother in North Carolina, Alexander attended private colleges in Delaware and Maryland for two years. In 1756, during his twenty-second year, he moved to Newark and entered the junior class at the newly-formed College of New Jersey. In Newark he was instructed by President Aaron Burr, Sr., who was not only an outstanding preacher but was also gifted in classical languages and the liberal arts. When the College relocated to Princeton in 1757, Alexander became a member of Princeton's first graduating class. He took his degree from Princeton in the fall of 1757, just a few days after the unexpected death of President Burr.

After graduating from Princeton he went under care with the Rev. William Tennent of Freehold. He was licensed to preach in 1758 and was married to Mary Cumming that year. Mary was the daughter of a respected merchant who also served as the sheriff of Monmouth County.

In the late 1750's Newark's First Presbyterian Church was in turmoil and was without a permanent pastor for several years. For two years the church suffered from internal division, until they called Alexander to preach a sermon to them in June of 1759. The congregation immediately developed a fondness for him and called him to be their pastor that summer. He was ordained by the synod of New York and Philadelphia and was installed as pastor at the Newark church when he was twenty-five years old.

The First Presbyterian Church witnessed five revivals of religion during the years MacWhorter pastored the congregation. The first of these occurred during the winter of 1764-65 and served as an encouragement to him during a time of severe physical illness. In 1772 a second spiritual awakening began and was more extensive than the first, lasting for two years.[10] By the end of 1774 the membership rolls of the church had greatly increased, and plans were drawn up to build a larger sanctuary. A considerable sum of money and materials were collected for this purpose, but the outbreak of the Revolutionary War prevented the plans from being implemented at that time.[11]

The third revival under MacWhorter started in 1784 and lasted for two years. During that "glorious revival of religion" more than a hundred souls were added to the church. In his funeral message for Dr. MacWhorter, Edward Griffin described the events of that memorable season as follows:

> "In no period of the Doctor's ministry was he observed to be so deeply laden with a sense of everlasting things, and so ardent in his desire to win souls to Christ. Besides his labors on the Sabbath, he preached several times in the week, and spent a part of almost every day in catechizing, exhorting from house to house, or attending religious societies."[12]

As a result of Dr. MacWhorter's indomitable zeal and perseverance, the congregation began to build the present house of worship in September of 1787. Through the financial and volunteer labor contributions of the congregation, the new building was completed in three years and was officially dedicated for public worship on January 1, 1791. At the time of dedication it was the second largest congregation in America, with its membership exceeded only by the First Presbyterian Church in Philadelphia.

Two more revivals of religion under MacWhorter occurred in 1796 and 1802, during a period known as the Second Great Awakening.[13] The 1796 awakening added thirty or forty new members to the church and produced a greater interest in benevolent institutions to assist the growing number of immigrants and needy families in the community. The 1802 awakening resulted in one hundred and forty adults joining the church, including more than a hundred persons in one twelve-month period.[14]

Throughout his forty-eight year ministry Dr. MacWhorter gave strong support for charitable institutions in Newark. One of his early passions at the First Presbyterian Church was to become a subscriber to the Widow's Fund, which was established in 1761. Having grown up in a single-parent household, he had a burden for widows and those who were destitute for other reasons. He was a life-long subscriber to this fund and in later years served as its director.[11]

Following the spiritual awakening of 1802, his sermons gave increasing emphasis to the empowerment of women in leadership positions to care for the needy and disadvantaged. One of these initiatives, The Newark Female Charitable Society, was launched in 1803 and served the community for more than a century, as is described in Chapter Two of this book. His 1805 "Charity Sermon" set down principles of Christian charity that inspired Newarkers for several generations. In that address to the Newark Female Charitable Society he wrote,

> "God is ever pleased with the graces, virtues and duties of his people, but with none more than the manifestations of a public

> spirit, in doing public and general good. . . . In sacrificing something was parted with and given to God; so, in doing good to our fellow men, administering to the necessities of the poor, supporting the gospel, propagating it among the heathen etc., some of our worldly goods must be parted with and dedicated to God; this is offering Christian sacrifice. And such offerings are important duties incumbent upon all who are blessed with the good things of this world."

He continued by urging the members of his congregation to contribute generously to the relief of the poor:

> "The object of our present charity, is to assist a Female Charitable Society in this Town, for the relief and assistance of certain poor, who are in distress, and yet not so perfectly reduced as to cast themselves on the town. . . . Now they apply to this congregation and to the town for assistance. It is undoubtedly our duty to assist them. They have laid out their money with judgment and propriety. They have relieved the distressed, taken care of the poor sick, and are doing most important service in this place. Therefore, let us help them that they may help the poor."[16]

Through his leadership in benevolent institutions in Newark, his advice and encouragement to Washington and the Continental Army, and his prominent role in the General Assembly of the Presbyterian Church, he provided a "moral compass" that was greatly needed in the early days of the United States. This moral compass kept his ministry focused on Christian charity.

MacWhorter had a deep understanding of the history and destiny of Newark. He knew that the Founders had established the city to be a representation of the kingdom of God on earth, but he also knew that church and state had been separated in the 1740's and were not likely to be reunited into a Puritan theocracy again. Had God failed to achieve His purposes in Newark? Or was it possible that the Founders' conception of the kingdom of God was incorrect?

An illustration from ancient Greece may help to understand this dilemma. In the time of Homer (c. 850 B.C.) Greek sailing vessels navigated the sea with reference to the constellation Ursa Major (the "Big Bear"). It was thought that this constellation was "true north"—i.e., the solar object around which all other objects revolved. By 600 B.C., however, the Phoenicians became more skilled at navigating the seas than the Greeks because they navigated according to the "Phoenician constellation," which is referred to today as Ursa Minor (the "Little Bear"). At the top of Ursa Minor is Polaris, which we now know is the closest star to true north. By navigating according to Ursa Minor, the Phoenicians needed fewer mid-course adjustments than the Greeks did to reach their destination.[17]

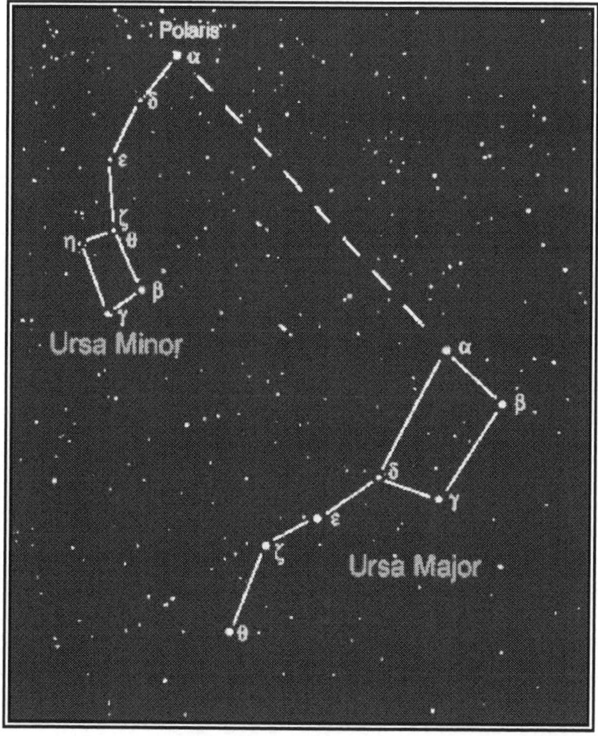

By 600 B.C. the Phoenicians had discovered that Ursa Minor includes Polaris—the "true north" for celestial navigation.

During Newark's first century its leaders implemented and enforced a government that combined church and state, under the impression that the kingdom of God was best implemented through a theocracy. This model worked fairly well during the 1600's, but by the time of the Constitutional Convention it was clear that the American government would be a republic rather than a theocracy. Moreover, at the local level the theocratic model failed when many second- and third-generation Newarkers refused to become church members. Since Newark's laws allowed only church members to vote and hold property, an increasing number of Newark residents had no representation in issues facing the town government.

MacWhorter's focus on charity rather than legalism represented an important "paradigm shift" for the Presbyterian church in Newark.

MacWhorter's focus on charity rather than legalism represented an important "paradigm shift" for the Presbyterian church in Newark. From 1800 to the present day, the emphasis of the church has been on Christian charity, character development, and the role of the family as a key social institution. Since the Second Great Awakening, a vast number of benevolent institutions have been established to care for the less advantaged members of society. MacWhorter's sermons, as well as his personal life, pointed toward the life of Jesus, not toward political or economic agendas. As he wrote in his "Charity Sermon,"

> "Love to our neighbor is the summary of the whole second part of religion; and our Lord, in the parable of the good Samaritan, has taught us that our neighbor is the whole family of mankind. Wherefore, when we are called and have an opportunity to give, let us do it with a Christian and a benevolent heart, and with a free, open, charitable and generous spirit. Let the god-like principle of benevolence to mankind, rule and reign in our minds. . . . Whatever we do, whether as it immediately respects God, ourselves, or our fellow man, ought

to be performed from a right temper, from proper views, and for a proper end."[18]

Alexander MacWhorter died on July 20, 1807, a week after his seventy-third birthday. In his own words, he had "lived to see two worlds die."[19] All of the Founding Fathers of America knew him, and he lived long enough to baptize the entire generation of Newarkers who were born after the end of the Revolutionary War. His ministry guided Newark—and Colonial America as well—through its darkest and most turbulent period.

In a very real sense he provided the spiritual leadership that supported Newark's growth from a small village into a modern industrial city that welcomed immigrants from Europe while expanding civil liberties for African-Americans and other groups. By the end of his lifetime New Jersey had passed legislation for the gradual elimination of slavery (in 1804). A generation later Newark churches were welcoming African-Americans to their services and providing resources for them to form their own congregations (such as the Fourth Presbyterian Church in Newark).

Harriet Tubman was a Maryland slave who was called by God to release more than three hundred fugitive slaves from captivity in the years leading up to the Civil War. Although she initially resisted God's call for her to proclaim freedom for the captives, she was confident that God would lead her every step of the way. She made nineteen return trips to the South to help slaves gain their freedom, and she claimed that "I never lost a passenger." When asked about the source of her strength for this ministry, she stated simply, I'm gwine [going] to hold stiddy on you, an' you've got to see me through."[20]

Tubman claimed that God told her to travel to freedom by night, following the North Star on the long journey to Canada, where the slaves would receive their freedom. On several occasions her night journeys brought her to Newark, where she and her fugitives took refuge in the basement of the First Presbyterian Church. Although her stays in Newark were never mentioned publicly, Pastor Jonathan Stearns certainly knew that the church's involvement in the Underground Railroad was contrary to the prevailing federal and state laws. Like Tubman, the First Presbyterian Church followed the moral compass of Jesus rather than the laws of government authorities.

We close this chapter with Harriet Tubman's poem, "The North Star," which poignantly summarizes how God guided her to lead fugitives to their freedom.

THE NORTH STAR

by Harriet Tubman

The North Star leads and guides my way.
O Lord show me favor now I pray,
For I'm walking to freedom day by day.
It's more than a fight, more than a dream,
It's the fact we're all created equal, so let
freedom ring.

So I'm not giving up, I'll keep fighting still
I'll die for this cause if that is Your will.
It is my hope for the next generation to see,
What it's like to truly be free.
So there's no time for worry, no time for fear,
For the light of independence is far too near! [21]

CHAPTER ELEVEN

Elizabeth Stryker Ricord (1788-1865): The Newark Orphan Asylum

Today, as we drive down Dr. Martin Luther King, Jr., Boulevard past Stevens Hall at the New Jersey Institute of Technology ("NJIT"), or on Ricord Street in the West Ward, we would do well to remember ELIZABETH STRYKER RICORD, who used her gifts in teaching and parenting to manage the first home for the growing population of orphans in New Jersey in 1847.

The Panic of 1837 caused considerable distress among Newarkers, particularly in lower-income families. Most of Newark's manufacturing firms closed down that year, after two decades of economic boom. While many workers who lost their jobs moved back to Europe in search of employment, other unemployed workers turned to alcohol to drown their sorrows. The demand for relief and health care services grew dramatically, and in 1840 city officials established the Newark Alms House to care for these poor and needy individuals.

The Alms House was built on Elizabeth Avenue with public funding. Official reports revealed that more than half of the inmates of the Alms House were admitted because of alcohol addictions. Data from 1851 revealed that many of the Alms House residents were "friendless, jobless, and penniless,"[1] In that year there was an occupancy level of fifty-five inmates and an alarming number of twenty-six deaths—a one-year mortality rate of almost 50%. In addition, three-quarters of the inmates that year were immigrants.

To make matters worse the Newark Alms House was "plagued by overcrowding, inadequate nutrition, filth, and primitive unsanitary facilities."[2] It was built adjacent to a meadow that was a prime breeding ground for malaria-carrying mosquitoes.

In describing the Alms House historian Stuart Galishoff writes,

> "A decrepit old almshouse located on the edge of the meadows, where its ignominy could not trouble the conscience of the community, housed the incapacitated. From a health standpoint, a worse site could not have been chosen. Damp, humid, and thick with mosquitoes, some species of which transmitted malaria, the almshouse was a nursery of sickness and death. Intended to provide indoor relief for the poor, the almshouse was in reality a dumping ground for the community's handicapped, dependent, and deviant members, a place where orphans, widows, the infirm, the feeble-minded and other luckless souls were indiscriminately herded together with drunkards and criminals, often two or more to a bed."[3]

Admission to the Newark Alms House, then, was not only hazardous to the incapacitated members who required care, but also to the well-being of their children.

In Newark and other East Coast cities the churches and synagogues began to realize that deacons' funds and almshouses could not solve the growing need for social services for orphans. In an 1835 sermon to the Boston Female Asylum for Destitute Orphans, an Episcopal rector named Jonathan Mayhew Wainwright stated,

> "Should any of you in your walks through the city during its inclement winter behold a child almost naked, shivering with cold and fainting with hunger, and did you learn that it had wandered unprotected from the home where its only surviving parent had just expired in all the wretchedness of poverty and disease, and finding its mother's voice silent, her hands that had cherished it cold, and her eyes closed, the little one had gone forth weeping and alone, would any of you refuse it a home and

> food and protection? It is this sacred duty which our Institution has performed for many such suffering and innocent beings. Where, if not to such an object, can the heart send forth its sympathies without restraint, and give itself to all the delights of a glowing generosity?"[4]

Rector Wainright reminded his congregation of their sacred duty to care for orphans, having pity especially on those children who never had the opportunity to say "father" or "mother" or to be embraced by loving parents.

Until the 1830's the primary model of caring for needy orphans was the indenture system. Indenture, which was also called apprenticeship or "binding out," involved releasing a youth to an adult employer, who was expected to act as a parental figure. (In Chapter One, we reviewed how Moses Combs trained a generation of apprentices in innovative techniques of shoemaking, while providing them instruction in education and in character development. His school was an outstanding model of how the indenture or apprenticeship system was intended to operate.) The cholera epidemic of 1832, and the subsequent Panic of 1837, however, overwhelmed the indenture system and required a new solution for the problem of orphanhood in Newark and other cities.

A number of leading Protestant women met in 1847 to establish the Newark Orphan Asylum, which became the first orphanage in New Jersey.

In response to this burden a number of leading Protestant women met in 1847 to establish the Newark Orphan Asylum, which became the first orphanage in New Jersey. Modeled after asylums in New York, Massachusetts, and Pennsylvania, the Newark Orphan Asylum sought to protect vulnerable orphans from the outside world while allowing parents to take back their children as their circumstances permitted. Like other orphan asylums, the Newark orphanage provided education, religious training, and practical skills such as sewing and job skills. These forward-looking women chose Elizabeth Stryker Ricord to be the first Directress of the Asylum.

Elizabeth Stryker Ricord

Elizabeth Stryker was the second of three children born to a Dutch Reformed pastor, Peter Stryker. He and his wife Sarah served a congregation in Perth Amboy, New Jersey, for twenty years before relocating to Geneva, New York, where he served as a missionary. As a child Elizabeth was described as:

> "'[A] real lady and a lovely Christian,' from whose lips was never heard 'a word of unkindness, harsh judgment, gossip or idle talk.' She was 'gentle, kindly, full of sweet reasonableness, patience, peace.'"[5]

In 1810 she married Jean Baptiste Ricord-Madianna, who was the son of a successful ship owner from the West Indies and the grandson of a distinguished physician from Marseilles, France. They moved to his family home town in Guadaloupe and had four sons, of whom only

Frederick and John survived to adulthood. Jean Baptiste studied medicine at the College of Physicians and Surgeons in New York but was more interested in music, painting, and history than in practicing medicine. He was a Roman Catholic, whereas Elizabeth was a pious evangelical with Calvinist persuasions. In 1823 they separated—perhaps due to differences in their religious beliefs and lifestyles—and Elizabeth returned to New Jersey with her sons.[6]

In 1829 she moved to Geneva, New York, to be closer to her parents and brother, James Stryker. To support herself and her family she opened a secondary school for women, which she called the Geneva Female Seminary. At that time secondary education for women was in single-sex academies and seminaries, most of which were privately funded. Elizabeth modeled her school after the Troy (New York) Female Seminary, an outstanding prototype that set the national standard for excellence in curriculum and methods for educating women by building upon the model developed by Emma Willard. Unlike most secondary schools for women at that time, the Geneva Female Seminary went beyond the usual offerings of music, painting, sewing, language, and social graces to offer rigorous core academic offerings:

> "Elizabeth was part of a growing group of women that believed that women should receive an education equal to that of men. She saw the primary purpose of her seminary as training teachers. With that in mind she designed a much more rigorous curriculum than what was offered at the majority of female seminaries. Besides sewing very few domestic subjects were offered. The core subjects were spelling, reading, geography, arithmetic, history (ancient and modern), science (astronomy, botany, geology, natural history, and chemistry), mental philosophy, moral philosophy, natural philosophy and composition. For an additional fee classes in Latin, Greek, Italian, French, music, drawing and painting were also offered."[7]

She personally taught innovative courses in 'mental philosophy' (psychology) and 'moral philosophy' (ethics) that were structured so as to "lead you to an acquaintance with the powers of your own minds, and be the first step in that most important part of your education, Self-Knowledge."[8] The textbook she developed for these courses was the first book on psychology or philosophy written by an American woman. It was also the first book-length academic work that described gender differences.[9]

One of her key insights was that nurture rather than nature causes young women to focus on "the minutiae of domestic concerns" and on receiving admiration and affection. For this reason many of her lectures focused on the importance of instructing young children, particularly by parents. She saw the woman's role as teacher of the young as particularly important:

> "For Ricord, the terms mother and teacher are practically synonymous. A mother is a teacher, and the most influential teacher is the mother. It is clear that Ricord expected her students to become mothers or teachers and that the self-knowledge she urged them to seek would prepare them for their life's task."[10]

The Seminary was highly successful and averaged 200 students per year for more than a decade. During the 1830's it was a hotbed of revival in Western New York, frequently hosting campaigns by Charles Finney and his associates. Ricord served as Principal of the Seminary until 1840 but then stepped down because of poor health. Two years later she closed the Seminary, which had faced continuing problems in generating endowment funding.

By 1845 her sons Frederick and John were grown and were developing successful professional careers. Frederick taught at a private school and invited his mother to come live with him in Newark. Accepting his offer, Elizabeth moved into his home and spent the final twenty years of her life in Newark.

Concerned about the increasing number of orphans needing assistance from the churches, a group of Protestant women organized the Newark Orphan Asylum on November 5, 1847. The Asylum accepted children of both sexes from two to ten years of age. In addition to full orphans the Asylum accepted fatherless, motherless, and illegitimate children. The Newark Orphan Asylum was located at 323 High Street (currently Dr. Martin Luther King, Jr. Boulevard), which is now Stevens Hall on NJIT campus. Today it is the oldest existing building at NJIT.

The opening of the Newark Orphan Asylum encouraged other religious and ethnic groups to start orphanages as well. In 1849 the Episcopal churches established the Protestant Foster Home at 284 Belleville Avenue in the North Ward. Roman Catholics opened up St. Mary's Orphan Asylum at South Orange Avenue and North Sandford St. in 1853. And Jewish leaders launched the Hebrew Orphan Asylum at 533-44 Clinton Avenue in 1861. All of these institutions sought to address six key challenges facing all orphanages:

1. How can we maintain a proper standard of health among the children at the institution?
2. How shall we give our children the education which fits for life?
3. By what means can the institution furnish its wards with a proper social life and wholesome education?
4. The problem of discipline: how shall we approach it?
5. How can we preserve the right relationship between the children and their relatives, so that the two should not become estranged?
6. The problem of 'after care,' i.e., how should the children be followed up after they leave the institution?[11]

Although we do not have any documents or personal correspondence from Elizabeth Ricord during her years in Newark, the time she spent as Principal of the Geneva Female Seminary undoubtedly prepared her to set up the Newark Orphan Asylum. It appears to have been one of the outstanding orphanages in the Northeast. A detailed description of the Asylum and its services appeared in a 1912 document published by the Newark Bureau of Associated Charities; see the excerpt on page 159 for details.

The Newark Orphan Asylum (now Stevens Hall)
323 Dr. Martin Luther King, Jr. Boulevard

This document indicates how the Asylum addressed the six key issues mentioned above. First, the medical issues were assessed by a physician who did an initial examination of the children referred to the orphanage. It is not explicitly stated that this physician provided continuing care to the orphans after admission, although this was quite possibly the case. Second, the educational curriculum for the children in the orphanage was likely designed by Ricord, given her outstanding credentials as a teacher and academic administrator. The 1912 writeup explicitly mentions that the children were schooled at the institution rather than sent to public grammar schools. Third, the 1912 document mentions a Country Home in Westfield, NJ, where the children were able to get out of the urban environment from May through October. At the Country Home they also learned practical skills in farming. The document does not specifically mention the issue of discipline, but Ricord's love of children and her experience as an educator undoubtedly addressed this issue. Fifth, in regard to relationships with natural family members, the document mentions that families were allowed to visit the Asylum on the first Friday of each month or by special permission.

The Newark Orphan Asylum Association (1912)

(Org. 1847; inc. 1849). 323 High Street. Telephone, 987R Market. Country Home, Westfield, N.J., to which Home the children are taken about May each year, returning to Newark in October. A Protestant Home for destitute orphans or half-orphans of both sexes. Children received from the age of two to ten years, subject to the physician's examination. Those able to pay for the admission of children are required to do so up to the maximum of about $4.00 per month for each child. Capacity, 110. Children are generally kept until the age of twelve. Relatives and friends may visit the Home on the first Friday in the month. Legal holidays are not visiting days except by special permission. Children are not sent to public school but are given instruction within the institution. There is no specific industrial or manual training at the Home in Newark. At the Country Home, however, the children are taught farming. Officers: First Directress, Mrs. F.S. Douglas; Secretary, Mrs. N.A. Merritt; Treasurer, Mrs. C.A. Woodhull; Chairman of Admission Committee, Mrs. N.A. Merritt, 137 Livingston Street, New Brunswick, N.J., telephone 4533L Market.[13]

Finally, the issue of after care is addressed by examining the data in Table 1. This is a table that the author compiled from an 1884 publication that provided statistical data on every orphanage in the United States. In this table the Newark Orphan Asylum is compared with five similar orphanages in New York and New Jersey (The Children's Friend Society in Jersey City, NJ; The Cayuga Asylum for Destitute Children in Auburn, NY; the Susquehanna Valley Home in Binghamton, NY; and St. Vincent's Male and Female Orphan Asylums in Albany, NY). From Table 1 it appears that the Newark Orphan Asylum compared favorably with these other orphanages in terms of educational offerings and placement services. Although all five institutions provided education in the "three R's" (reading, writing, and arithmetic), only the Newark Orphan Asylum and the Cayuga Asylum for Destitute Children offered training to students in drawing and music.

The biggest difference, however, was in terms of placement services. The Newark Orphan Asylum reported that orphans leaving their institution were "adopted, placed in homes, or returned to friends." The St. Vincent's Male and Female Orphan Asylums stated that orphans were "placed in homes or with friends." The other three comparison institutions, however, offered considerably less after care for children who left the institution. The Susquehanna Valley Home, for example, stated that the aftercare provision was "homes provided or children indentured," which could have been considerably less supportive than placement in a free home with adopted parents or friends. The Cayuga Asylum for Destitute Children said their after care provision was "given a suit of clothing," and the Children's Friend Society in Jersey City listed their after care provision as "none".[12]

In 1916 Miss A. J. Sutphen, a member of the Board of Trustees, summarized the achievements of the Newark Orphan Asylum in its first seventy-five years as follows:

> "Undoubtedly the main reason that children are in orphan asylums and other kindred institutions is that dependent children have been cared for in that way in our cities for the last seventy-five years. We have had the institutions and the

Table 1: Comparison of Six New York/New Jersey Orphanages

	Newark Orphan Asylum	Children's Friend Society	Cayuga Asylum for Destitute Children	Susquehanna Valley Home	St. Vincent's Male/Female Orphan Asylums
City	Newark	Jersey City	Auburn	Binghamton	Albany
State	New Jersey	New Jersey	New York	New York	New York
Year Founded	1848	1853	1833	1859	1832-M, 1849-F
Income	$6,555	--	$5,880	$9,909	$33,376
Age Limit	12	12	No limit	16	16
Present Inmates	98	39	79	87	400
Full orphans	37	8	11	12	133
Half orphans	61	30	56	38	287
Foundlings	0	1	0	1	0
Education					
Reading	82	35	70	85	346
Writing	36	35	50	85	255
Arithmetic	82	30	54	70	280
Drawing	50	--	30	--	--
Music	70	--	70	--	--
Provision for children who have left the institution	Adopted, placed in homes or returned to friends	None	Given a suit of clothing	Homes provided or children indentured	Placed in homes or with friends

Source: Report of the Commissioner of Education for the Year 1882-'83. Washington, D.C.: Government Printing Office, 1884, p. 766

people have been trained to support them, and those interested in dependent children have turned to them for a solution of their difficulties. . . .

The children in orphan asylums are always there, naturally, through the failure of the parents properly to protect and support them. In my experience this has not been due to alcohol and immorality as much as to misfortune and inefficiency."[14]

The summer home in Westfield was significant in that it allowed the children in the orphanage to spend several months a year in a relaxed, rural environment. Miss Sutphen described this facility as follows:

> "Some of the institutions in Newark have both a summer home and winter home. Our children are turned loose in a most attractive country home for six months of the year with their own gardens, a swimming pool in the good-sized lake they row on, farm animals, and fruit trees and everything that goes to make the country a happy place, with no confining fences. In the city this long country outing interferes with the public schooling of all but the five oldest children, who are in the evening high school, so a private school is maintained both in the city and in the country. Last year a Boy Scout leader was sent to Westfield several times a week and took the boys on hikes and established the "good-turn-a-day" code."[15]

This "Children's Country Home," as it was originally called, was located at the intersection of New Providence Road and Mountain Avenue in Westfield. It originally housed eight "underprivileged" children from the Newark Orphan Asylum and was converted into a year-round home for handicapped children in 1897. During the Twentieth Century this home merged with what is now the Children's Specialized Hospital in nearby Mountainside.[16]

Starting from the humble beginnings of the Newark Orphan Asylum in 1847, child welfare services have continued to expand in New Jersey throughout the Twentieth and Twenty-First Centuries. The Newark Orphan Asylum merged with the Protestant Foster Home in 1948, and the organization known as the Advocates for Children of New Jersey (ACNJ) was created in the late Twentieth Century.[17] Orphan asylums, which were the centerpiece of child welfare services in the U.S. until the 1920's, were gradually replaced by government social service programs during the Great Depression, bringing a shift to foster care and public assistance programs in modern times.[18]

Elizabeth Stryker Ricord left a rich legacy in New York and New Jersey. Today psychologists and philosophers remember her pioneering work in "mental philosophy" for women, which encouraged hundreds of young women to examine the cultural biases that prevented women from advancing in education, ministry, and other areas. Her 1840 textbook on this subject, ***Elements of the Philosophy of Mind, Applied to the Development of Thought and Feeling,*** is generally regarded as the earliest textbook that systematically addressed the psychology of women.

During the last two decades of Ricord's life her selfless work as Directress of the Newark Orphan Asylum set a regional standard for orphanages and contributed significantly to the growth of child welfare services in New Jersey. Finally, she took seriously her roles as a mother and a teacher at home. Her two surviving sons, John and Frederick, become prominent professionals during her lifetime. John studied law and became a noted lawyer and traveler.[19]

Frederick Ricord started his career as an educator at a private school in Newark. In 1849 he was appointed as librarian of the Newark Library Association. After that he became a member of the Newark Board of Education and later served as the State Superintendent of Schools. In 1865 he was elected as Sheriff of Essex County, and four years later he was elected Mayor of Newark, which position he held from 1870-74. A notable achievement during his term as Mayor was the 1872 Industrial Exposition, which drew national attention to Newark as a major U.S. center for manufacturing. After his two terms as Mayor he continued to serve as judge for Essex county courts and as librarian for the New Jersey Historical Society.[20]

In 1883 William H. Shaw interviewed Frederick Ricord in preparation for the monumental work, ***History of Essex and Hudson Counties, New Jersey:***

> "But it is in his study, among his books, by the midnight lamp, translating from his foreign brothers in literature, that Judge Ricord would best like to be remembered to the readers of this sketch. . . .

> Although in his sixty-fourth year, Judge Ricord is a man of vigorous health. He scarcely knows what sickness is, and has never taken a month's vacation for a period of more than thirty years, and during that time has never been absent from home more than ten days at a time, and that but twice or thrice. . . .
>
> [H]e will leave to his children what will be better than gold, because gold could not purchase it—the inheritance of an honorable record, and the recollection that in raising his fellows to a higher plane in culture, and setting them a shining example in political life, the State of New Jersey has been bettered by his residence within her borders."[21]

In summary New Jersey's current child welfare system is built upon the legacy of Elizabeth Stryker Ricord, who used her gifts in teaching and parenting to establish an institution to help Newark's orphaned children grow up in a safe, healthy, and nurturing environment.

CHAPTER TWELVE

Edwin Leahy (1945 -): Fighting Against the Street

For years the monks at Newark's Benedictine monastery struggled with the challenges of running a religious institution in the middle of New Jersey's largest city. Originally established to minister to German and Irish Catholics who had moved to Newark, the monastery was forced to reassess its mission and commitment to the city as these European ethnic groups left Newark and were replaced by African-American and Latino immigrants. The monastery's academic wing, St. Benedict's Preparatory School, faced enormous challenges in the years following the Newark civil disturbances in 1967, after which many of the monks felt that the School should close its doors and relocate to the Morristown Abbey.

Finally, on February 10, 1972, the community voted to suspend operations at St. Benedict's after more than one hundred years of service to the students of Newark. Four months later half of the faculty hired a moving van and left Newark as soon as St. Benedict's completed its graduation ceremonies.

Like hundreds of other Catholic schools across the country, St. Benedict's Prep faced serious financial woes, a declining neighborhood environment, a general move away from Catholic education, decreasing enrollments, and a lack of vocations in Catholic religious life. St. Benedict's demise brought sorrow to hundreds of students and thousands of alumni, who had received excellent educations at an affordable price throughout the previous decades.

A faithful remnant of monks, however, had a dream about a "new and greater St. Benedict's" and began planning to reopen the school with an enlarged vision for urban ministry. A year later, under the leadership of Father EDWIN LEAHY, St. Benedict's Preparatory School reopened with fifteen monks and ninety-three students who were committed to rebuilding the school based on their faith that God would guide to serve all racial and ethnic groups in the Greater Newark area.[1]

The United States branch of the Order of St Benedict's ("OSB") was founded in Pennsylvania in 1846 by Father Boniface Wimmer. Two key principles guided the development of Benedictine monastic life in the U.S.—*stability* and *adaptability*:

> "Benedictines are men of *stability*; they are not wandering monks; they acquire lands and bring them under cultivation and become thoroughly affiliated to the country and people to which they belong. Moreover, based on more than a millennium of experience, the Benedictine Order could 'very readily *adapt* itself to all times and circumstances.'"[2]

All Benedictine monks took vows of conversion of life, obedience, and stability of place. Under the vow of stability, they committed to be anchored to a specific location during their monastic service. In Newark's early days this was not a problem, because it was one of the most dynamic cities in America in terms of scientific innovation and job creation. By the late 1960's, however, racial and ethnic tensions in Newark climaxed, and the populations from which St. Benedict's traditionally recruited students were quickly moving to suburban Essex County and other surrounding communities. In 1967 Abbott Martin J. Burne, who directed the monks in both the Newark and Morristown monasteries, summarized the school's predicament as follows:

> "I feel that we, as a Community, are at a turning point in our history. Everyone among us realizes that American cities are in a real problem today, and even the dullest among us would be forced to admit that a monastery in the

middle of a city of over three hundred thousand people is bound to be affected by the changing conditions our cities are experiencing. The question that lies before us is this: do we wish to maintain a monastery in the middle of a rapidly changing city, or do we wish to withdraw from the city completely?"[3]

Abbott Martin, who himself was a St. Benedict's Prep graduate and was also a civil rights activist at the 1963 March on Washington, set about to establish the Newark community as an independent abbey. He cast a vision for St. Benedict's Prep that would continue the existence of the school while firmly anchoring it to the needs of inner city youth:

> "For the present, we shall continue to operate Saint Benedict's Prep as a secondary school that will draw, for the most part, perhaps, from suburbia. But increasingly we shall try to identify with the underprivileged, in order to render a service to our environs that the times seem to be demanding of us. If we really want to be part of the best trends in our culture, we shall not anticipate an all black or an all Puerto Rican population in our school. We shall try hard to conduct a school that reaches out to all races and colors and creeds, offering for the love of Jesus Christ whatever talents we have to the least of Christ's brethren as well as to the more fortunate."[4]

Abbott Martin's vision was embraced by many of the monks at the Newark community, but the tension between the ethnic groups that had traditionally sent their sons to St. Benedict's Prep and the new groups living in the neighborhood surrounding the school on High Street (now known as Dr. Martin Luther King, Jr., Boulevard) continued to cause frictions inside and outside the monastic community. These tensions remained unresolved until June 1972, when St. Benedict's Prep closed and many of the monks left Newark to relocate to the Morristown Abbey.

The minutes of the community's meetings regarding the closing noted that St. Benedict's was "suspending operations" because of declining enrollments, neighborhood changes, and the high cost of operations in the inner city, but forty years later Father Edwin Leahy offered a different perspective on this decision:

> "[St. Benedict's Prep closed] because of a lack of faith—a lack of trust in God who had accompanied us beginning on this journey just after the Civil War. The answer to the why is not finances, not decline in enrollment, not the number of blacks, but in the lack of faith, in the recognition that this work belongs to God and not to us. . . . It closed because monks began to take it for granted. Lay teachers at the time began to take it for granted. Some said, 'Give up the commitment to the city. Move out.'"[5]

"We were creating an alternative to the street, especially since many kids coming here in the 1970's and 1980's did not have experiences of community. We were creating it for them."

The fifteen monks who decided to remain at Newark in 1972 came to realize that the city's streets were the greatest obstacle to rebuilding the school. The lifestyle that the streets represented—drugs, guns, and violence—was hostile to the core mission of St. Benedict's Prep. Father Edwin summarized this challenge very well in the following statement:

> "St. Benedict's relentless adversary [was] the street, where drugs and lethargy [were] ubiquitious, and where de-emphasis on academics, its social and academic honor code, and its commitment to community stood in direct opposition to an anti-intellectual, dishonorable, and altogether individualistic street culture. We were creating an alternative to the street, especially since many kids coming here in the 1970's and 1980's did not have experiences of community. We were creating it for them."[6]

Through a series of meetings that summer and fall they recognized that St. Benedict's needed to establish a new community that gave hope to the young African-American and Hispanic men growing up in Newark. The school would need to provide a quality education to prepare them challenging careers in their field of interest. But how could this happen in downtown Newark, which was experiencing a decline of 70,000 jobs during the 1970's?

Having lost three of their last four headmasters to Morristown and the Delbarton School, the monks remaining in Newark also knew that they needed to create a new school that consisted of "all crew and no passengers." At a meeting in November they met to select a headmaster for the new school. After three ballots they chose twenty-six year-old Father Edwin Leahy as their new leader. Although he had recently been ordained and had no advanced degrees or administrative experience, his peers saw that he had the vision, drive, and energy that were needed to build the new St. Benedict's. He later reflected on his election as headmaster:

> "At that time I was clearly a big mouth. I had no clue what I was doing, but I knew the kids in the city needed something from us and we were going to do it. I had no idea how I was going to take care of all the details and finer points, but I knew I lived in a community with people that knew how to get things done. I never felt like I was alone so I'd say outrageous things knowing that I had smart people with me that could get it all done."[7]

At an offsite retreat in December 1972 thirteen of the Newark monks gathered in "a spirit of openness, sharing, and camaraderie" and established bylaws for the order that committed them to providing spiritual guidance and educating youth at what would become the new St. Benedict's Prep school. After that meeting Father Albert Holtz crafted a six-page proposal, which he modestly titled "A Possible School." This document included a three-semester school calendar, projections of faculty and student enrollments, and a rough budget for the school's finances. This document was approved by all the monks and became the blueprint for the new St. Benedict's Prep for the next four decades.[8]

The expansion to three semesters a year represented a conscious shift away from the traditional September-to-June schedule for two reasons. First, the St. Benedict's educators believed that the summer break caused students to forget much of what they had learned during the academic year, and they felt that the students' attention began to wane every May and June as they anticipated the long summer ahead. Moreover, the summer months had become increasingly dangerous in Newark, and the leaders at St. Benedict's felt the youth would be safer in an academic program that operated eleven months a year.

The second conscious shift for the new St. Benedict's Prep was the commitment to a diverse student body. In the old St. Benedict's there was a constant tension between "Benedictine insularity" and service to the inner city. The new St. Benedict's embraced a new understanding of the city. As Father Philip [James Waters] explained,

> "[Liberation theology] gave us a new model for understanding the inner city: we weren't dealing with a bunch of criminals that we were trying to insulate ourselves from, but we were in fact dealing with a community where God and the Spirit were at work."[9]

In short the Newark monks decided that St. Benedict's was to be "a place both in and of the city."

On July 2, 1973, Newark Mayor Kenneth Gibson gave the opening day address for the new St. Benedict's Preparatory School. "It is important that a school is opening up in Newark," the Mayor began, "But that a school is re-opening, that is doubly important."[10]

The school reopened with a lot of hope but very limited resources. At opening day there were only ninety-three students, compared with nearly five hundred a decade earlier. There were fifteen monks, two lay people, a maintenance man, and a secretary. Formal attire was no longer required, and there were few rules and regulations.

The faculty worked tirelessly to form relationships with the students and to develop a real sense of unity. They shot basketball hoops with the students and took them on field trips to New York City. The students appreciated the monks' personal concern for them and began to open up about their deepest hurts—rejection, abandonment, fear of the neighborhood, and the grip of drugs and alcohol on their families. Through these conversations the faculty came to understand that the students were struggling to live in two worlds:

> "The monks found out early that many young men had to navigate two worlds—school and street—which affected how they dealt with the issue of language. They insisted on the use of "Standard English" in all written work, but they also allowed for "Black English" in classroom discussions."[11]

Father Leahy emphasized that *listening* was the key to the early shaping of the school. This conscious focus on hearing the students' concerns helped to define his style as an effective school leader. In his own words,

> "I think one of the things we learned early on was to keep our mouths shut as much as we could and keep our ears open."[12]

The term "preparatory" was reinserted into the school's name after students and parents insisted on it. They wanted St. Benedict's to implement a college prep program, which they believed would maximize their chances to realize the "American dream." Father Leahy continued,

> "We wanted to bring a lot of different kinds of people together—city, suburban, rich, poor, black people, white people—all bound by the common interest that concerned parents have for their children."[13]

The monks believed that the 1500-year traditions of the Benedictine order would help to bridge the gaps that existed in contemporary society.

A group of loyal alumni was another key factor in the early success of the reopened school. Shortly after the reopening in 1973 one alum-

Father Leahy with St. Benedict's Students

nus, Bernard M. Shanley, Jr., sent a personal check to Father Leahy with a note saying, "Father Ed, use this where it will do the most good."[14] Shanley was one of several "guardian angels" who were committed to the school's successful relaunching. Others included John Magovern, the former president of the Mutual Benefict Life Insurance Company, and Adrian Foley, a former World War II veteran and successful New Jersey attorney. Foley, who had been a star quarterback at St. Benedict's, provided moral support for the school's athletic program.[15]

These and other "guardian angels" provided advice to the monks on legal and financial matters and encouraged them to pursue an aggressive financial campaign to cover the school's operating costs and capital expenditure program. In September 1973 Paul Thornton became the school's first director of development. He was an Ivy League educated layman who enhanced the school's reputation in academic circles. After his appointment as director the school soon began receiving millions of dollars in contributions from public and private donors.[16]

The revitalized St. Benedict's Prep graduated its first class of seniors in June 1975. At the graduation ceremony that year Father Edwin reflected on the first two years since the reopening:

> "Before this year we had no place to go but up. People didn't expect anything of us and said we'd never make it. Well, now we've gotten somewhere—state champs in track, reasonable showing in other sports, 500 people at a drama guild production—and all of a sudden we've got two directions we can go in. For the first time we can go either up or down. Let's be sure we put in the work it takes to go up. It gets harder the higher you go."[17]

During these two years the loose, free-flowing atmosphere at the school evolved into a more rule-bound, traditional Catholic school environment. Students began receiving detention for being late to classes or for uncooperative behavior. The monks began to monitor student performance and suspended students from activities if they did not perform well enough. In addition the monks began to monitor all aspects of a young man's life and took seriously the responsibility of turning them from boys into men.[18]

Based on these early successes, the school began doing long-range planning and grew the enrollment to 134 students that year, then to 168 students in the 1977-78 academic year. More and more applicants from the suburbs began to enroll in St. Benedict's, and the school joined a nationwide exchange program with twenty elite private and public high schools. During these years the sports teams began to win regional championships, and an excellent gospel choir began doing concerts and recordings throughout the Greater Newark area under the leadership of Father Albert Holtz. The group's signature song, "We've Come This Far by Faith," became the unofficial alma mater song.[19]

The new St. Benedict's first four-year class graduated on June 5, 1977, at a joyous commencement celebration. Father Albert Holtz remarked that this was "the end of the beginning" for the revitalized school. He cited the following differences between the new St. Benedict's and the last class that had graduated from the old school in 1972:

> "We're different in many ways from what we were then. Especially striking is the difference in outlook and attitude: no longer flailing just to stay afloat, we are now concentrating on very specific directions we want to go in; no longer lying awake at night wondering where the money's gonna come from, we now can spend more time wondering about more exalted things. We can look back on the events of 1971-73 as history already."[20]

The school's continuing emphasis on "all crew and no passengers" had helped to resurrect the once-dead St. Benedict's Prep School. The monks and students would never give up this can-do attitude about running a private religious school in the center of Newark.

In 1959 Monsignor Charles McCorristin of St. James Roman Catholic Church in Woodbridge wrote a note to the admissions office at St. Benedict's Prep School on behalf of Dennis Leahy, one of his parishioners who had just been rejected because of his poor scores in mathematics. The Monsignor wrote a short note to the admissions officers, saying,

> "I think the boy has a vocation. I wonder if you could do something for [him] and thus foster another vocation?"[21]

The St. Benedict's admission team changed their minds about Dennis after this strong recommendation from his local priest and admitted him into the class of 1963. Little did they know that Dennis would one day become Father Edwin Leahy, the longest-serving headmaster in the entire history of St. Benedict's, nor did they foresee his pivotal role in turning around the school a decade later. Whatever his deficiencies were in math, he more than made up for them with his outstanding people skills. On this matter author Thomas McCabe writes,

> "Leahy has made St. Benedict's feel like 'home' for thousands of other young men. His brilliant people skills allow him to feel

> equally comfortable with a teenager and an aging alumnus. According to one close friend, 'Edwin has an almost unlimited capacity to make and to maintain close friendships.' Father Edwin also possesses a magnetism that draws talented people and resources to his school. His ability to understand, command, and hold the rapt attention of various audiences is impressive. So is his ability to read various situations, whether in the life of an individual or of an institution. A hands-on headmaster, he labors tirelessly and without rest. His mother, a spry octogenarian, says he is incapable of taking time off, and her own active life suggests from where he gets his drive and energy."[22]

Father Leahy always seeks to develop in others three character strengths that he himself has: toughness, endurance, and moral strength. Like his father, Bill Leahy, he is a man of principle, believing that laws and rules—both religious and secular—must be obeyed. He attributes his sense of humor, stubbornness, and ability to get things done to his father.[23]

As a freshman at St. Benedict's Leahy was quickly drawn to two other strong father figures—football coach Joe Kasberger and his protégé, Johnny Allen. Although Leahy was only a third-string quarterback and saw little playing time, he credits most of his success as headmaster to the skills he learned from these two coaches. McCabe writes,

> "'I was never a great athlete, but I spent a lot of my life in locker rooms. I learned just being around great coaches—Joe K and Johnny Allen—and they taught me most of what I do in running a school.' Over the last three decades, the master team-builder has used convocation to 'huddle' his 'players and staff' each and every morning to cajole, criticize, or motivate. 'It's the most important thing we do. It's about building a team and it's critical to have them together at least once a day,' he said."[24]

Not surprisingly, one of Father Leahy's key initiatives as headmaster has been to build up the athletic programs at St. Benedict's. In the late 1970's he began assembling a highly competent coaching staff and broke ground for a new recreational complex on an urban renewal site, creating two playing fields, a cinder track, and two tennis courts. In an address to a panel of congressmen in 1980 he stated,

> "Strange as it may sound coming from a headmaster of a well-regarded prep school, I believe athletics are as important as academics for our students. For some students at certain stages, athletics are even more important than classes. That's not at all to say that schoolwork is neglected. Rather schoolwork can be tackled with greater confidence and success once a certain determination and toughness are present in a student. It's all too easy for a student to hide from a really tough challenge in the classroom.
>
> But activities like sports help a kid face certain responsibilities head on—in a clear way that neither he nor anyone else can ignore. . . . The demands are rapid, intense, clear, and the results are in right away. You have to meet the test, and pass or fail, almost instantly, and often alone."[25]

Over the years St. Benedict's has become an athletic powerhouse in sports including wrestling, track and field, swimming, basketball, and soccer. In the mid-1970's student Fred Smith learned valuable skills on the wrestling mats that prepared him for later success in life. In 1977 he became the seventh African-American—and the first Newarker—to win a prestigious Rhodes Scholarship to study at Oxford University in England. After excelling there in boxing and crew, he pursued a Harvard law degree and eventually became the first African-American partner at McCarter & English, Newark's most prestigious law firm at that time.[26]

In 1985 St. Benedict's hired Rick Jacobs as soccer coach. Under his coaching St. Benedict's won many state titles and six national championships. His teams produced some of America's most outstanding high school soccer players, including U. S. national champion Claudio Reyna. In recent years St. Benedict's teams have also won national championships in basketball, wrestling, and track. When Coach Jacobs retired after 25 seasons in 2009, one of his former students—Jim Wandling—took over as head coach for the soccer program. In his first two years St. Benedict's won back-to-back national titles and amassed an impressive 54-game winning streak.[27]

More recently, at the 2008 Summer Olympics St. Benedict's grad Cullen

Jones (Class of 2002) teamed up with Michael Phelps and two other swimmers to win an Olympic gold medal in the 4x100 meter swimming event in Beijing. At the 2012 Summer Olympics in London, Jones was part of a team that won a gold medal in the 4x100 meter medley relay and also won two silver medals in other swimming events.[28]

Father Leahy with Cullen Jones, 2008/2012 Olympic Medalist

The 6th Century Rule of St. Benedict of Nursia has been the prescriptive teaching of the school since its founding in 1870, but this Rule took on new meaning when St. Benedict's Preparatory School reopened in 1973. Recognizing that Newark lacked a sense of connectedness between diverse groups, the monks put increasing emphasis on St. Benedict's fundamental teaching about community: "Whatever hurts my brother hurts me." They adopted this motto for the new school and encourage the students to repeat this as a chant several times a day. It serves as a positive reminder that each student is an essential part of the larger community.

But "community" is more than a slogan at St. Benedict's—it's also a lifestyle. The monks are dead serious about turning boys into men. The boys do not simply participate in the community—they actually run important parts of the school. Seniors supervise freshmen, student leaders rather than priests run each morning's convocation, and students take attendance and follow up with absentees.[29]

In 2014 Marylou and Jerome Bongiorno produced a documentary movie called "The Rule," which describes how the revitalized St. Benedict's Preparatory School has become a national model for educational excellence. Today the school has 550 students, nearly all of whom will go on to attend college.[30]

St. Benedict's graduates have not only been admitted to each of the Ivy League schools, but they have also been successful in law, medicine, business, athletics, and countless other professions. During the fortieth anniversary celebration of the reopening of St. Benedict's, ***Star-Ledger*** columnist Bob Braun had these words to say about his alma mater and about Father Leahy:

> "I congratulate St. Benedict's Prep, my school, on the 40th anniversary of its reopening. I congratulate Father Ed for his leadership—and on the 50th anniversary of his graduation from the school. *Our 50th*, because we were classmates. Unlike too many people who get too much ink from the conventional media, Father Ed is an essential man. He is the man on the stairway.
>
> If, as Father Ed says, God works through history, the kid I met when I was 13—Dennis Leahy or 'DeLay'—is one of His agents. I know he sees both the wonder and the irony in that idea."[31]

Part Five

The Year of the Lord's Favor

The Year of the Lord's Favor:

Equality of Opportunity for All

In the Colonial period only male landowners were eligible to vote in elections and public referendums. Women, foreign immigrants, and racial minorities had very few civil rights until after the Civil War. The individuals highlighted in Part Five helped disadvantaged individuals to lead lives of dignity and hope.

MARCUS WARD (1812-1884) served as Mayor of Newark and was Governor of New Jersey after the Civil War. In 1862 he used his personal resources to fund the Ward Hospital for the care of wounded soldiers. This was the first hospital in Newark and provided training opportunities for a generation of healthcare workers in the city. Ward was also known as the "Soldier's Friend" for his tireless work to secure pensions for Civil War veterans.

MARY BURCH (1906-2001) was a philanthropist who dedicated her life to helping inner-city youth. She and her husband, Dr. Reynold Burch, established The Leaguers organization on Clinton Avenue and enabled hundreds of Newark children to receive improved educational opportunities and social services.

DONALD PAYNE, Sr. (1934-2012) was the first African-American from New Jersey to be elected to the U.S. House of Representatives. He helped countless Newarkers and others to gain access to better economic opportunities and expanded civil rights.

CHAPTER THIRTEEN

Marcus Lawrence Ward (1812-1884): Binding Up the Nation's Wounds

On April 20,1865, the citizens of Newark held a memorial service for President Abraham Lincoln, who had been shot down by an assassin a week earlier. The pall bearers at that service were headed by MARCUS LAWRENCE WARD, who was a personal friend of Lincoln and who had nominated him as the Republican candidate for President during the campaigns of 1860 and 1864. Just a month earlier, on March 4, 1865, Lincoln had stood on the East Portico of the U.S. Capitol and stated these words in his Second Inaugural address:

> "With malice toward none, with charity for all, with firmness in the right as God gives us to see the right, let us strive on to finish the work we are in, to bind up the nation's wounds, to care for him who shall have borne the battle and for his widow and his orphan, to do all which may achieve and cherish a just and lasting peace among ourselves and with all nations."[1]

Over a period of six weeks the President was re-inaugurated, the Civil War ended, and a speech was given about the promise of giving voting privileges to four million former slaves. Now the immortal Lincoln was dead, and it would be the burden of others to fulfill the dream he had laid out in March.

No one in America worked harder than Marcus Ward to achieve the three goals President Lincoln outlined in his Second Inaugural Address—*patriotism* ("to bind up the nation's wounds", leading to "a lasting peace among ourselves and with all nations"), *love* ("to care for him who shall have borne the battle and for his widow and his orphan", "with charity for all"), and *justice* ("with firmness in the right"). Ward's great mission was to serve Almighty God and his fellow man every day in these three areas.

Marcus was a descendent of John Ward, one of Newark's original Founders in 1666. He was born in 1812 and was the first of six children raised by Moses and Fanny Ward. His father was a successful candle and soap manufacturer whose business was located at 204 Market Street in Newark.

Marcus received a basic public school education and went to work for his father at an early age. He eventually partnered with his father and amassed a considerable fortune as a young man. By the 1840's he was devoting his energy to Newark civic affairs and philanthropic work. He sold the family business in 1846 and became a director at the National City Bank and later the executive chairman of the New Jersey Historical Society. During that decade he was also a founder of the Newark Library Association and the New Jersey Art Union.

He became active in politics at the age of forty-four and viewed politics as an instrument for social and moral reform. In 1858 he became interested in the abolition of slavery and traveled to Kansas to support the free-state cause. Although New Jersey was not yet ready to embrace the abolitionist position, he began working with leaders across the nation to promote freedom and equality for African-Americans. In 1860 Marcus was selected as a delegate to the Republican national convention in Chicago and was one of the strongest advocates of Abraham Lincoln for President.

Marcus married Susan Longworth in Newark in 1840 and had a happy marriage with her for forty-four years. During that time they had eight children, of which only two sons (Joseph and Marcus, Jr.) survived to adulthood. They bought a large and prominent home at 49 Washington Street and hosted a constant stream of friends and relatives throughout their married life. Today their property is owned and maintained by the Newark Museum. His biographer writes the following about his life and character:

> "His life, too, was very free from personal difficulties and anxieties. Accumulating by care and prudence a large fortune, his life was full of deeds of considerable charity

which were as numerous as they were blessed. Many a struggling artist received from him the generous order which did not degrade the spirit while relieving the necessity. His charities were frequently pursued for years unknown to the world, the result of the native kindness of heart which characterized him.

Few men ever brought to public duties a greater amount of conscientious principle. Every public act was governed by that law of justice and right which would stand the test of the closest scrutiny. Popular in the highest and purest sense of that term, he would not sacrifice his judgment or his convictions to the caprices of the multitude. His manners were unassuming and popular, but he reached position because he possessed the qualities which should command it. He 'preferred the true to the false, the substantial to the pretentious, and his life was one which may be studied by all who seek distinction and success in public life.'"[2]

1. WHO IS THE SOLDIER'S FRIEND?

Not he who dealt in language loud,
Heard only by the open crowd;
Nor he who read by costly lamps
And sighed o'er sufferings of the camps,
Then laid the mournful journal by,
Forgetting he had cause to sigh,
But he who, when the thundering guns
Made havoc 'mid our Union sons,
Was there with what the patriot needs,
When for his country's cause he bleeds;
Who, thro' the thick confusion pressed.
And took the dying to his breast—
There bathed his lips with tenderest care,
And caught his passing breath of prayer;
His last request, he bent and heard,
Then brought his dear ones every word.
Throughout the land, from end to end,
I hear you called the Soldier's Friend.[3]

In 1865 Thomas Buchanan Read wrote a poem about Marcus Ward, which he titled, "The Soldier's Friend." This first stanza of the poem is a fitting description of Ward's *patriotism* and his desire to be the friend of soldiers who sacrificed everything to serve in the Civil War.

Marcus Ward

At the outbreak of the Civil War in April 1861 most New Jerseyans thought the "rebellion" would be short-lived, given the North's overwhelming superiority in manpower and resources. After the Union army seized coastal fortifications in North Carolina, blocked river entrances in Tennessee, and made major advances in the border states, the New Jersey legislature approved an initial dispatch of 3,123 soldiers for the Union Army and issued several patriotic resolutions praising these triumphs.[4]

To support the cause Marcus Ward set up the Public Aid Committee of Newark in April 1861 and raised thirty-seven thousand dollars to "encourage enlistments and to support families of soldiers."[5] In January 1862 Ward set up an innovative system to transfer soldiers' pay to their families. His experience in running his father's business, and later as a director of the Newark National Bank, made him ideally qualified for this assignment, and it was reported that "not a dollar was ever mis-carried or was lost."[6]

The burden of caring for the financial payments to soldiers and their families grew rapidly as the war progressed and would have been an impossible assignment for anyone with less skill, determination, and honesty than Marcus Ward. The pamphlet just referenced above provides the following details:

> "In order to carry on his work of soldiers' aid properly and systematically, Mr. Ward at once opened an office in Newark, where clerks were at all times engaged in the multifarious labors undertaken by him, he giving the work his personal and careful supervision. So tremendous was the pressure of labor upon him, that even the sacred and refreshing relaxation and repose of the Sabbath was wrested from him, and with his son's assistance on that day, Mr. Ward has toiled Sunday after Sunday, in the wearisome and perplexing labors which to him were sacred duties. The system pursued in this office was a model of method, precision and dispatch.
>
> Some of the work here done may be briefly alluded to: Mr. Ward assumed the duty of securing and collecting the state pay, Government bounties and back pay of the soldiers both in the service and after discharge, and the enormously perplexing labor of examining into and adjusting the numberless complaints and difficulties arising among the soldiers. If a man got into trouble from any cause, to MARCUS L. WARD he turned as surely as a son to a father. . . . The great confidence reposed by the Government in the probity and justice of Mr. Ward enabled him better than any one else to perform this task."[7]

By the spring of 1862, however, it became clear that the war was not going well for the Union Army. On May 5 the Confederate army attacked General Ambrose Burnside's Union troops at Williamsburg, Virginia, and inflicted 2283 casualties, including 526 who were killed, wounded, or missing from the Second New Jersey brigade alone. That same day Ward received a disturbing telegram from Washington:

> "On a Sunday morning Mr. Ward received a telegram from Washington stating briefly that one hundred sick and wounded New Jersey soldiers were on their way by train to Newark. He set at once to work, secured the large brick building opposite the Centre Street Depot, known at that time as 'Nichol's Factory,' cleared it out and filled it up with cots, beds, and suitable accommodations.
>
> With such celerity was that whole task performed, that on Monday morning, twenty-four hours after the reception of the message, everything was in readiness. The patients were received, tenderly removed from the cars, and comfortably housed. Soon other assignments of patients, by steamboat and train, were received in like manner from the overflowing hospitals of Washington and Baltimore, and the walls of this structure soon became too circumscribed."[8]

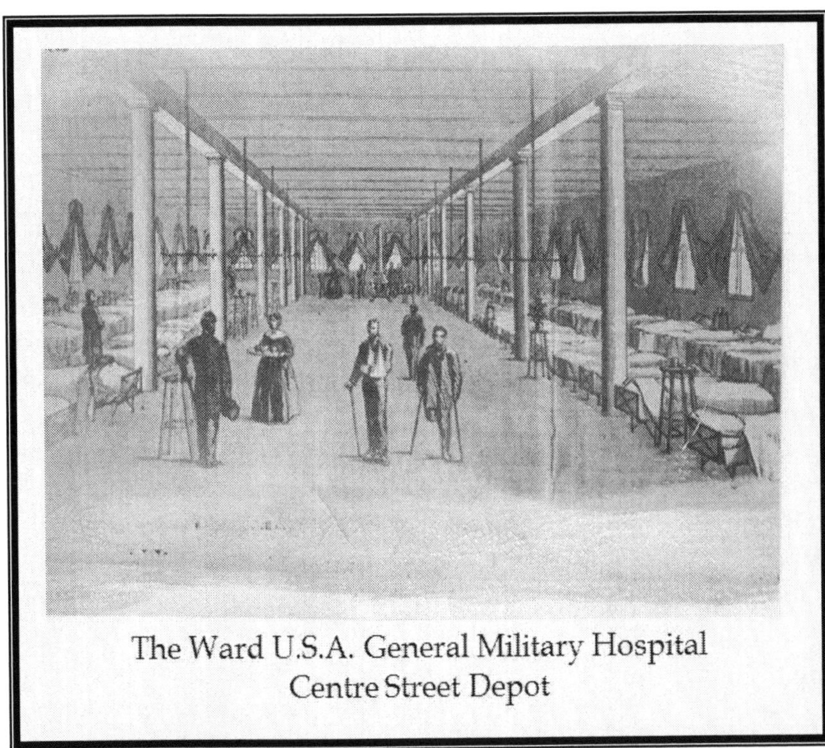

The Ward U.S.A. General Military Hospital
Centre Street Depot

In one weekend Marcus Ward established Newark's first hospital, which quickly became a model hospital for U.S. Government patients. It was appropriately named "The Ward U.S.A. General Military Hospital".[9] It was initially established to accommodate seven hundred patients. As the war escalated, however, the Ward Hospital quickly filled to overflowing and needed to be expanded. Four hundred new patients came to Newark by train from the James River in July 1862, and the following July six hundred and fifty wounded patients arrived in one day from the Battle of Gettysburg, most of whom had wounds in the head or upper extremities. An 1862 article from The New York ***Times*** praised the Ward Hospital as being one of the finest military hospitals in the country:

In one weekend Marcus Ward established Newark's first hospital, which became a model military facility. It was appropriately named "The Ward U.S.A. General Military Hospital."

"Mainly through the efforts of a benevolent and highly esteemed citizen of Newark, Marcus L. Ward, Esq., there is now in successful operation in that city, one of the most complete army hospitals yet extemporized, capable of accommodating about seven hundred patients. The buildings are situated at the Centre-street Depot, fronting on the river, and are so located that wounded or sick soldiers brought by either the cars or the boats, may be landed in their beds with but one change.

There are in all, three edifices, three stories and basement high, and covering about 100 square feet of ground. They were erected for a large manufacturing house, at a cost of over $100,000. On the reception of the news of the battle of Williamsburg, Mr. MARCUS L. WARD conceived the idea of having these spacious rooms converted, under the auspices of the State of New Jersey, and particularly of the vicinity of Newark. Arrangements for this purpose were partially made, and in connection with other benevolent gentlemen, and a number of volunteer lady nurses, the hospital was started."[10]

The Ward Hospital closed at the end of the Civil War in 1865, after providing medical care for approximately 80,000 soldiers.[11]

2. WHO IS THE SOLDIER'S FRIEND?

Not him who sat in slippered ease
While wintry storms assailed the trees,
Sounding like the orphan's wail,
Where widows sobbed their mournful tale—
Where weeping mothers, gray and old,
The sorrows of a lifetime told.
The fireless homes, where swept the storm
He did not see—his own was warm;
The famished wife, the children's cry,
He did not heed, but passed them by.
But not so thou—for every haunt
Which told its piteous tale of want,
In spite of storm, or sun or shade,
They bounty there dispensed its aid.
Therefore, the land, from end to end,
Has christened thee the Soldier's Friend.

The second stanza of "The Soldier's Friend" talks about Ward's *love* not only for soldiers but also for their widows and orphans. As was mentioned in the first stanza, Marcus Ward went out to visit the troops on a regular basis, and he literally "took the dying to his breast." But his love for the soldiers also extended to their widows and orphans. The previously mentioned pamphlet written by the New Jersey Union Executive Committee describes his compassion for the soldiers' families:

> "Mr. Ward's care for the soldier ceased not with his death. To him the widow and orphan looked for the collection of back pay, bounties and other claims, and never looked in vain. It is ascertained from an authoritative source that Mr. Ward has

> secured back pay, etc. to a vastly larger amount *than all other agencies for the purpose in New Jersey combined.* The welfare of the soldiers' *families* was as carefully looked after as that of the soldier himself. Did a wife want to learn the whereabouts of a long silent husband; did a widow or mother of a dead soldier want to know where the precious dust was laid, and to recover it, or, if that were impossible, to secure such mementoes as however trifling are inconceivably precious to the heart of affection—to Mr. Ward they went, and the work was done, if in the power of man to do. No detail of care for the New Jersey soldier or his loved ones, however important, or however trivial, but was carefully and religiously executed by this good friend."[12]

Years later, when he was a U.S. Congressman representing New Jersey, he sponsored a bill by which the federal government would pay a "bounty" to any widow or orphan who could claim to be a dependent of a Civil War soldier.[13]

3. 'Tis fitting, then, the grand old State,
Whose battles turned a nation's fate,
Whose many a storied field still shows
Where met the patriots and their foes—
Should seat thee in the Ruler's chair
And blessed the hour that placed thee there.
I need not bid thee, *still be true*—
What Heaven has done naught can undo.
Thy wisdom, truth and gentleness,
No breath can soil—no hand make less.
This is the verdict, East and West,
Indorsed in every patriot's breast.
And still I hear their voice ascend—
"God bless the Soldier's generous friend."

Thomas Buchanan Read

The third and final stanza of "The Soldier's Friend" alludes to Ward's desire to implement *justice* through governmental institutions. His constant desire was to help all who were destitute—the poor, the afflicted, the widow, the orphan, and victims of racial discrimination. During his visit to "bleeding Kansas" in 1858 he became acutely aware of the evils of slavery and spent years as a public official—as Governor of New Jersey, then later as a U.S. Congressman—working to end involuntary servitude and to extending voting rights to naturalized U.S. citizens.

New Jersey, like other border states, was divided on the issue of slavery during the Civil War. New Jersey was the only Northern state that voted against Abraham Lincoln in the elections of 1860 and 1864, and the mid-term elections of 1862 were widely seen as a rejection of Lincoln's Emancipation Proclamation that year.[14]

In Newark the press reactions to the Emancipation Proclamation on September 22, 1862, were mixed:

> "Lincoln's decree left moderate Republican politicians both reassured and unsettled. They supported it, but anxiously, and defended it as the logical, indeed inevitable extension of the Second Confiscation Act. They rejoiced that presidential decision and determination had finally replaced vacillation and indecision. Yet the Newark ***Advertiser*** was unsure whether history would regard this proclamation as a mighty landmark or would mock it as an empty pronouncement inaugurating a fruitless experiment. Some stunned conservative Republicans, who earlier had opposed extension of slavery, refused to endorse wholesale abolition. The Newark ***Register,*** however, regarded Lincoln's edict as one of transcendent importance. The ***Unionist*** went further, declaring, "It is the greatest event in our history." In the words of the Trenton ***Gazette***, Lincoln's proclamation of emancipation combined necessity with a 'great act of justice.'"[15]

Throughout the Civil War most New Jersey Democrats were strongly in favor of preserving the Union but were opposed to the Thirteenth Amendment, which set forth the elimination of slavery. Historian William Jackson sums up this issue as follows:

> "Opponents in New Jersey, led by Governor [Joel] Parker, clung to the old constitutional argument that states should decide the matter of slavery for themselves. Unlike the Radical Republicans, he believed that the slave states had not left the Union and still had the 'right' to decide the issue for themselves. And emancipation, its opponents believed, should be undertaken only gradually, just as it had been in New Jersey. The Thirteenth Amendment issue became the locus for the expression of race-based fears."[16]

The political landscape shifted dramatically, however, as the Civil War wound down in 1865. The U.S. House of Representatives passed the Thirteenth Amendment on January 31, 1865, after which the bill went to the individual states for ratification. When the War ended in April of that year, the former Confederate states of Virginia, Louisiana, Tennessee, and Arkansas ratified the Amendment, and they were followed by Alabama, North Carolina, and Georgia in the first week of December. The Thirteenth Amendment became part of the Constitution when Secretary of State William Seward declared it officially ratified by 27 of the 36 U.S. states on December 18, 1865.[17]

New Jersey, however, rejected the Amendment on March 16, 1865, and was the only Northern state that had not ratified it when it became law. After the majority of the former Confederate states voted in favor of the Thirteenth Amendment, leaders from other states began to question whether New Jersey was really a Northern state. A cartoon in ***Harper's Weekly***, for example, heaped scorn on New Jersey Democrats for blocking ratification of the Amendment.[18]

On September 2, 1865, New Jersey Union Party politicians [Republicans] met in Newark to nominate Marcus Ward as their candidate for Governor. On that occasion the Union Party put out a call to "the citizens of Newark and vicinity, desirous to aid in vindicating the good name of New Jersey, and redeeming the State administration from the control of the proslavery opposition," to meet at Concert Hall at 8PM that evening. Senator Frederick T. Frelinghuysen was the first speaker on that occasion and made the following opening remarks:

"That great physical battle for civil liberty, preparatory to which had been all the contests, privations and hardships of past ages, had been fought, and, thank God, the physical victory was on the side of victory. [Applause] Through the prowess of the soldier, the anguish of bereaved hearts, the wager of battle had adjudged that in America man shall be free. [Applause] . . .

The State of New Jersey [has] been under an odious rule too long; now was the time for reformation. . . . [W]hile the physical victory was achieved, the political victory was not, and would not be till slavery was eradicated. [Applause] As in the dark days of the Revolution, it was on the field of New Jersey that it might be, to the honor of New Jersey, that by her vote she eradicates forever from the American Constitution the system of American slavery. . . .

[W]e invite all men, of whatever past party faith, to unite with us in a sublime endeavor for the redemption of our State, and the overthrow of all doctrines and all organizations which stand in the way of the nation's complete and perfect deliverance."[19]

After Senator W. R. Kinney from Kentucky urged the delegates to "endorse the amendment to the Constitution, rendering slavery in the country impossible," the Union Party voted to nominate Marcus Ward as their candidate for Governor of New Jersey.

Ward defeated Theodore Runyon for Governor in the fall election, receiving strong support from returning soldiers, previous abstainers, and Democrats who had voted against Lincoln in the 1864 Presidential election. In his Inaugural address in Trenton on January 19, 1866, he began with a statement of his personal goals as Governor:

"Gentlemen of the Senate and of the General Assembly:

In assuming the responsible and important duties devolving on me as the Chief Magistrate of this State, I desire to invoke the guidance of Almighty God that I may be enabled to administer my Office as to redound to the welfare and happiness of the people, and to the honor of the State.

> While I bring little experience in governmental affairs to the discharge of the duties of the position, which by the generous suffrages of the people of my native State I have been called to fill, I pledge an honest endeavor to meet its obligations to the best of my ability, and with a single eye to the general good."

After acknowledging the momentous events of 1865—the end of the Civil War, the elimination of human slavery across the land, and the death of Abraham Lincoln—Ward told the New Jersey Senators and Congressmen that his first request as Governor would be to ask them to ratify the Thirteenth Amendment:

> "I have received from the Honorable the Secretary of the State of the United States an official copy of the joint resolutions which were passed on the first day of February last, proposing an amendment to the Federal Constitution, and requesting that I would cause the decision of the Legislature to be taken on the subject. The resolutions are in the following words:
>
> ***ARTICLE XIII, SECTION 1. Neither slavery nor involuntary servitude, except as a punishment for crime, whereof the party shall have been duly convicted shall exist within the United States, or any place subject to their jurisdiction.***
> ***SEC.2. Congress shall have power to enforce this article by appropriate legislation.***
>
> The Constitution of the United States provides that the concurrence of three-fourths of the States shall be necessary to ratify an amendment to that instrument before the same can go into effect.
>
> The required number of States is supposed to have already adopted the Amendment and the vote of New Jersey may not be necessary to the ratification. But for the honor of our State and people, we should avail ourselves of the occasion which is here afforded us, of giving the weight of our endorsement to the extinguishment forever of human slavery in our land. The

> people of the State, by their late action at the poll, have spoken clearly and emphatically in favor of this measure, and demand its prompt passage, which I know you will gladly accord. No argument is needed from me to secure your cordial support of this measure, which it is my high privilege to make the subject of my first recommendation."[20]

On January 20 the New Jersey legislature voted to ratify the Thirteenth Amendment, and Governor Ward signed it into law the same day.

Marcus Ward left a vast legacy in Newark, which impacted all of New Jersey and indeed the entire nation. Arguably the three major components of his legacy are health care, veterans homes, and liberty and social justice for all.

First, his extraordinary skill in mobilizing public and private resources to build the Ward U.S.A. General Military Hospital in 1862 not only provided quality medical treatment for 80,000 soldiers—an amazing accomplishment by itself—but also served as a prototype for the development of the first four private hospitals in the Greater Newark area. As more and more trains and boats arrived with wounded soldiers, the people of Newark rose to the occasion time after time. Doctors and nurses were hired from leading medical centers, and a support team of volunteers provided the food, clothing, social services, and financial resources that the military could not supply by itself. Many of these leaders were Newark women, who found permanent positions in the healthcare field after the Ward Hospital closed in 1865. Within the following decade four major hospitals were opened in the Newark area: St. Barnabas (Episcopal, 1867), St. Michael's (Roman Catholic, 1867), the German Hospital (Lutheran, 1870), and the Orange Memorial Hospital (public, 1873).[21]

The second major component of his legacy was the establishment of New Jersey's first home for disabled veterans. In 1866 Ward opened the New Jersey Home for Disabled Veterans, which was built on a portion of the property purchased for the Ward Military Hospital four years earlier. During the remaining eighteen years of his life he served as Treasurer of the Board of Managers of the Home, and he visited the sick and dying almost every Sunday. Although the New Jersey Home was smaller and less well funded than many other veterans homes across the United States, soldiers from those other homes frequently requested to be transferred to the Newark facility when space became available, because of the quality of care and proximity to family members for New Jersey veterans.

Finally, Newarkers—indeed, all New Jersey residents—should never forget Marcus Ward's commitment to liberty and social justice for all. He felt a moral obligation to look out for the welfare of others, and he viewed government as "a means to material and moral progress."[22]

Although Abraham Lincoln did not live long enough to "bind up the nations wounds," all New Jerseyans should be thankful that Marcus L. Ward was elected to the office of Governor in 1865 and spearheaded the ratification of both the Thirteenth Amendment (which ended slavery) and the Fourteenth Amendment (which stated that all persons born or naturalized in the U.S. are citizens). To his dying day Ward continued to fight for soldiers, widows, orphans, and former slaves. He did these things not for personal gain, but rather because he viewed labor as worship, a sacred trust from his God. After signing the Thirteenth Amendment in January 1866, Governor Ward declared,

> "But for the honor of our State and people, we should avail ourselves of the occasion which is here afforded us of giving the right of our endorsement to the extinguishment forever of human slavery in our land."[23]

CHAPTER FOURTEEN

Mary Beasley Burch (1906-2001): The Leagurers

During Newark's 300th Anniversary celebration in 1966, President Lyndon B. Johnson spoke in Newark and reflected on the city's rich history. In that same year the Essex County Community College completed a $10 million construction program, which is memorialized in the "Essex County Community College, Founded 1966" inscription in the overpass on Dr. Martin Luther King, Jr., Boulevard. Today, however, many people are unaware of the hot political debate that surrounded the establishment of the College. Without the strong advocacy of MARY BEASLEY BURCH, the Essex County Community College would not be in Newark today.[1] Moreover, the philanthropic work that she and her husband REYNOLD E. BURCH did through The Leaguers provided educational and social opportunities for more than 25,000 young people during the latter half of the Twentieth Century.[2] In this chapter we focus on Mary Burch's pioneering work with The Leaguers, which was the first nonprofit organization established to improve educational opportunities for African-American youth in Newark.

Mary Allison Beasley was born in Lewistown, Pennsylvania, on August 5, 1906. She was the only child of Charles Henry Beasley and Elsie Amelia Williams Beasley. Charles was a cabinetmaker from Virginia, and Elsie was the daughter of a middle-class family from Lewistown. Elsie's mother, Alice Williams, was from an Amish background and married an African-American man who worked in Lewistown.[3]

Mary's parents divorced when she was a child, after which her mother went to work as a governess for a family in Philadelphia. At that time Mary remained in Lewistown and lived with her grandmother, Alice Williams. Alice had a deep love for Mary and encouraged her to pursue in a career in teaching.

After her graduation from Lewistown high school Mary enrolled at Shippensburg State College in Pennsylvania, where she majored in education. At that time Shippensburg had only a small number of African-American students, and Mary was the only black student in her class. Although she was light-skinned, she had few friends in her class and was often lonely. At lunchtime, for example, she typically sat by herself on the back steps of the cafeteria.[4] She persevered, however, and earned her undergraduate degree in education from Shippensburg State. When she graduated from college she accepted an elementary school teaching position in Camden, New Jersey, and lived with her mother in Philadelphia.

One night she went on a blind date and met Reynold E. ("Buster") Burch, who was a charming young medical resident at a hospital in Harlem. After that initial date Mary began going to Harlem on weekends to see him. According to her friend Irma Dryden, who was a nurse at that hospital,

> "With another couple, we would get together socially or go out to dinner. Mary was teaching then and had many wonderful stories to tell about her students. They were her main topic of conversation."[5]

Mary and Buster were married in 1942 during World War II. As the needs for medical personnel increased, Buster volunteered to enter the Air Force and received training to be a flight physician. At that time Mary resigned from her teaching position in Camden to be with him during his period of military service.

While he was a medical student Buster Burch wrote an article describing the shortage of African-American physicians in the United States. He stated,

"It is estimated that at present there are 3500 colored physicians in the country—approximately one to every 3500 persons. There is one white physician for every 743 persons. The ideal rate is considered to be one physician for every 1000 persons.

Despite the inadequacy of hospitals and clinics, there are not enough medical graduates to fill the available internships and residencies.

The decrease in the number of colored students [from 1928 to 1941] may be attributed to the inability of the average student to finance his medical training and the refusal of many medical schools to train colored physicians."[6]

Mary Burch

At that time he developed a strong interest in increasing opportunities for African-Americans in medicine and other fields. The Burches' mutual interest in educating young people began during that time—a period in which new career opportunities for minorities opened up in the military, health care, and other critical fields.

Shortly after their marriage Reynold was assigned to the air corps and was sent to the Air Force School of Aerospace Medicine in Texas for flight training. After completing this training he was promoted to Captain in the Air Force and was assigned as a flight surgeon and medical examiner for the prestigious 744th Bomb Squadron, which was stationed at Selfridge Army Air Field in Michigan.[7] Now, for the first time in her adult life, Mary Burch was separated from her work with children. Freed now to spend her time as she wished, she turned her attention to the needs of the less fortunate.[8]

At the end of World War II Dr. Burch retired from the Air Force with distinction and opened a private practice in pathology and surgery in Newark. The Burches' first Newark residence was an apartment at 102 South Fourteenth Street, which was located in a neighborhood that had many troubled youth. While Reynold established his private practice and developed a specialty in gynecology and obstetrics, Mary began to reach out to needy adolescents in their neighborhood. Her goal was to help them get their lives moving in a positive direction. She said,

> "We had too many ruffians in the neighborhood. We didn't need more."[9]

Mary started by inviting ten young people to their home. After a while she encouraged these ten to invite their friends to their weekly meetings. The Burches' home group quickly began to attract so many other young people that they needed to move to a larger facility. These young people decided to call their group the "Junior Leaguers", and they began holding meetings in various buildings around the city. Sometimes they met at the Jones Street YMCA or at the Monmouth Street School. Other times they would meet at one of the local churches.[10]

The group grew rapidly as the word spread that something remarkable was happening on Fourteenth Street. In 1949 the Burches incorporated their home-based agency as "The Leaguers" and decided to purchase a larger, permanent headquarters for the organization at 750 Clinton Avenue. Until that time the Burches had funded the Junior Leaguers out of their personal assets, but now they needed outside funding to expand The Leaguers. According to Barbara Kukla, Mary had a brilliant inspiration about how to raise the necessary funds:

> "Pushing her ingenuity into overdrive, Mary Burch came up with a novel idea for raising the money needed to buy the house and the corner lot that went with it: Let the community buy it, brick by brick. Although it was a tedious fund-raising campaign, it was a success, as she recruited every living soul—from teenage members of The Leaguers to her corporate friends—to donate to the cause at the nominal cost of one dollar per brick."[11]

Years later Mary wrote a book describing the challenges they faced in the early years of The Leaguers:

"Mary Burch . . . is writing a Leaguer book named 'The House That Chicken Built,' referring to the birth pangs of The Leaguers when youths and maidens fried chickens, aided by their mothers, and then peddled the food to customers along Clinton Avenue, all this to enable the organization to survive."[12]

One of the first members of The Leaguers was Donald M. Payne. By 1950 he had become the President of The Leaguers, which greatly expanded his social network and provided valuable social and educational skills that he had not learned at home. Many years later, when he was a U.S. Congressman, Payne cited Mary Beasley Burch as an outstanding role model for himself and other Newark youth:

"Mrs. Burch was a visionary who implemented programs long before the federal government ever thought of them. . . . She taught us that just because we were black and poor it had nothing to do with our dignity and respect." – Hon. Donald M. Payne, Sr.

"Belonging to The Leaguers opened up a whole new world for young people like myself, a world from which we otherwise would have been excluded. Never before had we been able to have the opportunity to wear formal attire when I was a young boy, to learn the waltz and to attend Cotillion dances in a ballroom. It was an uplifting experience which taught us about social graces and made us feel special.

The Leaguers sponsored many innovative programs. I recall as a teenager my excitement over my first real trip as a high school student away from home, to visit Philadelphia through a Leaguers exchange program. Later, the student I visited, Joe Wade, stayed at my home in Newark. Forging friendships and relationships with young people from different cities was exciting, it was novel, and it was a great experience."[13]

In 1952 Donald Payne became The Leaguer's first scholarship recipient, enabling him to attend Seton Hall University. He explained how important Mary Burch's mentoring and financial support had been to him and to countless other Newark youth:

> "Mrs. Burch was a visionary who implemented programs for young people decades before the federal government ever thought of them. She got us assistance for school long before college grants and loans became possible. . . She taught us that just because we were black and poor it had nothing to do with our dignity and respect."[14]

As we shall see in Chapter 15, Donald Payne never forgot the lessons he learned through involvement in The Leaguers. After his election to the U.S. Congress in 1988, he dedicated the rest of his life to improving educational and vocational opportunities for disadvantaged young people in America and abroad.

The Leaguers's first formal ball, or "Cotillion", began in 1951. This was a gala event in which the girls and boys danced in formal attire and practiced their etiquette and social graces, which Mary saw as important stepping stones to success.[15] At each Cotillion the "debutantes" were high school seniors, with the girls wearing white gowns and the boys formally dressed with suits and top hats. Underclassmen were also invited but were dressed in pastels (girls) and tails (boys). The Cotillion typically began with a program that included raising funds for college scholarships. Barbara Kukla describes how the evening progressed from there:

> "After the program, the debutantes, seated at the back of the room, would come forward, escorted by their father or some other important male figure in their lives, to do a short dance together. The boys danced next. 'They were always a favorite with the audience because they looked so nice in tails,' [Yvonne Counts] Lowen said. Eventually, they also wore top hats and carried canes. After dances by the subdebs [juniors] and predebs [freshmen and sophomores], the debutantes danced alone and

then with their escorts. 'All the songs were waltzes,' said Lowen. 'The one many of us remember is "Now Is the Hour."'"[16]

But the Cotillion was not just an annual ball that was held one night in June. Starting in January every year the students not only rehearsed the dances but also learned the finer points of etiquette, such as setting up a table and mastering how to behave in various social situations. Carolyn Ryan Reed, the former director of the East Orange Public Library, reflected about the Cotillion with the following words:

> "The Cotillion was more about education than the ball itself. The preparation that went into it—learning the social graces and learning to work as a team—provided us valuable lessons that helped us later on in life."[17]

An entire generation of Newark leaders was involved in The Leaguers. In 1986 the authors of reference book, ***Past and Present: Lives of New Jersey Women***, the Women's Project of New Jersey, Inc., summarized the impact of The Leaguers as follows:

> "The Leaguers . . . has helped more than 25,000 people, particularly Newark's African-American youth. Poets, musicians, artists, scientists, doctors, teachers, public servants—all are represented in The Leaguers' alumni. They have served their city, state, country, and their own community. Today Leaguers' programs include tutoring and volunteer work in hospitals, in addition to their principal efforts in education and recreation."[18]

Singer Dionne Warwick received her first scholarship at the 1959 Cotillion and attributed much of her success in life to her involvement with The Leaguers. In a 1986 ***Star-Ledger*** interview she stated,

> "If it wasn't for Mrs. Burch and The Leaguers, I don't know where I would be today."[19]

Other notable Leaguers alumni include former Assemblyman William Payne, former Energy Secretary Hazel O'Leary, State Senator Ronald

Rice, Essex County Community College Vice President Dr. Robert Spellman, State Assembly leader Sheila Oliver, poet Amiri Baraka, and countless other prominent Newarkers.[20]

Mary Burch (2nd from right) and Leaguers Board of Directors, 1965*

---

*Left to right: George J. Haney, Co-Chairman; Mrs. Robert A. Johnson, Chairman; Mary Beasley Burch; and William Payne, Chairman Board of Trustees. 1966 photo from the Newark ***Evening News***.

In addition to her groundbreaking work with The Leaguers, Mary Burch was involved in many other civic organizations. In 1949 she formed the United Women's League of Newark, which encouraged women to take an active interest in state and local politics. The next year (1950) she became the first black woman to serve on the Newark Board of Education and was elected as president. During the 1950's and 1960's she was also a delegate to the State Federation of District Boards of Education, secretary of Newark State College (now Kean College) Board of Trustees, and an executive board member for both the NAACP and the Urban League of New Jersey. She also served a critical role on the Davis Commission, which was the planning committee for the establishment of the Essex County Community College. Because of Mary's connection with Seton Hall University, the University's property at 50 Clinton Avenue because the first official home of the College.

Long-term President Dr. A. Zachary Zamba felt that Mary Burch's strong advocacy was crucial in the establishment of Essex County Community College in Newark. During the Davis Commission planning effort in the early 1960's suburban representatives became concerned about student protests in Newark and wanted to build the College in Verona. But according to Zamba,

> "Mary Burch wouldn't let that happen. She fought vigorously against the move to Verona. Because of her struggle, it never happened. The college stayed right here in Newark."[21]

Dr. Robert Spellman, who worked closely with Burch as one of the College's Vice Presidents, agreed with Zamba's assessment:

> "If it hadn't been for Mrs. Burch, we'd be up there in Verona. From my perspective, keeping the college in Newark was one of her greatest contributions to our city."[22]

Buster conducted a busy medical practice in Newark for more than four decades and always treated his patients like family. In one of her letters Mary reflected on his career as a physician:

> "No matter how late it was at night, my husband would make house calls if one of his patients was sick. Most of his patients were poor. Some couldn't afford to pay anything. So they'd give him things like food to bring home."[23]

In addition to his private practice and serving on the medical staff at the University of Medicine and Dentistry of New Jersey, Buster broke a major racial barrier by becoming the first African-American to serve on the board at Public Service Electric & Gas ("PSE&G"), New Jersey's largest public utility company. Buster and Mary also attended many of the major social functions and fundraising events sponsored by Newark's prominent leaders. At the same time they were also world travelers, visiting China, Nigeria and other countries on humanitarian missions.

Buster's health, however, began to fail in the late 1970's, when he developed symptoms of Alzheimer's disease. Although he was still handsome and charming, his mind declined rapidly. Recognizing in 1981 that he could no longer do his daily rounds and attend social functions, he resigned from his position at the hospital and his many civic endeavors. The Burches decided it was best to move to Silver Spring, Maryland, where Buster's niece was living. They spent their retirement years there and enjoyed summers at their lakefront cottage in Gardiner, Maine, where Buster had grown up.

After Buster's death in 1993 Mary moved into a smaller apartment in Silver Spring but continued to keep in contact with her friends from Newark and other cities. A young nurse named Connie Thompson had taken care of Buster as his health declined and lived with them for several years. After Buster's death, Connie described what it was like living with Mary:

> "Mary was starting to slow down, yet in many ways she was still very youthful. Into her nineties, she was full of vitality and as tenacious as the bulldog she owned when she and Dr. Burch lived in Meeker Avenue in Newark. She was a brilliant woman, far ahead of her time."[24]

Mary made her last trip to Newark in 2000, when she was invited to the fiftieth anniversary celebration of The Leaguers. At that time she was in poor health, having suffered several heart attacks, and she did not even have enough strength to attend the opening night event. During that celebration the Essex County Board of Chosen Freeholders had a special luncheon for her and held an evening event to honor her at the Newark Club, a private restaurant in one of Newark's tallest buildings, which features a panoramic view of New Jersey and New York City.

After that trip she returned home and spent her final days at the Adventist Hospital in Gaithersburg, Maryland. Although her body was declining, her mind was sharp until the end. In the summer of 2001 she suffered a series of strokes that left her incapacitated. She died at the Adventist home on August 9, 2001, and was buried next to Buster at the Arlington National Cemetery in Virginia.[25,26]

In September 2001 friends, family, and past and present Leaguers gathered in the Mary B. Burch Theater at Essex County College for a memorial service. Donald M. Payne, Hazel O'Leary, Amiri Baraka, and others came to give their regards to the Burches and recalled their experiences with The Leaguers during the past half century. Barbara Kukla gives the following account about that evening:

> "The highlight of the tribute came when Sesser Peoples and Shirley Jenkins, joined by another couple, danced to "Now Is the Hour," bringing new meaning to the Cotillions of their youth. As a special tribute, a children's dance ensemble performed against a backdrop of hundreds of photos of Ma Burch, a display that included many images of the young men and women who had passed through The Leaguers over the years. . . .
>
> For those in attendance, the program was far more than a memorial. It was a reunion of the minds, a flashback to the days when they too were young, idealistic, and about to take their places in the world with the support of Mary and Buster Burch."[27]

Mary and Buster's legacy continued to grow long after they left Newark in 1981. In 1985 the National Conference of Christians and

Jews honored them as "outstanding citizens in the practice of brotherhood."[28] Then in 1994 Congressman Donald M. Payne, Sr., gave a congressional tribute to Mary Burch as she approached her ninetieth birthday:

> "Mr. Speaker, over the years I have had the privilege of working with young people as teacher, advisor, mentor, and friend. Working with our young people is one of the most important jobs I have held. I am sure my sense of commitment and dedication to our young people—our future—stem from my acquaintance with people like Mrs. Burch.
>
> Mrs. Burch is a woman of courage, conviction, and high standards. She has given of herself in a tireless, unselfish way. She chose to invest her time, her energy, her money, and other resources in the development of youth. Mrs. Burch, on behalf of the generations who have gone before and those who will be, I want to thank you for having the courage and foresight to take some of the troublesome youth into your home and arms, and nurture them into fine and productive men and women."[29]

In her will Mary Burch donated more than $600,000 to charitable organizations, including The Leaguers, the Essex County Community College, and Shippensburg State University.[30] In 2009 The Leaguers used some of this money and federal resources to build a $23.5 million dollar building at 405 University Avenue in Newark. This building includes a 22,000 square foot Head Start and community services facility, commercial office space, and underground parking.[31]

Starting from humble beginnings in the Burches' home in 1946, The Leaguers today serves 1095 families and children a year in Newark, Irvington Township, Elizabeth, Roselle, and Union Township as well as the Burch Charter School of Excellence in Irvington.[32] Perhaps the best summary of the Burches' legacy comes from a 1986 interview she had with the Women's Project of New Jersey, Inc.:

> "We have the family of Leaguers—past, present, and future—and we have the satisfaction of knowing that because all of us believed, we inspired, motivated, and liberated some of the most beautiful people on earth—young, gifted and black."[33]

CHAPTER FIFTEEN

Donald M. Payne, Sr. (1934-2012): The Power of a Dream

On March 26, 1988, DONALD M. PAYNE, SR. officially announced that he was running for the U.S. House of Representatives seat for New Jersey's 10th District, which included most of Newark plus parts of Jersey City and Elizabeth. This was the fulfillment of a dream that started on that same day twenty years earlier, when he listened attentively to Dr. Martin Luther King, Jr.'s speech at Newark's South Side High School. As he recalled from King's message that evening, "He told the youth to burn the midnight oil to learn."[1] Dr. King was assassinated in Memphis, Tennessee, eight days later, but the dream he shared with the South Side High School audience that day came to fruition in the life of Donald Payne, Sr.

In November 1988 Payne was elected as Congressman with 77% of the popular vote, becoming New Jersey's first black federal lawmaker. His dream—to break New Jersey's color barrier in Congress—had come true by the formula he received from Dr. King—education, hard work, and an unswerving commitment to "uplifting the human condition worldwide."[2] Payne's election to Congress was a monumental victory for Newark and for all African-Americans. At the time of his election there were only fifteen African-American members of Congress, compared with forty-three today. He described why he worked so hard for more than a decade to get elected to national office:

> "I want to be a congressman to serve as a role model for the young people I talk to on the Newark street corners. . . . I want them to see there are no barriers to achievement. I want to give them a reason to try."[3]

In another interview that year he summarized his quest for a congressional seat with these words:

> "Nothing is as powerful as a dream whose time has come. Sometimes a political leader is marching a little in front or a little behind the people. But once in a while the marcher and the drumbeat are in exactly the same cadence, and then, finally, good things happen."[4]

"Nothing is as powerful as a dream whose time has come. Sometimes a political leader is marching a little in front or a little behind the people. But once in a while the marcher and the drumbeat are in exactly the same cadence, and then, finally, good things happen."

Donald Payne was the youngest of three children and was born to William Evander Payne and Norma Garrett Payne in 1934. His father was a chauffeur, elevator operator, and dock worker who struggled to afford the cost of their cold-water flat on High Street (now Dr. Martin Luther King, Jr., Boulevard) in the North Ward. His mother was a domestic worker who died of cancer in 1943 when Donald was only eight years old. After her death Donald and his siblings, Bill and Kathryn, went to live with their grandmother in her home at 94 Peabody Place.[5]

Although the Payne family's circumstances were extremely modest by most people's standards, they never considered themselves to be poor. When he was running for Congress in 1988, a New York ***Times*** reporter asked him to describe the neighborhood he grew up in. Payne responded,

> "Everyone, whites and blacks, worked for low wages, although we didn't think of it as living in poverty, and there was a real sense of neighborhood, depending on one another."[6]

When one of the Payne children said they needed some extra spending money, they were told to go out and earn it. Based on this advice Donald took his first job as a ***Star-Ledger*** paperboy, earning ¾ of a cent for each paper he delivered. During his teenage years he built up his route from 50 to 500 customers and saved enough money to buy clothing items for himself.

He became an avid reader of the ***Star-Ledger*** and developed an interest in public service through this newspaper. He described how this happened in a congressional tribute to Peter Rodino in 2005:

> "From my personal experience growing up in Newark, New Jersey, I was inspired to enter public service after reading stories in the newspaper I delivered as a youngster, the ***Star-Ledger***, about the work of my local Congressman, Peter Rodino, and the passion he brought to the job. We felt proud to have such a hardworking and dedicated public servant representing our interests in Washington, especially since I lived in the neighborhood in the old North Ward of Newark where he served and lived."[7]

During those years Donald joined a group called "The Leaguers," which provided social, educational, and work activities for inner-city youth. In 1950 he became the President of the Leaguers, which introduced him to many prominent leaders in Newark and across New Jersey. As described in Chapter Fourteen, the founders of the Leaguers, Dr. Reynold and Mary Beasley Burch, also helped him to get a four-year college scholarship at Seton Hall University, where he received a degree in social studies in 1957. From there he went on to complete a masters degree in education from Springfield College in Massachusetts.

His first professional job was as an English and social studies teacher at Barringer High School. Payne taught in the Newark public school system for seven years, during which time he married Hazel Johnson and started raising a family. As a teacher he developed a burden to help troubled inner-city youth and became an organizer and coordinator of after-school youth programs at the Newark YMCA. He worked with the toughest but most popular kids and gave them new fraternity or sorority names to help them form new identities. He also established a youth council that taught civic responsibility and skills in debating. Cardell Cooper, a former mayor of East Orange, New Jersey, recalled that Payne set up social events to keep the kids off the streets and out of trouble:

> "He had a youth council. We held elections and he taught us civic responsibility—not politics, civic responsibility. Where did I learn Robert's Rules of Order? From Donald Payne. He taught us that, when we debated, we were supposed to be strong and take a strong position, but we were supposed to practice civility when we spoke to each other."[8]

Hazel died of cancer in 1963, leaving Donald alone to care for his three children. At that time he decided that he would raise the children by himself, rather than putting them in the care of grandparents or other relatives. He left the field of teaching and took a management position at Prudential Insurance Company while continuing his extensive volunteer work at the Newark YMCA.

During the 1960's Payne served as a father to countless Newark youth through the local YMCA. ***Star-Ledger*** columnist Joan Whitlow writes,

> "In the 1960's Payne's youthful followers were legion. He took them on bus trips and field trips, exposed them to the possibility of college, told them how to apply and how to get financial aid. He celebrated with them, as happy as any of them when they got accepted to college."[9]

YMCA leaders around the country quickly realized that Payne had extraordinary leadership skills, and he quickly rose in the management ranks of their national organization. In 1970 he was named the national president of the YMCA—the youngest person as well as the first black person ever to hold that position. Three years later the YMCA elected him chairman of their World Refugee and Rehabilitation Committee, which gave him the opportunity to visit YMCA projects in more than eighty countries. Through these YMCA positions he gained international recognition, and they also helped him to understand that his calling in life was to help other people.

In 1970 Bill and Donald Payne launched their Newark Democratic party headquarters at 1009 Bergen Street. Donald became the South Ward party chairman that year and held that position until he was elected to Congress in 1988. He served as campaign manager for Bill when he ran for Newark City Council, and both Payne brothers helped Sharpe James and several other Democratic leaders to gain political offices in Newark and elsewhere in Essex County.

Donald was elected to his first political office in 1972, when he became one of the Essex County Board of Chosen Freeholders. He held that position until 1978, when he decided to run for U.S. Congress in the 10th District. He lost that election to Peter Rodino in 1980 but was not discouraged by his showing against the popular Congressman. He believed that African-Americans needed a representative in Congress that would do for them what Rodino had accomplished for Newark's Italian-Americans, who had also suffered from discrimination for many decades.[10]

In 1982 Payne was elected as a member of the Newark City Council after receiving strong backing from Jesse Jackson. This turned out to be another stepping stone in fulfilling his dream of getting elected to Congress. When Peter Rodino announced that he was not running for another term in Congress in 1988, Payne successfully ran as the Democratic candidate for the 10th Congressional seat and became New Jersey's first African-American congressman by defeating the Republican Michael Webb, a public school teacher from West Orange.

He described his historic quest to be a congressman in a 1989 Black History Month address to students at Lincoln School:

> "You have to earn your right to be a congressman. I had a goal and I never gave up on that goal. I had a dream for a long time."[11]

In that same address he told the Lincoln School students that they needed to set goals and reach them by earning them. He told them about how he had taken a paper route as a fourth grader and continued to meet new goals by hard work, by listening to his parents, and by saying no to street kids who were looking for trouble. He also emphasized that successful adults should serve as role models to young people:

> "It's important that people who have achieved certain goals

encourage other people to 'reach for the stars'" . . . . A dream to some people seems far away. You have to keep encouraging them to keep reaching for it."[12]

After recounting some of his own setbacks in politics and other areas, he finished his address by reminding the Lincoln School students that there was nothing wrong in losing as long as they kept trying.

Donald M. Payne, Sr.

Donald Payne never forgot his Newark roots after he went to Washington, D.C. He had spent more than a decade of his life seeking to become a congressman, and his first priority in Congress was to improve educational opportunities for young people in Newark and other American cities. One of his colleagues, Congressman Gregory Meeks of New York, stated,

"Donald Payne knew what his purpose was. He found and was determined to get to this House of Representatives so that he

> could make a difference in so many lives. Once he came here, he never changed his focus, and he never changed his purpose. He knew that he wanted to deal on the international scale. He knew he wanted to take care of the people of Newark, and he knew he was focused on education. So when he had the opportunity to go on the powerful Appropriations Committee, he was so focused on what his mission was that he said "no" to Appropriations and stayed on Foreign Affairs and stayed on Education because that is what he wanted to do."[13]

Through the Education Committee, and later as Chairman of the Congressional Black Caucus, he worked tirelessly to improve the quality and affordability of education for disadvantaged children and youth. He was a leading advocate for better K-12 public school education, for passage of the College Cost Reduction and Access Act, the Expanded Learning Time Act, the Prescribe a Book Act, and the Youth Financial Education Act. Through these and many other initiatives disadvantaged young people realized improved opportunities to enter the workforce with marketable skills.[14]

His second key priority was foreign affairs. Throughout his distinguished career in Congress he was recognized as a champion for democracy and human rights in nations across the globe. Congressman Keith Ellison of Minnesota described some of his key achievements in foreign affairs:

> "He joined with his colleagues to introduce a measure which was subsequently approved by Congress to strengthen the Microenterprise Act, providing small business loans to people in developing nations. Representative Payne was recognized as having the most supportive record in Congress involving the Northern Ireland peace process. He was successful in passing a resolution condemning genocide in Darfur, Sudan. He authored the Sudan Peace Act to facilitate famine relief efforts and a comprehensive solution to the war in Sudan, which was approved by Congress.
>
> On the global health front, he co-founded the Malaria Caucus, which was launched at an event with former First Lady Laura Bush. He successfully secured $50 million for prevention, con-

> trol, and treatment of drug-resistant tuberculosis. Representative Payne also helped secure passage of a bill authorizing $50 billion for HIV/AIDS, tuberculosis, and malaria under the historic PPFAR Program, which assists individuals primarily in Sub-Saharan Africa."[15]

One of his greatest foreign affairs achievements was working with Paul Simon on the Water for the Poor Act. Through this Act the U.S. government committed to a four-year goal of cutting in half the number of people around the world who lacked access to safe drinking water and sanitation facilities. This was America's first cohesive policy toward meeting the water and sanitation needs of the world's poor people, and it literally saved millions of lives because of Payne's forceful leadership in this area.[16]

His third great passion was for social and economic justice at home and abroad. Throughout his career he kept the spirit and philosophy of Dr. Martin Luther King, Jr., and was a personal friend of Nelson Mandela from South Africa, Gerry Adams of Northern Ireland, and every U.S. President from Bill Clinton to Barack Obama. He personally advised Bill Clinton, George Bush, and Barack Obama on U.S. policies to numerous African nations. Frequently ignoring the advice of the U.S. State Department, he traveled to war-torn nations to negotiate peace settlements or bring messages of hope from the United States. In 2009 his plane was shot at by terrorists as he traveled to Mogadishu, Somalia, to meet with the president of that nation. As he met with President Sheikh Sharif that day he said,

> "I believe that a stable Somalia is really a key to a stable Africa. . . . I think if we support the new government that we would see a decline in piracy. I think that it would be a dollar certainly well spent, because President Sharif feels that you can stop piracy on the ground. Once they get out into the water, it gets very difficult."[17]

Donald Payne was more than a politician—he was truly a statesman. He always remembered the great principles on which the United States was founded, and he remained committed to these principles. This point was well stated by Congressman Steny Hoyer of Maryland:

> "[T]hroughout his life, he was focused on making sure that America kept the faith with people around the world, that its values, that its hopes, its visions for ourselves were also the hopes and visions for others."[18]

In February 2012 Payne announced that he was diagnosed with colon cancer and would seek treatment while attending his congressional duties. He succumbed to this disease on March 6, 2012, at St. Barnabas Hospital in Livingston, New Jersey. His death led to an outpouring of sympathy locally as well as from leaders around the world. Newark Mayor Cory Booker ordered flags to be flown at half-mast in honor of the man whom he called an icon and a hero. Booker said,

> "He's a guy who walked into a room and he was immediately someone that people respected; he could change the temperature and the tone. He had a gravitas about him the only the humblest of leaders do. . . . He was a true gentleman."[19]

Dignitaries from across America assembled to attend his funeral service at Metropolitan Baptist Church in Newark the following week. At that service former President Bill Clinton remarked that Payne was a friend and colleague to him and also to Hillary when she served as Secretary of State. Clinton admitted, "He made her a better Secretary of State and he sure made me a better President."[20]

The Rev. Al Sharpton stated that Payne could be gentle and quiet because he was secure in who he was, and that was why "Newark still stands today" for him. He added,

> "What made him loved is he was not only global but grounded. Donald Payne never forgot why Newark sent him to Trenton and to Washington. We never worried when Donald Payne was in the room."[21]

New Jersey Governor Chris Christie said he was struck by Payne's constant desire to be a role model to the young people on the streets of Newark, and by "his gentle power":

"As we celebrate his life today and as we say goodbye, we thank him for his gentle grace. . . . Standing up for those who had trouble standing up for themselves. To make us a better people—he did that for New Jersey, he did that for America. Donald Payne changed the world."[22]

Not surprisingly, Payne's quiet demeanor was a reflection of his inner spirituality. He was a lifelong member of the Bethlehem Missionary Baptist Church in Newark's North Ward. His pastor, the Rev. Toney Jackson, Sr., summarized his outlook on life this way:

"His greatest value was for God, then for family, and then for people."[23]

His children fondly remember the values he taught them after Hazel's death in 1963. His daughter Nicole Payne recalled that he always wanted to be a role model for others:

"Titus 2:7: 'And you yourself must be an example to them by doing good works of every kind. Let everything you do reflect in the integrity and seriousness of your teaching.'

This verse embodies the legacy of my father. As our family moved through the process during the final days with him, I was fluttered with pleasant memories of how he lived life and loved to live. My first rollercoaster ride was with my father. I realized going through the process that the ride was analogous to life. It was a life lesson of how to enjoy the ride we call life through the peaks, the valleys, the scary times, and the points of exhilaration, and to truly enjoy the ride.

Known as a gentle man, he was also a fighter, but not to destroy—to edify. He was passionate about compassion and he had to fight for what was right. He could not rest until it was done."[24]

Wanda Payne, his younger daughter, had similar memories about him being a positive role model to her:

"My father was like a mother and a father to me because as you

> know my mother passed away when I was 2 and my brother was 4. He never remarried so he raised us on his own and he did a good job.
>
> He always encouraged me to do whatever I wanted to do just as long as I was happy and good at it. I am a pre-K teacher and I love my job. He never pushed me to do anything else because you have to be happy with what you do or you're not going to be effective."[25]

Donald Payne, Jr., also remembered how his father served as a role model:

> "When I was very young, I came across a book of poetry from my father. I will never forget a quote from that book that read, 'A father wants his son to be a better, brighter man than he.' I always remembered that as I grew up. Among the many lessons my father taught me, he taught me that in whatever I do, to be the best at it—to work hard, to always be respectful, to be proud of whatever I do. This has made me a better person."[26]

Donald Jr., also recalled a poem that his father taught the children about how to understand and regard other people:

Whether you have blonde fleecy
locks or black complexion;
It cannot forfeit nature's claim;
Skin may differ in black and white,
But it is all just the same.

Were I so tall as to reach the poles,
Or span the oceans with my hands,
I must be measured by my soul,
The mind is the standard of a man.[27]

Six months after his death in 2012 a 500-pound bronze statue of Donald M. Payne, Sr., was dedicated in the plaza between the Essex County Veterans Courthouse and the Essex County Leroy F. Smith Public Safety Building. It was called the Congressman Donald M. Payne, Sr. Statue and was designed by artist Jay Warren from Oregon, who had previously created Newark statues of Althea Gibson and Supreme Court Justice William F. Brennan, Jr. The statue was funded by donations from several New Jersey-based corporations and nonprofit organizations. At the dedication Essex County Executive Joseph N. DiVincenzo, Jr., said,

> "Congressman Payne was a legendary figure and will have a prominent place in the history of Essex County. He dedicated his life to public service, serving as a public school teacher, Newark City Councilman, Essex County Freeholder and U.S. Represenative. . . . At home, he was a staunch advocate for issues involving education, children and addressing poverty. Abroad, he was a peacemaker and a champion of human rights."[28]

Additional accolades for Donald Payne, Sr., have subsequently been given by other local organizations. In November 2013, for example, Berkeley College invited two hundred legislators, dignitaries, family members and friends to a dedication of its new Donald M. Payne, Sr., Library. Dr. Dario A. Cortes, President of Berkeley College, stated:

> "The library is the heart and soul of the institution. It is a safe haven where information, culture, history, research and learning converge. Today, Berkeley College dedicates the Donald M. Payne, Sr. Library, a fitting tribute for a man who left a global legacy of humanity and a love for education."[29]

Another accolade for Payne occurred in a 2015 lecture given at his alma mater, Seton Hall University. On that occasion National Security Advisor Susan E. Rice fondly remembered working with Payne and was particularly impressed by his strength of character:

> "He prided himself on being a role model—to make sure young people knew that nothing was off limits for them, no mat-

Donald M Payne, Sr. Statue

ter where they grew up or what their background. That was true for his own children—who he raised as a single father, and to whom he was devoted. It was true for the kids he met on the streets of Newark—Congressman Payne wanted them to look at him and see that 'there are no barriers to achievement.' And, it was true for the children he met throughout Africa, in camps for refugees and displaced people, and whom he worked tirelessly to help."[30]

His brother, former state Assemblyman Bill Payne, summed up his brother's legacy with the following words:

"Donald was a gentle giant. He was a guy who really felt very deeply about people. That's why he worked so hard for as long as he could to uplift people in Africa and elsewhere. And he never asked for anything in return."[31]

Today Bill Payne is retired from political office and dedicates his time to keeping his brother's dream alive through the Donald M. Payne Global Foundation.[32] The Foundation's charter is this:

> "The mission of the Donald M. Payne, Sr. Global Foundation is to continue the work of New Jersey's first African-American Congressman, who used his global influence to work toward eradicating health and education disparities, promoting peace and youth development, and uplifting the human condition worldwide."[33]

NOTES

CHAPTER ONE: Moses Combs

[1]"George Washington Describes the Continental Army's Needs," Digital History ID 126, www.digitalhistory.uh.edu/disp textbook.cfm

[2]Jean-Ray Turner and Richard T. Koles, ***Newark, New Jersey***. Charleston, SC: Arcadia Publishing, 2001.

[3]Susan E. Hirsch, "From Artisan to Manufacturer: Industrialization and the Small Producer in Newark, 1830-60, in Stuart W. Bruchey, ***Small Business in American Life***. Washington, DC: Beard Books, 2003, p. 85.

[4]William H. Shaw, ed., ***History of Essex and Hudson Counties, New Jersey***. Philadelphia, PA: Everts & Peck, 1884, p. 571. See also Guy Sterling, ***The Famous, the Familiar, and the Forgotten.*** Bloomingon, IN: Xlibris, 2014, p. 31.

[5]Frank John Urquhart, ***A History of the City of Newark, New Jersey: Embracing Nearly Two and a Half Centuries, 1666-1913***. New York: Lewis Historical Publishing Company, 1913, pp. 518-19.

[6]Shaw, ***History of Essex and Hudson Counties***," pp. 572-73.

[7]Urquhart, ***A History of the City of Newark,*** pp. 514-15.

[8]Urquhart, ***A History of the City of Newark,*** pp. 517-18.

[9]Urquhart, ***A History of the City of Newark,*** p. 519.

[10]Urquhart, ***A History of the City of Newark,*** p. 519.

CHAPTER TWO: Rachel Bradford Boudinot

[1]Mrs. A. F. R. Martin, ***The history of the Newark Female Charitable Society; from the date of organization, January 31st, 1803, to January 31st, 1903: a century of benevolence, 1803-1903.*** Newark, NJ: The Society, 1903. Reprinted in 2012 by Nabu Press.

[2]Newark Town Records, 1784. See ***The Collections of the New Jersey Historical Society,*** Volume VI, 1864, p. 161.

[3]Quaker women started the Female Society of Philadelphia for the Relief and Employment of the Poor in 1793. This was the first benevolent society in America. The second oldest benevolent society was the Boston Female Asylum, which was founded in 1803. See Page Putnam Miller, ***A Claim to New Roles***. Metuchen, N.J., and London: Scarecrow Press, Inc., 1985, p. 14. See also Rosemary Skinner, ed., ***Encyclopedia of Women and Religion in North America***, p. 13.

[4]Bradford Papers, quoted in The Women's Project of New Jersey, Inc., ***Past and Present: Lives of New Jersey Women***. Metuchen, NJ and London: The Scarecrow Press, 1990, p. 10.

[5]The Women's Project, ***Past and Present***, p. 11.

[6]Dr. Alexander MacWhorter, "A Century Sermon preached in Newark, New Jersey, January 1, 1801; containing a brief history of the Presbyterian Church in that town." Newark, NJ: O.W. Tuttle & Co., 1807.

[7]Martin, ***The history of the Newark Female Charitable Society***, p. 11.

[8]Martin, ***The history of the Newark Female Charitable Society,*** pp. 102-03.

[9]Martin, ***The history of the Newark Female Charitable Society***, p. 174.

[10]Martin, ***The history of the Newark Female Charitable Society***, p. 176.

[11]Martin, ***The history of the Newark Female Charity Society***, pp. 176-77.

CHAPTER THREE: Seth Boyden

[1]Frank John Urquhart, ***A History of the City of Newark, New Jersey: Embracing Nearly Two and a Half Centuries, 1666-1913***. New York: Lewis Historical Publishing Company, 1913, pp. 466-67.

[2]Urquhart, ***A History of the City of Newark***, p. 487. The monument mentioned on the marker was never built.

[3]Borglum was a prominent American artist and sculptor who lived from 1867 to 1941. He dedicated the Wars of America statue in 1926. This was the last and greatest of the four public works he created in Newark. The other three works were the "Seated Lincoln" (1911), the "Indian and Puritan" (1916), and a bas-relief titled "First Landing Party of the Founders of Newark" (1916). Borglum is best known for his Mount Rushmore monument in South Dakota and for Stone Mountain in Georgia.

[4]John Cunningham, "Seth Boyden, the Uncommercial Inventor," Stories of New Jersey, Bulletin Number 10, 1939-40. Sponsored by the New Jersey State Library and the New Jersey Guild Association, 6 pages.

[5]Anonymous, "Recollections of the Late Seth Boyden," ***The Manufacturers' Gazette***, Newark, New Jersey, March 1871, Vol. II, No. 3, p. 1.

[6]Brad R. Tuttle, ***How Newark Became Newark: The Rise, Fall, and Rebirth of an American City.*** New Brunswick, NJ and London: Rivergate Books, 2009, p. 27.

[7]Tuttle, ***How Newark Became Newark,*** p. 27.

[8]Newark Public Library, ***Seth Boyden of Newark: The story of his life, with tributes to and appreciations of his genius and of the value of his inventions and discoveries in Newark, to New Jersey and to all the world.*** Pamphlet published November 2, 1925, p. 4.

[9]Newark Public Library, ***Seth Boyden of Newark***, p. 4.

[10]Anonymous, "Belleville Man, last of Seth Boyden's Employees, Tells of Genius's Eccentricities and of the Time the Ghost Appeared in High Street Foundry," Newark ***News***, undated. Available in the Seth Boyden clippings file at the Newark Public Library.

[11]Cunningham, "Seth Boyden, the Uncommercial Inventor."

[12]Newark Public Library, "Seth Boyden of Newark,' p. 5.

[13]Dr. Sanford B. Hunt, editor of the Newark ***Daily Advertiser.*** "Biography of a Famous Newarker Written in 1879." Published in the June, 1870 issue of the ***Hours at Home*** magazine. Reprinted in the Newark ***Sunday Call,*** November 10, 1980.

[14]Newark Public Library, ***Seth Boyden of Newark,*** pp. 6-7.

[15]Shaw, ***History of Essex County***, New Jersey, 1884, p. 592.

[16]Seth Boyden editorial in the Newark ***Daily Advertiser***, June 10, 1864.

[17]Tuttle, ***How Newark Became Newark,*** p. 63.

[18]Edison Innovation Foundation, "Edison Patents," http://www. thomas edison.org/index.php/education/edison-patents/

[19]For a detailed description of the many products created in Newark, see Ezra Shales, ***Made in Newark: Cultivating Industrial Arts and Civic Identity in the Progressive Era.*** New Brunswick, NJ and London: Rivergate Books, 2010.

[20]William Rankin and William C. Wallace, "Seth Boyden: Newark's Foremost Mechanic and Inventor; some reminiscences of old Newark." Newark, NJ: Advertiser Printing House, 1890, 64 pp.

[21]Anonymous, "Newarker Developed Many Ideas," Newark ***News***, October 7, 1951.

[22]Grace V. Halsey, in "Seth Boyden: Newark's Foremost Mechanic and Inventor," p. 43.

CHAPTER FOUR: Theodore Frelinghuysen

[1]"Senator Frelinghuysen on Indian Removal," April, 9, 1830. From Paul F. Prucha, Paul F., ***Documents of United States Indian Policy***, 1990, University of Nebraska Press, pp. 49-52.

[2]See Anthony F. C. Wallace, ***The Long, Bitter Trail: Andrew Jackson and the Indians***. New York: Hill and Wang, 1993.

[3]Robert J. Eells, ***Forgotten Saint: The Life of Theodore Frelinghuysen; A Case Study of Christian Leadership***. Lanham, MD: University Press of America, 1987, pp. 1-4.

[4]Eells, ***Forgotten Saint***, p. 7.

[5]Eells, ***Forgotten Saint***, p. 7.

[6]Talbot W. Chambers, ***Memoirs of the Life and Character of the Late Hon. Theodore Frelinghuysen***. New York: Harper & Brothers, 1863, pp. 7-8. Quoted by Cortland Parker in 1844.

[7]Chambers, ***Life of Frelinghuysen***, p. 47.

[8]Chambers, ***Life of Frelinghuysen***, p. 5.

[9]Chambers, ***Life of Frelinghuysen***, p. 31.

[10]Eells, ***Forgotten Saint***, p. 38.

[11]Eells, ***Forgotten Saint***, pp. 39-40.

[12]Eells, ***Forgotten Saint,*** p. 83.

[13]Eells, ***Forgotten Saint***, p. 37.

[14]Eells, ***Forgotten Saint***, p. 37.

[15]Eells, ***Forgotten Saint***, p. 85.

[16]Eells, ***Forgotten Saint***, p. xiv.

[17]Eells, ***Forgotten Saint***, p. 106.

CHAPTER FIVE: Joachim Prinz

[1]Quoted by Susan Starkman in "Joachim Prinz: I Shall Not Be Silent," Teacher Resource Package prepared for the Toronto Jewish Film Festival. Toronto, Ontario: Ontario Trillium Foundation, April 2014. Available at: tjff.com/media/Joachim_Study_Guide.pdf . The complete speech by Rabbi Prinz is available online at http://www.usconstitution.net/dream.html.

[2]Michael A. Meyer, ***Joachim Prinz: Rebellious Rabbi***. Bloomington and Indianapolis: Indiana University Press, 2008, p. 4.

[3]Meyer, ***Joachim Prinz: Rebellious Rabbi,*** pp. 29-30.

[4]Meyer, ***Joachim Prinz: Rebellious Rabbi,*** pp. 22-23.

[5]Meyer, ***Joachim Prinz: Rebellious Rabbi***, p. 35.

[6]Meyer, ***Joachim Prinz: Rebellious Rabbi***, p. 37.

[7]Meyer, ***Joachim Prinz: Rebellious Rabbi***, p. 71.

[8]Meyer, ***Joachim Prinz: Rebellious Rabbi***, p. 72.

[9]Meyer, ***Joachim Prinz: Rebellious Rabbi***, p. 81.

[10]Meyer, ***Joachim Prinz: Rebellious Rabbi***, p. 101.

[11]Excerpt from ***Wir Juden***, http://joachimprinz.com/books.htm.

[12]Meyer, ***Joachim Prinz: Rebellious Rabbi,*** pp. 126-27.

[13]Meyer, ***Joachim Prinz: Rebellious Rabbi***, p. 165.

[14]"The First 150 Years, a historical perspective created in celebration of B'nai Abraham's 150th Anniversary in 2003." Weblink: http://www.tbanj.org/who-we-are/our-history.

[15]Meyer, ***Joachim Prinz: Rebellious Rabbi***, p. 211.

[16]Meyer, ***Joachim Prinz: Rebellious Rabbi***, p. 213.

[17]Meyer, ***Joachim Prinz: Rebellious Rabbi***, p. xxxi.

[18]Meyer, ***Joachim Prinz: Rebellious Rabbi***, p. 222.

[19]Rachel Nierenberg Pasternak, Rachel Eskin Fisher, and Clement Price, "Rabbi Joachim Prinz: The Jewish Leader Who Bridged Two Journeys, From Slavery," Moment Insider Blog, November 2014. http:/www. momentmag.com/rabbi-joachim-prinz-jewish-leader-bridged-two-journeys-slavery.

[20]"Joachim Prinz: I Shall Not be Silent," by R-Squared Publications, 2013. http://www.prinzdocumentary.org/.

[21]The ***High Holiday Prayer Book*** was created for B'nai Abraham's services in 1951. This excerpt is taken from the website http://joachimprinz.com/ books.htm.

CHAPTER SIX: E. Alma Flagg

[1]New Jersey History Partnership, "Newark and the Great Migration." http://www.kean.edu/~NJHPP/proRef/greatMigr/pdf/greatMigrLesson.pdf.

[2]Linda Caldwell Epps, ***From Zion to Brick City: What's going on? Newark and the legacy of the sixties.*** Madison, NJ: Drew University doctoral dissertation, 2010. Reprinted in 2011 by BiblioBazaar.

[3]"Dr. E. Alma Flagg: Pioneering Educator," in Barbara J. Kukla: ***Defying the Odds: Triumphant Black Women of Newark.*** West Orange, NJ: Swing City Press, 2005, pp. 59-60.

[4]Gladys P. Graham, "Dr. Alma Flagg wins honors," ***The Afro-American***, July 20, 1968, p. 8.

[5]Kukla, ***Defying the Odds***, p. 60.

[6]Kukla, ***Defying the Odds***, p. 61.

[7]Kukla, ***Defying the Odds***, p. 61.

[8]Kukla, ***Defying the Odds***, p. 61.

[9]Kukla, ***Defying the Odds***, p. 62.

[10]Kukla, ***Defying the Odds***, p. 62.

[11]Fanny Jackson Coppin, ***Reminiscences of School Life, and Hints on Teaching.*** Philadelphia, PA: 1913, 149-50. Quoted in "Library Exhibits: James M. Baxter, Jr.," Villanova University Falvey Memorial Library. https://exhibits.library.villanova.edu/institute-colored-youth/graduates/james-m-baxter-jr-bio/.

[12]Kathleen O'Brien, "Black History Month: Newark project honors influential city educator James Baxter," NJ Advance Media for NJ.com, February 5, 2010. Available online at www.nj.com.

[13]O'Brien, "Black History Month."

[14]"Colored Instructor Dead: J. M. Baxter Was Dean of Newark School Principals—Served 45 Years," ***The New York Times***, December 29, 1909.

[15]Kukla, ***Defying the Odds***, pp. 65-66.

[16]Kukla, ***Defying the Odds***, p. 66.

[17]Kukla, ***Defying the Odds***, p. 66.

[18]Kukla, ***Defying the Odds***, p. 67.

[19]Kukla, ***Defying the Odds***, p. 56.

[20]Kukla, ***Defying the Odds***, p. 56.

[21]Kukla, ***Defying the Odds,*** p. 68; and Donald M. Payne, Sr., "Dr. E. Alma Flagg—Role Model," Congressional Record, May 2, 1995. Washington, D.C.: U.S. Government Printing Office, 1995, p.E928.

[22]Kukla, ***Defying the Odds***, p. 69.

[23]Kukla, ***Defying the Odds***, p. 71.

[24]Kukla, ***Defying the Odds***, p. 71.

[25]Dr. E. Alma Flagg, ***Lines, Colors, and More: A commemorative edition of the poems of E. Alma Flagg.*** Metuchen, NJ: Upland Press, 1998, pp. 58-59.

[26]Gladys P. Graham, "Dr. Alma Flagg wins honors," p. 8.

[27]Kukla, ***Defying the Odds***, p. 72.

[28]Charles Smith, letter to Lloyd Turner, April 18, 2016.

[29]Kukla, ***Defying the Odds***, p. 72.

[30]Adamu Shaibu Braimah, "Tribute to Dr. E. Alma Flagg," no date. Weblink: http://www.poetry.com/historical_users/1356504-Adamu%20Shaibu%20Braimah/6860565--Tribute-to-Dr-E-Alma-Flagg-

CHAPTER SEVEN: Edgar Holden

[1]Galishoff, Stuart, ***Newark: The Nation's Unhealthiest City, 1832-1895***, p. 122. New Brunswick and London: Rutgers University Press, 1988.

[2]Galishoff, ***Newark: The Nation's Unhealthiest City***, p. 117.

[3]Galishoff, ***Newark: The Nation's Unhealthiest City***, p. 122.

[4]Galishoff, ***Newark: The Nation's Unhealthiest City***, p. 118.

[5]Galishoff, ***Newark: The Nation's Unhealthiest City,*** p. 203.

[6]Adams, Graham, Jr., review of "Newark: The Nation's Unhealthiest City, 1832-1895," ***Urban History Review***, February 1, 1990.

[7]Galishoff, ***Newark: The Nation's Unhealthiest City***, p 97.

[8]Galishoff, ***Newark: The Nation's Unhealthiest City***," p. 87.

[9]Frederick L. Hoffman, "The General Death Rate of Large American Cities, 1871-1904." Publications of the American Statistical Association 10, No. 73 (March 1906), 5, 49. Quoted in Galishoff, ***Newark: The Nation's Unhealthiest City***, p. 96.

[10]Galishoff, ***Newark: The Nation's Unhealthiest City***, p. 167.

[11]Galishoff, ***Newark: The Nation's Unhealthiest City***, p. 169.

[12]Galishoff, ***Newark: The Nation's Unhealthiest City***, p. 167.

[13]Sandra W. Moss, ***Edgar Holden, M.D., of Newark, New Jersey: Provincial Physician on a National Stage.*** Xlibris: 2015, p. 15.

[14]Moss, ***Edgar Holden, M.D.***, p. 12.

[15]"Pingry School," in Wikipedia, https://en.wikipedia.org/wiki/Pingry_School.

[16]"A Short History of the Class in College," in ***The Decennial Record of the Class of 1859***, p. 15. Quoted in Moss, ***Edgar Holden, M.D.***, p. 35, fn. 67.

[17]Moss, ***Edgar Holden, M.D***., p. 24.

[18]Moss, ***Edgar Holden, M.D***., pp. 34-35.

[19]Moss, ***Edgar Holden, M.D***., p. 53.

[20]Moss, ***Edgar Holden, M.D***., p. 78.

[21]Moss, ***Edgar Holden, M.D***., p. 80.

[22]Mindell, David A., ***War, Technology, and Experience Aboard the USS Monitor.*** Baltimore: Johns Hopkins University Press, 2000, p. 62. In Moss, ***Edgar Holden, M.D.***, p. 90, fn. 25.

[23]Moss, ***Edgar Holden, M.D***., p. 90.

[24]Moss, ***Edgar Holden, M.D***.,p. 110.

[25]Moss, ***Edgar Holden, M.D***.,pp. 121-23.

[26]Moss, ***Edgar Holden, M.D***.,p. 146.

[27]Moss, ***Edgar Holden, M.D***.,p. 284.

[28]Edgar Holden, "House-heating and Its Dangers," ***Sanitarian*** 14 (1885), p. 55. Quoted in Moss, ***Edgar Holden, M.D***., p. 285, fn. 63.

[29]Holden, Edgar, ***Mortality and sanitary records of Newark, New Jersey, 1859-1877: A report presented to the president and director of the Mutual Benefit Life Insurance Company***, January 1880. Newark, NJ: 1880, pp 113-114.

[30]Quoted in Galishoff, ***Newark: The Nation's Unhealthiest City***, p. 123.

[31]***Sunday Call***, May 23, 1880. Quoted in Galishoff, ***Newark: The Nation's Unhealthiest City***, p. 172.

[32]Quoted in Galishoff, ***Newark: The Nation's Unhealthiest City***, p. 98.

[33]Galishoff, ***Newark: The Nation's Unhealthiest City***, p. 99.

[34]Quoted in Galishoff, ***Newark: The Nation's Unhealthiest City,*** p. 100.

[35]Galishoff, ***Newark: The Nation's Unhealhiest City***, p. 99.

[36]Glenn R. Modica, "The History of the Newark Sewer System," American/ Local History Network, ca 2000, http://usgennet. org/usa/nj/state/ EssexNewarkSewer.atm.

[37]"Dr. Holden's Service to Newark," unknown Newark newspaper, 1909; collection of mounted newspaper clippings of published obituaries of Edgar Holden, Birdsall family collection. Quoted in Moss, ***Edgar Holden, M.D.***, p. 372.

[38]City of Newark, New Jersey, ***Thirty-Sixth Annual Report of the Department of Health for the year ending December 31, 1920***, p. 14.

[39]Moss, ***Edgar Holden, M.D***., p. xiii.

[40]"Edgar Holden, Jr., '95", obituary in ***The Princeton Alumni Weekly***, May 15, 1936, p. 715.

[41]"Dr. Edgar Holden Dies; Prominent Newark Physician Was a Grandson of a Continental Officer," The New York ***Times***, July 20, 1909.

[42]"Holden, Edgar, Physician," Alumni Records, Undergraduate, Box 116, Class of 1859, Folder "Holden, Edgar," Princeton University Alumni, PUA-RBSC, SMML. Quoted in Moss, ***Edgar Holden, M.D.***, p. 458, fn. 7.

CHAPTER EIGHT: Earnest Mae McCarroll

[1]Barbara Kukla, ***Defying the Odds: Triumphant Black Women of Newark.*** West Orange, NJ: Swing City Press, 2005, p. 82.

[2]Zena Martin, "Through Zena's Eyes–Black History Month 2011, February 27, 2011. http://zmblackhistorymonth2011.blogspot.com/201/02/feb-27-dr-john-kenney-jr-medical-pioneer.

[3]Jasmyn Belcher and Michael Garofalo, "From the Son of Ex-Slaves, the Gift of a Hospital," National Public Radio broadcast, February 25, 2011. http://npr.org/2011/02/25/134042852/StoryCorps.

[4]***Report of the New Jersey State Temporary Commission on the condition of the urban colored population to the Legislature of the State of New Jersey : created by chapter 393, Laws of 1938***. Trenton, NJ: The Commission, 1939.

[5]Kukla, ***Defying the Odds***, p. 85.

[6]Kukla, ***Defying the Odds***, p. 89.

[7]"Earnest Mae McCarroll, ca. 1898-," in The Women's Project of New Jersey, Inc., ***Past and Present: Lives of New Jersey Women***. Metuchen, NJ and London: The Scarecrow Press, 1990, pp. 355-56.

[8]Kukla, ***Defying the Odds***, p. 82.

[9]Kukla, ***Defying the Odds***, p. 82.

[10]Kukla, ***Defying the Odds***, p. 83.

[11]Kukla, ***Defying the Odds,*** p. 86.

[12]Kukla, ***Defying the Odds***, p. 86.

[13]Kukla**,** ***Defying the Odds***, p. 87.

[14]Kukla, ***Defying the Odds***, p. 90.

[15]Kukla, ***Defying the Odds***, p. 90.

[16]Kukla, ***Defying the Odds***, p. 89.

[17]Kukla, ***Defying the Odds***, p. 97.

[18]Lucy Santos, "Proctor's Palace, once a grand theater and now a forgotten treasure," AXA Digital Group, 2006-2015. http://www.examiner.com/article/ proctor-s-palace-once-a-grand-theater-and-now-a-forgotten-treasure.

[19]Kukla, ***Defying the Odds***, pp. 92-93.

[20]"A Black Mass," ***Wikipedia,*** https://en.wikipedia.org/wiki/A_Black_Mass.

[21]Kukla, ***Defying the Odds***, p. 92.

[22]W. Montague Cobb, M.D.,"E. Mae McCarroll, A.B., M.D., M.S.P.H., 1898—, First Lady of the NMA," ***Journal of the National Medical Association*** 12/1973, 65(6), pp 544-45.

[23]Alfonso A. Narvaez, "New Jersey Journal," The New York ***Times,*** April 25, 1982. http://www.nytimes.com/1982/04/25/nyregionnew-jersey-journal-094564.html.

[24]Kukla, ***Defying the Odds***, p. 95.

[25]Kulka, ***Defying the Odds***, pp. 94-95.

[26]Kukla, ***Defying the Odds***, pp. 95-96.

CHAPTER NINE: Clara Louise Maass

[1]The material in this section is taken from Chapter 2 of Mildred Tengbom's book, ***No Greater Love: The Gripping Story of Nurse Clara Maass.*** St Louis, MO: Concordia Publishing House, 1978, pp. 20-26 passim.

[2]Tengbom, ***No Greater Love***, pp. 38-39.

[3]Tengbom, ***No Greater Love***, p. 50.

[4]Tengbom, ***No Greater Love***, pp. 46-47.

[5]Tengbom, ***No Greater Love,*** pp. 53-54.

[6]John T. Cunningham, ***Clara Maass: A Nurse, a Hospital, a Spirit***. Cedar Grove, NJ: Rae Publishing Company, 1968, p. 42.

[7]Nancy Steinbach and George Grow, "Six Medical Research Heroes: Jesse William Lazear, Clara Maass, Joseph Goldberger, Matthew Luk-

wiya, Carlo Urbani and Anita Roberts." Voice of America, "Science in the News," n.d., http:www.manythings.org/voa/people/ Medical_ Researchers.html.

[8]Tengbom, ***No Greater Love***, pp. 129-30.

[9]Tengbom, ***No Greater Love***, p. 139.

[10]Tengbom, ***No Greater Love***, p. 139.

[11]Tengbom, ***No Greater Love***, p. 141.

[12]Cunningham, ***Clara Maass: A Nurse, a Hospital, a Spirit***, p. 76.

[13]"Clara Maass Medical Center: About Us." http://www.barnabas health.org/ Clara-Maass-Medical-Center/About-Us.aspx.))

CHAPTER TEN: Alexander MacWhorter

[1]Karen DeMasters, "On the Map: With Roots in Earliest Newark, This Tree has Seen it All," The ***New York Times***, October 14, 2001.

[2]Thomas Paine, ***The Crisis Papers,*** 1776. Available at http://www.ushistory.org/Paine/crisis.

[3]Joseph Atkinson, ***The History of Newark, New Jersey*** (Newark, NJ: William B. Guild, 1878, pp. 91-93.

[4]S. P. Sullivan, "Washington Crossing the Hackensack: One man's journey retracing the 'Retreat to Victory,'" ***The Star-Ledger***, November 15, 2012.

[5]Frank John Urquhart, ***Newark: The Story of Its Awakening, 1790-1840.*** Newark, NJ: The Free Public Library of Newark, 1905, p. 10.

[6]Urquhart, ***Newark: The Story of its Awakening***, p. 10.

[7]"The Reverend Alexander MacWhorter on British Brutality," ***Pennsylvania Evening Post***, April 26, 1777.

[8]Edward Dorr Griffin, "A Sermon Preached July 22, 1807, at the Funeral of the Rev. Alexander MacWhorter, D.D." Newark, NJ: S. Gould, 1807.

[9]Griffin, "A Sermon Preached on July 22, 1807."

[10]Stearns, Jonathan French, ***First Church in Newark: Historical Discourses Relating to the First Presbyterian Church in Newark Originally Delivered to the Congregation of That Church During the Month of January, 1851.*** Newark, NJ: The Daily Advertiser Office, 1853, p. 227.

[11]Griffin, "A Sermon Preached on July 22, 1807."

[12]Griffin, "A Sermon Preached on July 22, 1807."

[13]The Second Great Awakening occurred from 1792 through the 1830's. For an excellent overview of this spiritual awakening see Chapter 7 of Edwin Gaustad and Leigh Schmidt, ***The Religious History of America: The Heart of the American Story from Colonial Times to Today.*** San Francisco, CA: HarperCollins, 2002, pp. 139-61.

[14]Griffin, "A Sermon Preached on July 22, 1807."

[15]Alexander MacWhorter, "A Charity Sermon Delivered for the Female Charitable Society; Instituted for the Relief of Poor and Distressed Widows and for the Instruction of Poor Children." Newark, NJ: W. Tuttle & Company, 1805, p. 16. Originally delivered as a sermon at the First Presbyterian Church in Newark in October of 1805.

[16]MacWhorter, "A Charity Sermon," pp. 14, 15.

[17]Ian Ridpath, "Ursa Minor: The Little Bear," at http://www.ianridpath.com/startales/ursaminor.htm.

[18]MacWhorter, "A Charity Sermon," p. 16.

[19]Griffin, "A Sermon Preached on July 22, 1807."

[20]"Harriet Tubman: The 'Moses' of Her people," ***Christian History***,

August 8, 2008. Available at http://www.christianitytoday.com/ch/131christians/ activists/tubmn.html. See also "Follow the Drinking Gourd," ***Pathways to Freedom: Maryland & the Underground Railroad.*** Baltimore, MD: Maryland Public Television, 2015. http://www.pathways.thinkport.org/secrets/ gourd1.cfm.

[21]This poem is available at: http://www.powerpoetry.org/poems/ harriet-tubmans-prayer

CHAPTER ELEVEN: Elizabeth Stryker Ricord

[1]Tuttle, Brad R., ***How Newark Became Newark: The Rise, Fall, and Rebirth of an American City***. New Brunswick, NJ and London: Rivergate Books, 2009, p. 33.

[2]Moss, Sandra M., ***Edgar Holden, M.D., of Newark, New Jersey: Provincial Physician on a National Stage***. Xlibris: 2015, p. 222.

[3]Galishoff, Stuart, ***Newark: The Nation's Unhealthiest City, 1832-1895***, pp. 24-25. New Brunswick and London: Rutgers University Press, 1988.

[4]Jonathan Mayhew Wainwright, "A Sermon Preached on the Anniversary of the Boston Female Asylum for Destitute Orphans, September 25, 1835. Boston: Dutton & Wentworth, 1835, p. 9.

[5]Muir, A F., "John Ricord," Southwestern Historical Quarterly 79 (1949), p. 49. Quoted in Scarborough, Elizabeth, "Mrs. Ricord and Psychology for Women, Circa 1840," ***American Psychologist*** 47 (1992), pp. 274-280.

[6]Scarborough, "Mrs. Ricord and Psychology for Women," p. 276.

[7]Lippincott, Kerry, "Mrs. Ricord's Geneva Female Seminary," Geneva Historical Society, 2013. http://genevahistoricalsociety.com/general/ mrs-ricords-geneva-female-seminary.

[8]Ricord, Elizabeth, ***Elements of the Philosophy of Mind, Applied to the Development of Thought and Feeling***. Geneva, NY: John N. Bogert, 1840, p. 1.

[9]"Ricord, Elizabeth Stryker (1788-1865), ***Dictionary of Early American Philosophers***, ed. by John R. Shook. New York, NJ: Bloomsbury Academic, 2012, pp. 889-891.

[10]Scarborough, "Mrs. Ricord and Psychology for Women," p. 279.

[11]Charles C. Rubens, Superintendent Hebrew Orphan Asylum. Newark, New Jersey: ***Conference on Charities and Correction, Fifteenth Annual Meeting, April 30-May 2, 1916***. Trenton, NJ: McCrellish & Quigley Co., State Printers, 1916, pp. 150-51.

[12]***Report of the Commissioner of Education for the Year 1882-'83***. Washington, D.C.: Government Printing Office, 1884, p. 766.

[13]MacDougall, A. W., ***The Resources for Social Service, Charitable, Civic, Educational, Religious of Newark, New Jersey: A Classified and Descriptive Directory.*** Newark, N.J.: Bureau of Associated Charities, 1912, p. 59.

[14]A. J. Sutphen, "Why Are Children in Orphan Asylums?" ***Proceedings of the New Jersey Conference on Charities and Correction, Fifteenth Annual Meeting, April 30-May 2, 1916***. Trenton, NJ: MacCresslish & Quigley Co., State Printers, 1916.

[15]A. J. Sutphen, "Why Are Children in Orphan Asylums?" pp. 148-49.

[16]Scott Daniels, "Can We Save the Original Children's Country Home?" In ***From the Hetfield House***, published by the Mountainside Restoration Committee, November 2013, p. 3. www.mountainside history.org.

[17]"ACNJ History, Advocates for Children of New Jersey," 2015. http://acnj. org/about-su/acnj-history.

[18]Timothy A. Hacsi, ***Second Home: Orphan Asylums and Poor Families in America***. Cambridge, MA and London: Harvard University Press, 1997, p. 45.

[19]"Frederick William Ricord," in ***Wikipedia,*** June 21, 2015.

[20]"Frederick W. Ricord," obituary in the ***New York Times***, August 13, 1897.

[21]William H. Shaw, ***History of Essex and Hudson Counties, New Jersey.*** Philadelphia, PA: Everts & Peck, 1884, p. 657.

CHAPTER TWELVE: Edwin Leahy

[1]Thomas A. McCabe, ***The Miracle on High Street: The Rise, Fall, and Resurrection of St. Benedict's Prep in Newark, N.J.*** New York, NY: Fordham University Press, 2011, pp. 183-89.

[2]McCabe, ***The Miracle on High Street***, p. 13.

[3]Archbishop Augustine J. Curley, OSB, "Monks and the City—A Unique New Experience." South Orange, NJ: Seton Hall University, Archibishop Gerety Lecture, November 15, 2006.

[4]Curley, "Monks and the City."

[5]Father Edwin Leahy, "Reflections of St. Benedict's Closing in 1972—40 Years Later," message delivered on the 40th anniversary of the reopening of St. Benedict's Preparatory School, September 2013. https://www.youtube.com/watch?v=qhf8dPm6PTc.

[6]McCabe, ***The Miracle on High Street***, p. 233.

[7]McCabe, ***The Miracle on High Street***, p. 195.

[8]McCabe, ***The Miracle on High Street***, p. 200-02.

[9]McCabe, ***The Miracle on High Street***, pp. 211-12.

[10]McCabe, ***The Miracle on High Street***, p. 208.

[11]McCabe, ***The Miracle on High Street***, p. 212.

[12]McCabe, ***The Miracle on High Street***, p. 212.

[13]McCabe, ***The Miracle on High Street***, p. 212

[14]McCabe, ***The Miracle on High Street***, p. 215.

[15]McCabe, ***The Miracle on High Street***, p. 129.

[16]McCabe, ***The Miracle on High Street***, pp. 218-19.

[17]McCabe, ***The Miracle on High Street***, p. 220.

[18]McCabe, ***The Miracle on High Street***, pp. 220-21.

[19]McCabe, ***The Miracle on High Street***, p. 221.

[20]McCabe, ***The Miracle on High Street***, p. 223.

[21]McCabe, ***The Miracle on High Street***, p. 227.

[22]McCabe, ***The Miracle on High Street***, pp. 227-28.

[23]McCabe, ***The Miracle on High Street***, p. 229.

[24]McCabe, ***The Miracle on High Street***, p. 230.

[25]McCabe, ***The Miracle on High Street***, p. 247.

[26]McCabe, ***The Miracle on High Street***, pp. 247-48.

[27]Ed Murray, "At St. Benedict's, a life of stability and amazing soccer in Newark," ***The Star-Ledger***, July 24, 2013.

[28]"Cullen Jones," bio in Wikipedia, https://en.wikipedia.org/wiki/ Cullen Jones.

[29]Steven Malanga, "It's Hard to be Saints in the City," ***City Journal***, September 2, 2014. http://www.city-journal.org/2014/bc0902sm.html.
[30]Maylou and Jerome Bongiorno, "The Rule." Newark, N.J.: Bongiorno Productions in association with KTWU, 2014.

[31]Bob Braun, "The school in the city and the priest on the stairway," ***The Star-Ledger***, August 4, 2013. http://www/bob braunsledger.com/ the-school-in-the-city-and-the-priest-on-the-stairway.

CHAPTER THIRTEEN: Marcus Lawrence Ward

[1]"The Assassination of Abraham Lincoln," Old Newark Events webpage, http://www.oldnewark.org/events/ lincoln.php.

[2]Francis Bazley Lee, ***Genealogical and Memorial History of the State of New Jersey, Volume 1.*** New York, NY: Lewis Historical Publishing Company, 1910, p. 268.

[3]Thomas Buchanan Read, ***The Soldier's Friend.*** Philadelphia, PA: The United States Sanitary Commission, 1865. Available in the Marcus L. Ward Papers at the New Jersey Historical Society, box 21.

[4]Richard F. Miller, ed., ***States at War, Volume 4: A Reference Guide for Delaware, Maryland, and New Jersey.*** Lebanon, NJ: University Press of New England, p. 615.

[5]William J. Jackson, ***New Jerseyans in the Civil War: For Union and Liberty.*** New Brunswick, NJ and London: Rutgers University Press, 2000, p. 45.

[6]The New Jersey Union Executive Committee, ***Marcus L. Ward, "The Soldier's Friend."*** Paterson, N.J.: Criswell & Wurts Press Office, 1865, p. 7. Available in the Marcus L. Ward Papers at the New Jersey Historical Society, box 51.

[7]The New Jersey Union Executive Committee, ***Marcus L. Ward, "The Soldier's Friend***," p. 8.

[8]John Younglove, ***Marcus L. Ward, The Soldiers Friend***, pp. 17-18.

[9]Richard F. Miller, ed., ***States at War, Volume 4***, p. 617.

[10]"The Model Hospital in Newark: Wholesale Accommodations for the

Sick and Wounded, One of the Finest Hospitals in the Country, Room for Over Seven Hundred Patients, Rules and Regulations," The New York ***Times***, July 10, 1862.

[11]"Home Front Hospitals: Marcus Ward's U.S. General Hospital," in ***Struggle Without End: New Jersey and the Civil War***. https:/www/ libraries. rutgers.edu/rul/exhibits/struggle_without_end, 2014.

[12]The New Jersey Union Executive Committee, ***Marcus L. Ward, "The Soldier's Friend,"*** p. 8.

[13]***Congressional Record: Proceedings and Debates of the United States Congress,*** "Bounties", Vol. 3, Part 2, February 8, 1875, p. 1068. Bill H. R. 4667 was read as follows, "*Be it enacted &tc.,* That the heirs of any soldier who was killed or died while in the military services of the United States, in the line of duty, during the war for the suppression of the rebellion, whose period of enlistment, was for less than one year, or who shall have since died by reason of wounds received or disease contracted while in such service, shall be entitled to receive the same immunities as if said soldier had enlisted for three years: *Provided,* That the heirs so entitled shall be such only as are named in the first section of the act of July 11, 1862: *And provided further,* That nothing in this act shall authorize the payment on account of any soldier who has received bounty from the Government of the United States."

[14]Willliam Gillette, ***Jersey Blue: Civil War Politics in New Jersey, 1854-1865.*** New Brunswick, NJ: Rutgers University Press, 1995, pp. 197-199.

[15]Gillette, ***Jersey Blue***, p. 197.

[16]Jackson, ***New Jerseyans in the Civil War***, p. 215.

[17]"The Thirteenth Amendment: Ratification and Results," in Harpers Thirteenth Amendment site, http://13thamendment.harpweek.com/hubpages/CommentaryPage.asp.

[18]""The Thirteenth Amendment: Ratification and Results."

[19]"The Campaign in New Jersey: Enthusiastic Meeting at Newark, Speeches of Hon. F. T. Frelinghuysen, Hon. W. R. Kinney of Kentucky, Gov. McAllister, and Others," The New York ***Times***, September 2, 1865.

[20] "Gov. Ward's Inaugural," ***The Orange Journal***, Orange, N.J., January 20, 1866. Document available from the Marcus Ward Papers, New Jersey Historical Society, Box 51.

[21]William D. Sharpe, M.D., "'Women are Proverbially Hopeful:' Newark's Voluntary Hospitals, 1867-1890," ***Bulletin of the New York Academy of Medicine*** 62:4, May 1986, pp. 349-358.

[22]Michael J. Birkner, Donald Linky, and Peter Mickulas, ***The Governors of New Jersey: Biographical Essays***. New Brunswick: Rutgers University Press, 2014, p. 137.

[23] "Gov. Ward's Inaugural," ***The Orange Journal***, Orange, N.J., January 20, 1866.

CHAPTER FOURTEEN: Mary Beasley Burch

[1]"Mary Beasley Burch, Philanthropist: 1906-2001," in Barbara J. Kukla: ***Defying the Odds: Triumphant Black Women of Newark.*** West Orange, NJ: Swing City Press, 2005, p. 172.

[2]"Georgetta Merrill Campbell and Daryl Boylan, "Mary Allison Beasley Burch, Philanthropist: 1906—," in The Women's Project of New Jersey, Inc., ***Past and Present: Lives of New Jersey Women.*** Metuchen, NJ and London: Scarecrow Press, 1990, pp. 247-48.

[3]Kukla, ***Defying the Odds***, p. 160.

[4]Kukla, ***Defying the Odds***, p. 162.

[5]Kukla, ***Defying the Odds***, p. 162.

[6]This article by Reynold E. Burch appeared in the January 1941 issue of the ***Association of Medical Students Journal.*** It was quoted by Clarence Tolliver in "The Point is This," in ***The Afro-American***, March 8, 1941, p. 9.

[7]David R. Jones, Leroy P. Gross, and Roslyn Marchbanks-Robinson, ***United States Army Aeromedical Support to African-American Flyers,***

1941-1949: The Tuskegee Flight Surgeons. Brooks City Base, TX: United States Air Force School of Aerospace Medicine, Clinical Services Division, April 2007, p. 82, p. 127.

[8]Campbell and Boylan, "Mary Allison Beasley Burch, Philanthropist," pp. 247-48.

[9]Quoted in Kukla, ***Defying the Odds***, p. 158.

[10]Kukla, ***Defying the Odds***, p. 158.

[11]Kukla, ***Defying the Odds***, pp. 158-59.

[12]Harry B. Webber and Maria Martinez, "Jersey Happenings," ***The Afro-American***, July 27, 1985.

[13]Donald M. Payne, "Recognizing the Achievements of Women of Color," ***Congressional Record—House***, March 24, 1999, p. 5487.

[14]Amy Schapiro, ***Millicent Fenwick: Her Way***. New Brunswick and London: Rutgers University Press, 2003, p. 118.

[15]Schapiro, ***Millicent Fenwick: Her Way***, p. 118.

[16]Kukla, ***Defying the Odds***, p. 165.

[17]Kukla, ***Defying the Odds***, p. 165.

[18]Campbell and Boylan, "Mary Allison Beasley Burch, Philanthropist," p. 248.

[19]Newark ***Star-Ledger***, November 6, 1986. Cited by Campbell and Boylan, "Mary Allison Beasley Burch, Philanthropist," p. 248.

[20]"The Leaguers Inc.: Serving Newark Children and Families for 60 Years," ***The Positive Community***, Winter Issue 2009.

[21]Kukla, ***Defying the Odds***, p. 172.

[22]Kukla, ***Defying the Odds,*** p. 172.

[23]Kukla, ***Defying the Odds***, p. 173.

[24]Kukla, ***Defying the Odds***, pp. 176-77.

[25]Kukla, ***Defying the Odds***, p. 178.

[26]"Mary B. Burch." http://wsdev.billiongraves.com/pages/cemeteries/Arlington-National-Cemetery/108373.

[27] "Reynold E. Burch, January 17, 1995, Bates College, ME, alumni obituaries. http://abacus.bates.edu/pubs/S95Notes/obituaries.html.

[28]Kukla, ***Defying the Odds,*** p. 179.

[29]"Tribute to Mary B. Burch—Hon. Donald M. Payne (Extension of Remarks – November 24, 1994, ***Congressional Record, 103rd Congress (1993-1994),*** p. E23106. Washington, D.C.: U.S. Government Printing Office.

[30]Pegi Adam, "Newark's Bold and Courageous Women," ***Newark Bound VG***—2 014 Winter/ Spring. http://editiondigital.net/article/Newark%E2%80%99s+Bold+and+Courageous+Women/1584705/0/article.html.

[31]Chanta L. Jackson, "Leaguers break ground in downtown Newark," ***The Star-Ledger***, June 3, 2008.

[32]***Annual Report 2014-2015,*** The Leaguers, Inc., Newark, NJ. http://www.leaguers. org.

[33]Campbell and Boylan, "Mary Allison Beasley Burch, Philanthropist," p. 248.

CHAPTER FIFTEEN: Donald M. Payne, Sr.

[1]Reginald Roberts, "Payne stakes his claim as Rodino successor," ***The Star-Ledger***, March 27, 1988.

[2]Taken from the mission statement of the Donald M. Payne, Sr. Global Foundation. Weblink: http://allafrica.com/sories/201304291966.html.

[3]"Rep. Donald Payne (1934-2012): Remembering New Jersey's First African-American Member of Congress," ***Democracy Now***, March 7, 2012.

[4]Raymond Hernandez, "Donald M. Payne, First Black Elected to Congress from New Jersey, Dies at 77," ***The New York Times***, March 6, 2012.

[5]"Payne victory gives urban poor a voice in Congress," ***The Star-Ledger***, November 9, 1988. See also Guy Sterling, ***The Famous, the Familiar, and the Forgotten.*** Bloomingon, IN: Xlibris, 2014, p. 114.

[6]Joseph F. Sullivan, "A Victory in Jersey's Primary: From Coach to Congress Race," The New York ***Times***, June 9, 1988, page B1.

[7]Donald M. Payne, "Tribute to Peter Rodino," ***Congressional Record,*** Vol. 151, pt. 10, June 20 to June 27, 2005, p. 13262.

[8]Quoted in Joan Whitlow, "Remembering the man whose roots grew from Newark," ***The Star-Ledger***, March 16, 2012.

[9]Joan Whitlow, "Remembering the man whose roots grew from Newark."

[10]Raymond Hernandez, "Donald M. Payne, First Black Elected to Congress from New Jersey, Dies at 77," The New York ***Times***, March 6, 2012.

[11]Tom Canavan, "Payne: Goals have to be earned," ***Vailsburg Leader***, March 2, 1989. Available from the Donald M. Payne Papers at the Seton Hall University Library.

[12]Tom Canavan, "Payne: Goals have to be earned."

[13]"Memorial Addresses and Other Tributes Held in the House of Representatives and Senate of the United States together with Memorial Services in Honor of Donald M Payne, Late a Representative from New Jersey," ***House Hearing, 112th Congress.*** Washington, D.C.: U.S. Government Printing office, March 6, 2012, p. 68.

[14]See remarks by Congressman Keith Ellison in "Memorial Addresses

and Other Tributes," p. 59.

[15]Remarks by Congressman Keith Ellison in "Memorial Addresses and Other Tributes," p. 59.

[16]Remarks by Congressman Earl Blumenauer in "Memorial Addresses and Other Tributes," p. 55.

[17]Deirdre Walsh and Dana Bash, "U.S. lawmaker safe after plane fired on in Somalia," CNN.COM, April 13, 2009.

[18]Remarks by Congressman Steny Hoyer in "Memorial Addresses and Other Tributes."

[19]David Cruz, "Donald Payne Remembered as Single Dad and Political Hero," NJTV News, March 6, 2012.

[20]"Leaders mourn Congressman Donald Payne at funeral in Newark church," ***The Star-Ledger,*** March 14, 2012.

[21]"Leaders mourn Congressman Donald Payne at funeral in Newark church."

[22]"Leaders mourn Congressman Donald Payne at funeral in Newark church."

[23]Mark Bonamo, "Payne Sr. Documentary," Cablevision, 2014. This video is available for view at the Donald M. Payne Special Collection at the Seton Hall University Library.

[24]Remarks by Nicole Y. Payne in "Memorial Addresses and Other Tributes."

[25]Remarks by Wanda M. Payne in "Memorial Addresses and Other Tributes."
[26]Remarks by the Honorable Donald M. Payne, Jr, in "Memorial Addresses and Other Tributes."

[27]Remarks by the Honorable Donald M. Payne, Jr, to the Congressional Black Caucus, in the ***Congressional Record—House***. Washington,

D.C.: U.S. Government Printing Office, July 22, 2013, p. H4853.

[28]"Essex County Executive DiVincenzo Dedicates Congressman Donald M. Payne statue at Essex Couny Hall of Records Complex," http://www.essexcountynj.org/index.htp?section=pr/print/110812.

[29]Hene Greenfield, "Berkeley College Dedicates Donald M. Payne, Sr. Library. Berkeley College press release, November 8, 2013. http://newsroom.berkeleycollege.edu/news/berkeley-college-dedicates-donald-m-payne-sr-library.

[30]Remarks by Susan E. Rice at the Donald M. Payne, Sr., Global Foundation Lecture Services – As Prepared for Delivery, Seton Hall University, April 30, 2015.

[31]In Bonamo, "Payne Sr. Documentary."

[32]Max Pizarro, "Bill Payne, the 1966 South Ward Race, and the Rise of Donald Payne and Sharpe James," ***Politiker.com***, July 15, 2015. http:// politickernj.com/2015/07/bill-payne-the-1966-south-ward-race-and-the-rise-of-donald-payne-and-sharpe-james/.

[33]See http://www.paynelegacy.com for additional information about the Donald M. Payne, Sr. Global Foundation.

INDEX

Adams, Gerry 216
Adams, John 34
Adams, John Quincy 54
Allen, Johnny 175
Arthur, Chester 59
Atherton, Uriah 34
Baraka, Amiri 118, 204, 207
Basham, Charles 15
Bates, Julia 115
Baxter, James 80–82, 86, 112
Baxter, Leroy 111, 115, 116
Bayard, Samuel 24
Beasley, Charles 197
Beasley, Elsie 197
Benedict of Nursia, Saint 177
Benton, Thomas Hart 48
Berry, Bert 89
Bongiorno, Jerome 178
Bongiorno, Marylou 178
Booker, Cory 217
Borglum, Gutzon 33
Boudinot, Catherine 24
Boudinot, Elias 25
Boudinot, Elisha 21, 25
Boudinot, Rachel 1, 21–31
Boyden, Seth 1, 33–44
Boyden, Susan 34
Bradford, Susan 24
Bradford, William 24
Braimah, Adamu 90
Braun, Bob 178
Brennan, William, Jr. 220
Broadbent, Levi 37
Brown, Jeffrey R. 2
Brown, John 143
Brown, William 89
Burch, Mary 2, 197–208, 211
Burch, Reynold 198, 199, 200, 205, 206, 207, 211
Burne, Martin 166, 167
Burnside, Ambrose 185
Burr Sr,, Aaron 143
Burrell, Cornelia 111
Bush, George W. 216

Bush, Laura ... 215
Caesar, Howard ... 89
Calhoun, John ... 48
Carroll, Charles ... 34
Carver, George Washington .. 110
Christie, Chris ... 217
Clay, Henry ... 52, 56, 57
Clinton, Bill ... 216, 217
Clinton, Hillary ... 217
Coe, Benjamin ... 23
Combs, Moses .. 1, 13–19, 22, 41, 153
Cooper, Cardell ... 211
Cooper, Gwen ... 112
Cornwallis, Charles . 14, 139, 141
Cortes, Dario ... 220
Corwin, Margaret ... 115
Craster, Charles ... 120
Cross, Carol ... 116, 118
Crutchfield, Eleanor ... 83
Curley, Augustine ... 241
Cyprian, Bishop of Carthage . 130
Dallas, George ... 57
Dalton, John ... 98
Dana, John Cotton ... 44
Dargan, Ruth ... 116
DiVincenzo, Joseph, Jr. ... 220
Edison, Thomas ... 42, 44, 117
Ellison, Keith ... 215
Fenderson, Grace ... 88, 112
Finley, Robert ... 49
Finney, Charles ... 156
Fisher, Rachel ... 76
Flagg, E. Alma ... 1, 77–90
Flagg, Thomas ... 83
Flagg, Thomas Lyle ... 83, 84
Foley, Adrian ... 172
Foley, Luisa ... 85
Francis, Gladys ... 86
Franklin, Benjamin ... 142
Frazier, David ... 28
Frelinghuysen, Ann ... 49
Frelinghuysen, Charlotte ... 58
Frelinghuysen, Frederick (brother of Theodore) ... 53
Frelinghuysen, Frederick (father of Theodore) ... 49, 50
Frelinghuysen, Frederick T. (nephew of Theodore) ... 58, 191
Frelinghuysen, John ... 50
Frelinghuysen, Theodore ... 47–59
Frelinghuysen, Theodore Jacobus ... 49
Frost, Timothy ... 29
Galishoff, Stuart ... 95, 152
Garrison, William Lloyd ... 58
George III, King ... 140, 141
Gibson, Althea ... 220
Gibson, Kenneth ... 119, 170

Gillis, Thelma.......................... 77
Goldmann, Felix................ 64, 65
Gorgas, William 129–33
Griffin, Clifford S.................... 58
Griffin, Edward Dorr.. 22, 24, 25, 53, 144
Guinther, Leopoldine 133, 134
Guiteras, Juan........................ 131
Halsey, Grace V. 43
Halsey, William....................... 55
Haney, George....................... 204
Harris, Gloria............................ 1
Haskin, Aaron............... 119, 120
Henderson, Joan 78
Herbert, Arthur...................... 134
Herzl, Theodor 66
Hitler, Adolf 68
Holden, Ana 96
Holden, Asa 96
Holden, Edgar............. 1, 93–107
Holden, John........................... 96
Holden, Jr., Edgar.................. 106
Holden, Katharine 100, 101
Holte, Gennie 2
Holtz, Albert................. 169, 173
Homer (Greek poet) 147
Hoyer, Steny.......................... 216
Hunt, Sanford B....................... 39
Hunter, Bob 116, 117
Jackson, Andrew..................... 47
Jackson, Jesse 213
Jackson, Mahalia 61
Jackson, Toney 218
Jackson, William 191
Jacobs, Rich 176
James, Sharpe 213
Jefferson, Thomas................... 34
Jenkins, Shirley..................... 207
Johnson, Lyndon................... 197
Johnson, Mrs. Robert........... 204
Jones, Cullen......................... 177
Kasberger, Joe 175
Kennedy, Robert..................... 88
Kenney, John 109
King, Jr., Martin Luther... 62, 63, 75, 88, 209, 216
Kinney, W. R. 192
Knowles, Mrs. Joseph............ 29
Koch, Robert........................... 94
Kukla, Barbara. 80, 84, 111, 119, 120, 200, 202, 207
Lazear, Jesse 130
Leahy, Edwin............. 2, 165–78
Lee, Rosetta 114
Lee, Taylor.............................. 59
Lehlbach, Charles 127, 128
Levy, Julius.................. 120, 121
Lincoln, Abraham 181, 190, 192, 193, 195

Lindbergh, Charles.................. 74
Lister, Joseph 94
Maass, Clara................... 123–35
Maass, Clara Louise................. 1
Maass, Helwig....... 126, 132, 133
Maass, Robert 126
MacWhorter, Alexander 2, 17, 22, 24, 25, 26, 139–50
MacWhorter, Hugh 142
MacWhorter, Jane 142
MacWhorter, Mary 144
Magovern, John.................... 172
Mandela, Nelson 216
Marshall, Thurgood...... 112, 115, 116
McCabe, Thomas 174
McCarroll, Earnest Mae.. 1, 109–21
McCarroll, Francis 111
McCorristin, Charles............ 174
McGrath, Patrick.................. 117
Meeks, Gregory.................... 214
Moon, Betty 3
Morse, Samuel F. B. 38
Moss Sandra......................... 105
Mulford, Irene 81
Nightingale, Florence... 124, 125, 127, 128
O'Leary, Hazel............. 203, 207
Obama, Barack..................... 216
Obamedo, Jacobs.......................4
Ogden, John............................26
Paine, Thomas 139
Parker, Joel 191
Pasternak, Rachel 76
Pasteur, Louis 94
Payne William Evander.........210
Payne, Donald M., Sr. 2, 201, 202, 207, 209–22
Payne, Donald, Jr. 219
Payne, Hazel.................211, 212
Payne, Kathryn 210
Payne, Nicole 218
Payne, Norma 210
Payne, Wanda.......................218
Payne, William 203, 204, 210, 212, 221, 222
Peoples, Sesser 207
Pingry, John............................96
Polk, James.............................57
Potts, Nathaniel 89
Powell, Carrie 86
Prinz, Dorothea.......................64
Prinz, Hilde.......................68, 71
Prinz, Joachim 1, 61–76
Prinz, Joseph.....................63, 64
Prinz, Lucie 67, 68
Prinz, Nina..............................63
Rackwitz, Arthur 69

Rahl, Johann 49
Read, Thomas 184, 189
Reed, Carolyn 203
Reed, Walter 129, 130
Rice, Ronald 204
Rice, Susan 220
Ricord, Elizabeth 2, 151–64
Ricord, Frederick...156, 163, 164
Ricord, John 156, 163
Ricord-Madianna, Jean Baptiste 154, 155
Rodino, Peter 211, 213
Runyon, Theodore 40, 192
Schanck, John 98
Scott-Rountree, Louise 1
Seeber, Anna 123–26
Sellers, Robert 120
Seward, William 191
Shanley, Bernard 172
Sharif, Sheikh 216
Sharpton, Al 217
Shaw, William 163
Sherman, Abigail 35
Silberfield, Julius 72
Sims, Geraldine 88
Smith, Charles 4, 88
Smith, Fred 176
Smith, Leroy 220
Spellman, Robert 204, 205
Spring, Gardiner 54
Stearns, Jonathan 150
Sterling, Guy 223
Stockton, Richard 50
Stryker, James 155
Stryker, Peter 154
Stryker, Sarah 154
Sutphen, A. J. 160, 162
Tappan, Lewis 57
Tennent, William 143
Thayer, A. A. 41
Thompson, Ernie 90
Thornton, Paul 172
Tubman, Harriet 149, 150
Urquhart, Frank 16, 18
Van Arsdale, Jacob 141
Wade, Joe 201
Wainwright, Jonathan 152
Ward, Fanny 182
Ward, John 182
Ward, Marcus 59, 181–95
Ward, Moses 182
Ward, Susan 182
Warren, Jay 220
Warwick, Dionne 203
Washington, Booker T. 110
Washington, George 13, 139, 146
Waters, James (Father Philip) 170
Webb, Michael 213

Webster, Daniel.................48, 57
Weston, Edward................42, 44
Wilberforce, William..............48
Wilkins, Roy................112, 115
Wilks, Bernard.....................2, 9
Wilks, Keith...............................3
Willard, Emma......................155
Willard, Joseph.......................26
Williams, Alice............197, 198
Williams, Caroline............77, 78
Williams, Hannibal..................77
Williams, Hannibal Allen........77
Wilson, Andrew......................35
Wimmer, Boniface................166
Wise, Stephen....................71, 72
Witherspoon, John..................49
Yates, Henry............................93
Zamba, Zachary.....................205